"...This book captures the
Odhiambo, with wholesome
once again congratulate this a
effort."

— **HON. ENGINEER PHILIP OKOTH OKUNDI**

Commissioner, National Cohesion and Integration Commission.

"...Easy and enjoyable reading ... highly recommended to be read by students, professionals and laypeople. It is full of simple and solid prescriptions and anecdotes for every generation and age. *Aluta continua!*"

— **DR. ROBERT OKELLO ARUNGA**

Former Managing Director, Kenya Industrial Research and Development Institute (KIRDI).

"...Remarkable...an inspirational story of an indomitable spirit surmounting massive odds. I have had the privilege of sharing part of this history as a younger colleague for whom he has been an inspiration and a mentor, from the struggles we shared at KNH and the medical school to KCS and PASCAR, where I followed his footsteps into leadership. It is delivered in that punchy style that is typically Peter."

— **PROF. ELIJAH OGOLA**

MB ChB, M. Med, FACC.

President, PASCAR. Specialist Consultant and Cardiologist.

"*Making the Cut* ... highlight[s] the vast challenges that surgeons in Kenya face ...Truly, an eye opener offering insights to young surgeons and definitely a must-read."

— **PROF. JULIUS M. KYAMBI**

Professor of Surgery and Paediatric Surgery.

'I met Peter Amollo Odhiambo around 1965/66 during his undergraduate days at Kolkata Medical College ... I and my friend Ratna Sen had gone to cover a function of the African Students Association (ASA-India), Kolkata branch. He was one of the organizers. He delivered a fluent speech about his country and the African continent. My take was that here was a leader in the making, inside and outside his medical education.

His autobiography, *Making the Cut*, wades through his life in an inspiring and thought-provoking style of his own. The story includes his fight against communicable and non-communicable diseases, and tobacco, in very engaging reading.

The entire journey of this friend, who does not know how to boast about his successes and achievements, is a must-read, not only in Africa and other developing countries, but also all over the world."

— **MRS. ALPANA GHOSH**

Author, Retired Teacher, Freelance Journalist, Food Writer and Historian.

"I first met Peter Amollo Odhiambo in 1963 as a fellow student at the Calcutta Medical College in India. Even then, I was amazed by Amollo's striking imagination and often wondered why he chose to be a medical practitioner. Surely, he would feel more fulfilled in a profession that could value his storytelling capabilities. But time has shown me that Amollo is not a man of a singular profession, and his profession is not limited to his convocation. As *Making the Cut* now stands testimony, Amollo has utilised his powerful imagination to capture his life into these pages, all the while successfully managing to keep the essence of its magnitude alive.

Making the Cut shows us that Amollo has lived an inspired and inspiring life soaking up every little stimulus life has thrown at him and treating it as the motivation for a new, engaging challenge. And what amazes me is how he has managed so many challenges together at all – simultaneously and successfully. Yet when describing each life stage in the book, Amollo's style of narration remains modest, humble and engaging. At no point in the process does the reader feel overwhelmed or insignificant while standing across Amollo's tall achievements. He patiently holds his reader's hand through the various chapters in a way that will make even someone who has never met Amollo feel the same sense of familiarity and pride that I feel, reading about a friend I have known for 50 years.

Making the Cut is not just another book about a successful man and his journey, but an effective manual on how to brave life itself with an unwavering moral compass and a can-do attitude. Success and accolades are only by-products of that perspective. I would highly recommend this book to anyone who wants to enrich their lives with a continuous process of learning and helping the community."

— **DR. MOHAMMED YASIN**

MBBS, DOMS(Cal), MD(AIIMS), FORCE.

Assistant Professor.

MAKING THE CUT

MAKING THE CUT

The Autobiography of Kenya's First Thoracic and Cardiovascular Surgeon

Peter Amollo Odhiambo

PUBLISHED JOINTLY BY UPDATE PUBLISHERS AND WRITEMOTIVE

"MAKING THE CUT" – A double-barrel idiom meaning:
1. Facing and overcoming a challenge or challenges, and
2. The actual undertaking of a surgical operation.

First jointly published in Kenya by Update Publishers and Write Motive in 2018.
This edition published in 2023 by Update Publishers and Write Motive.
ISBN 978-9914-49-142-5

Cover design by Z.O.A. Odhiambo.
10 9 8 7 6 5 4 3 2
Revised Edition

DEDICATION

To my parents,
Jaduong' Mzee Tukiko Odhiambo Asuke: Teacher, Chief, Counsellor

and

Mama Zipporah (Mireri) Owiti Odhiambo: Mama Hygiene, Mama *Biblos.*

and

To my sons and daughters, the Princes and Princesses of Ong'eche-2, Omboga, Kendu Bay, Kenya.

To my teachers, from primary school to my post-tertiary days. I particularly recall the late John Koko Okal, who on my first day at Intermediate School (today's Upper Primary) admonished new entrants with words of wisdom. He gave a coin to an older male student who remembered what he had said in Dholuo the previous year: ***"Los ngima mar nyathi mondo ngima mar jaduong' obed maber," ("Prepare, nurture and protect the life of the child so that the life of the old man may and shall be good!")*** This was advice to us children, to look after ourselves so that we would be well, safe, and prosperous in old age.

I also remember the late Professor Anthony Harding-Raines, commenting on my research in micro-vascular surgery on pigs at Charing Cross Hospital: ***"For the sake and safety of your patient, you can try [research] anything!"***

To my immediate family, for always having faith in me.

To my relatives and friends, for always praying for me.

To my patients, whose contribution will forever be etched in my journey: From artist Saradindu Ghosh in what was then Calcutta (now Kolkata; 1969/70) to Mzee Naftali Matoke Matagaro (1993), who now has five grandchildren pursuing careers in the health profession because of his faithfulness, compliance and commitment as a patient, as well as his leadership as a patriarch. He was among my longest operated survivors of carcinoma of the oesophagus, despite a proven malignant deposit (3x3 cm) on his right forearm and a much larger (4x4) but benign lymph node in his left axilla (armpit)! I removed both more than three years after the main operation, which was an oesophagectomy and oesophago-gastrostomy. He lived for 17 more years and died of other natural causes!

Among the others were Francis Kiiyo, the late Mrs. Elizabeth Gitau, and the late Professor, Father Charles Nyamiti.*

To my former classmates, the 1963 batch of medical students at Calcutta Medical College, Calcutta, India, who wrote a poem about me in our memory book:

Writer and debater, Peter's a pride,
Any topic he can take in his stride,
A Kenyan, he is loved by all,
Bosses or students, big or small.

*See Chapter 26, Ties that Bind

1963 BATCH OF MEDICAL COLLEGE BENGAL

HUMILITY IS
THE
ALTER-EGO
OF
GREATNESS!

ACKNOWLEDGEMENTS

I ACKNOWLEDGE AND GIVE THANKS to the Almighty God, without Whom none of this would be possible. I also acknowledge the immense contribution of the following:

1. My parents.

2. My entire family.

3. My office staff, past and present.

4. My patients.

5. My colleagues.

6. My journal and book printers.

7. All hospitals, both public and private, where I have worked over the years; in particular, my 'Home Ward' at the Kenyatta National Hospital – Rahimtullah Wing Ground Floor, which became Ward 12 in the new Tower Block, which soon became Ward 4B, the latter two of which were on the fourth floor of KNH Tower Block.

8. The University of Nairobi, particularly the School of Medicine, before and after its re-organization to become the composite College of Health Sciences.

9. All who sponsored this project both directly and indirectly, both in cash and in kind.

10. Any and all individuals and organizations who have helped me in one way or another, but whom I have not mentioned above!

11. You, the reader, for sparing your precious time to read any part, or all, of this book about me! I apologize to you for the delay in its publication after I announced it more than two years ago!

FOREWORD

I HAVE HAD the opportunity of knowing Professor Peter Odhiambo for about sixty years, from around 1962. I was ahead of him in school, but we attended the same University in New Delhi and Calcutta.

His ambition and drive were evident early on when he was elected the leader of the African Student Association (ASA–India), and his leadership reflected his desire to contribute to the common good as a student representative of the African students during our time.

That was just the beginning. Over the sixty years that I have known him, in school and during his career, he has been driven by a strong will to make a difference; his leadership skill set, hard work and ambition have enabled him to undertake different and challenging tasks and achieve them all.

The author rose from a poor and underdeveloped rural village called Kanyaluo, Karachuonyo in Homa Bay County to be an accomplished surgeon and a well-known African author and scientist. The struggles that he has undergone and overcome are an inspiration.

From his leadership days in ASA—India, he went on to bigger things and founded the Kenya Cardiac Society and was an integral part of its Pan-African equivalent. These are landmark efforts and are an important marker in both Kenya and Africa's medical history.

This is an interesting and important book to read. Interesting because it documents the real and difficult life that most young people in Africa have gone through for centuries. Important because it is an inspiration to young, up-and-coming boys and girls in Africa, who are pursuing their goals; while the commonly faced hurdles present in Africa have forced many to simply give up, many young Africans require these documented examples for inspiration and guidance in facing and overcoming their everyday struggles. I want to say here that autobiographies such as this one are important because it is a fact that every life has something good to be copied or emulated as well as the bad that should be heeded or avoided. My greatest admiration for the author is his serious and commendable efforts to stop tobacco consumption and his handling of the bribery and persuasive tactics of the tobacco barons – he has stood, time and again, for the common good and not merely for a few pieces of silver. It confirms his unquestionable and strong sense of industry and integrity that he has always possessed and that I have observed in all my years of knowing him. This book is a commendable effort and takes you on a journey of an extraordinary life well lived; he has made the cut with tenacity, hard work and self-discipline.

PROF. G. B. A. OKELO
MD, FRCP, MRCP, MBBS, DTM&H.
Professor of Medicine.
Secretary, African Academy of Sciences.
Former Chairman, Department of Medicine, UoN.
Former Dean, School of Medicine, UoN.
Former Director of Medical Services, Ministry of Health, Kenya.

INSIGHT

MAKING THE CUT, the autobiography of the first Kenyan heart surgeon, Professor Peter Amollo Odhiambo, is a captivating read for all who want to know a good part of the history of medical professional and academic development in Kenya. Peter outlines his background in titillating reading. He tells the story of his family and early schooling in a memorable way. He then talks about his secondary school at Kisii High School and his assumed involvement in the school strike that led to his being sent home. The strike reminds one of how national events shape the youth and the citizens in their perception of growth and development. As he narrates it himself in the book, the precipitating factor here was that some two European teachers (an acting Principal and another) brought it on by expelling a very innocent Form III student after escalating time spent on the school farm and drastically reducing teaching and library hours in typical colonial style!

The time he was being expelled from school coincided with the wave of pre-independence politics that brought prominence to early educated Africans like Kwame Nkrumah, Dr. Kamuzu Banda, Mr. Sékou Touré, Mr. Ghamal Abdel Nasser, Mr. Habib Bourguiba, Mzee Jomo Kenyatta and others who led the fight for independence in the continent. The colonial government expropriation of land from Kenyan Africans and the subjugation of the African citizens led to the rebellion and uprising by the natives against the whites. The political awareness movement was championed by leading political fighters of freedom in Kenya.

The arrival of Jomo Kenyatta from the United Kingdom gave impetus to national resistance. He, together with five other political leaders, namely Paul Ngei, Fred Kubai, Achieng' Oneko, Kung'u Karumba and Bildad Kaggia were arrested and detained when Senior

Chief Waruhiu was shot and killed by the *Mau Mau*. The stalwarts like Oginga Odinga, Tom Mboya and Dr. Gikonyo Kiano continued the leadership of political campaigns during the trial and detention of the "Kapenguria Six," as the six detainees came to be later known. As fate would have it, two of them (Fred Kubai and Bildad Kaggia) were much later to become the author's friends and patients! Even the late Jaramogi Oginga Odinga passed through his clinical fingers briefly.

Between 1958 and 1961 Tom Mboya with his American friends, and Kenyan politicians like Dr. Gikonyo Kiano, Dr. Munyua Waiyaki and others, organized student airlifts to the United States of America. The two events caught the imagination and fascination of the youth who dreamt of taking Kenya's leadership baton and dared to embrace the challenge of leaving their parents and friends behind to go to foreign countries for higher education.

The author tells his story of how he missed going to America and Canada but managed to go to India. Traveling by aeroplane or sailing by ship was unheard of in his locality in those days for ordinary folk. Getting such an opportunity to go abroad was an experience which Prof. Odhiambo vividly narrates. At the same time that Tom Mboya was organizing the student airlift to America, Jaramogi Oginga Odinga was clandestinely sending Kenyan students to the Soviet Socialist Republic of Russia. Although this airlift and other forms of travel are not widely talked about in the media, it managed to train approximately 2000 Kenyans who returned to serve their country in various capacities in the public and private sectors in the country. Before I leave the story of airlifts or travelling by ship, one is reminded of the story of US ex-President John F. Kennedy's speech about landing an American on the moon before the end of the nineteen sixties (1960s) decade. It became a clarion call for the American youth to aim high and this propelled the United States of America into technological and economic global leadership. True leadership shapes the future and the nation.

Living in a foreign country whose citizens speak a language you do not understand can be very vexing, especially if you have not learnt the language spoken by host country. It is also very trying when the culture of the people is different from your own people's culture. Despite these challenges, Peter describes his studies in India with some admiration. He excelled in college and finished his first degree in medicine quite in time. While studying in India, he either formed or joined students' organizations and displayed his leadership abilities by being Secretary-General, Vice Chair or President of the students' organizations. He tells the story of how the Kenyan High Commissioner to India persuaded him not to remain in India, thereby rescuing him from being Kenyan brain drain to India. Upon his return home, the leadership and organization abilities he acquired in India served him well. On that return to Kenya, he was employed by the Ministry of Health and soon posted to Murang'a District Hospital where he, with little training and experience in surgery, found himself compelled to operate on his patients who all survived. He learned quickly and decided to join the University of Nairobi for further training. He and his fellow Kenyans feel proud of the narration of many challenging surgical operations he had done at Kenyatta National Hospital. The frustrations of operating a scientific and medical professional institution with poor governance and insufficient resources are given in examples he narrates. The conflict between newly independent educated Kenyans with the white Kenyan civil servants is well illustrated in the book.

The tobacco industry is well established as a global enterprise. The players in East Africa, like British American Tobacco (BAT), Mastermind, Phillip Morris, Japan Tobacco and others are not simply established but actually entrenched as powerful companies in Kenya. However, tobacco is a known leading killer of people through cancer. The tobacco industry in Kenya was not going to be restricted in its sales without a fight. The story of passing legislation in Kenya's Parliament, recognizing the ills of smoking and introducing regulations on sales or putting warning signs on tobacco packages, was won by Peter and his team. This battle is half-won when one considers, for example, the recently proposed legislation in the United States of American Congress on further restricting the types of tobacco smoking allowed in that country.

I wish to conclude by mentioning the professionalization of medicine in Kenya which Peter narrates in detail in his book and gives clear picture on how it was done in an admirable fashion. He was a leader in the fight for international and internal recognition of African medical doctors as well-trained and qualified to do any operation on human beings as done anywhere in the world. This is a valuable book that is worth reading, but also an educational book in giving the life stories of Kenya's first heart surgeon.

PROF. SHEM OYOO WANDIGA
FRSC, D.Sc. h.c.
Professor of Chemistry.

MAKING THE CUT

CONTENTS

Dedication	*i*
Acknowledgements	*vii*
Foreword	*ix*
Insight	*xi*
Prologue	*xxi*
Introduction	*xxiii*
1. The Beginning	*1*
2. Strike Trek	*15*
3. Bird In Hand: A Date With Hippocrates of Cos	*31*
4. Ice to Break and a Skill to Sharpen	*48*
5. '*Kwaheri ya Kuonana!*' Exit India – Home Again	*62*
6. Hunting for the Cancer Bug	*72*
7. Starting a Family	*80*
8. Bowater Corporation and Bowater Benevolence	*96*
9. Pioneer Times, Plus	*103*
10. Snow in New York, Storm in Detroit: An Ambulance, One Patient and One Doctor	*130*
11. From Tripoli to Lusaka	*137*

12. Overcoming a Nightmare *143*

13. A Bullet Named 'Asthma' and General China *157*

14. From Kabati in Kandara, Murang'a, to Nairobi in a 504 Pick-Up Van with Shujaa Bildad Kaggia *162*

15. Deanship *169*

16. My Brief Look at Surgery in Kenya *227*

17. Thoracic and Cardiovascular Surgery: Where Do We Go From Here? *238*

18. The 'Orphan' State of Some Kenyan Heart Patients and the Salvage: "Kenya Heart Patients' Association *251*

19. Drums of War, or Just Another Fatalistic African Rehearsal? *254*

20. Walking and Lobbying *257*

21. Serving on School and Other Boards *283*

22. Memorial Lectures *300*

23. Writer and Debater *304*

24. Lake "Taku," Not "Victoria" *310*

25. Bereavements

I. Bye-Bye Mum *324*

II. Another Shock *328*

III. Jim, Big Jim – "Jordan" *331*

26. Ties That Bind *340*

27. Pending and Suspended Dreams *369*

28. Ancestry and Roots *405*

29. The Final Motion *411*

Epilogue

I. Fifty-four Years a Medical Doctor (1968–2022) *414*

II. Planet Earth Named Environment (Translating Policy into Practice) *416*

III. Leadership in Health *420*

Summary *421*

PROLOGUE

LAW. ENGINEERING. MEDICINE. WHICH ONE?

Secondary school would soon be behind me. I needed to decide fast. I had limited my career options to three, but was still not sure exactly which course would be the best option for me to study.

Would it be Law? I was a good debater, and I could contribute to changed lives by defending the downtrodden and speaking out against societal ills.

Perhaps Engineering was a better idea. Specialisation options abounded in this field of study. Planes were fast becoming a more-common form of travel. The country's infrastructure needed major work. If I wished to, I could also gain expertise in the area of the production, transformation and transportation of chemicals, materials and energy.

Our country was in need of doctors, too. I could change the lives of families by helping their people get well. My paternal granduncle, Ojung'a, son of Odhuno of Kothidha, Kanyada (Homa Bay County) was, after all, an *ajuoga* – a traditional medicine-man, a doctor.

Which would it be? I consulted my eldest brother-in-law, Benson Ochieng Nyangoro, who was already employed as a clerk-typist, having left the prestigious Bugema College, Uganda, in Form One due to lack of fees.

We discussed the matter at length. I identified the triad of career counselling and career choices, based on interest, aptitude and opportunity. He left me to make the final decision. Sadly, he was killed in an intra-clan land feud more than a year after I had left the country to pursue my degree of choice:

Medicine.

INTRODUCTION

THIS BOOK IS ABOUT ME, written by me; it will not read like any other autobiography or *mémoires* that you might read. I have deliberately avoided any templates, however palatable. I shall, both directly and indirectly, touch upon the environment in which I was born, bred, worked and lived.

I have kept the order of the different sections and chapters quite simple, based on time sequence, sectors, disciplines, places and themes, without being sure of what to add for 'the sake of completeness.'

It has not been easy to include everything! To deal with that, I have set out to be very flexible, should there be need for a second edition. Nevertheless, I hope that the many pictures, photographs and sketches will serve that purpose and compensate for as many words!

There were things that I did, or that happened to me. Thought processes can be both limitless and endless. There were also things that I thought and still think about. For the latter particularly, I have given myself the additional liberty in this book to say it as I saw and still see it; for you, the reader, I ask that you just bear with me! Like anthropologist Ashley Montagu summarises it upfront, in the first sentence of the introduction of his small but influential and captivating 'one hour' book, *On Being Human*, ***"To be human is to be in danger...."***

But what I want to share more with you at this stage, my reader, is found in the middle of page 2 of the same introduction, that ***"Every human being is a problem in search of a solution!"*** No doubt, I am just another human being! Take it easy with me, ha-ha, but take it!

There are people, inside and outside my circles (family and all) mentioned in this book, about whom I could be expected to write volumes; this book is not about them as such. Once again, therefore, please bear with me. Just read about me, of what *I recall about me*, and move on, as you also search for your own solution or solutions, ***which you must***!

I have depended on my editorial and publishing supporters for ultimate formatting and necessary technicalities, but I know I must have influenced them somewhat, somewhere, somehow, in this territory of [modified] self-publishing. Again, the buck stops with me: I take responsibility for any lapses detected in the pages of my autobiography!

My final submission regards my headache with which photographs to include, and which ones to exclude from here. I cannot say more than that, but must apologize to those whose photographs I should have included but did not, as reasoning it out is itself also hard!

On a general, historical and common ground, I want to ask you to join me in taking serious note of the point and the fact that these are the **"Dark Ages"** of the Continent of the Black Man and Woman, which have engulfed us in three phases, namely:

a. **The slave trade** – That was an unforgivable assault! May the good God cleanse the souls of those affected, rest them in everlasting peace and bless their offspring.

b. **Colonialism and unwarranted subjugation** – That was a calculated belligerent invasion.

c. **'Independence' and post-'Independence,' on the threshold of a century and ongoing** – This has been like an attempted suicide, where bad political leadership, corruption and impunity are reigning supreme! Writers have written about the miseries, but more to entertain than to cleanse battered minds and mindsets. These require direct (naked) analysis, interpretation, and remedial guidance towards sustainable self-regeneration.

That is where I am writing from; it is where most of you will be reading from! Let us hope, pray and work hard so that the fourth phase emerges and sees us as the purest continent that never converted fellow human beings, human blood and human flesh into commercial fodder, a continent of human angels!

My very dear reader, welcome to my microcosm! You may learn something from my botched solutions. I am sure you will also learn something from my humble successes, and, indeed, my mistakes and failures! Take care! Good luck! And join me in moving my motion in Chapter 29 below!

1

THE BEGINNING

I WAS BORN on 2nd September 1940, at Kendu Mission Hospital, Kendu Bay, in Karachuonyo, Homa Bay County. Our home was right in the middle of the Omboga school-church complex, in the Kamenya part of Kanyaluo in Karachuonyo, hence the pet name "*Amollo Wuod* (son of) *Omboga.*" My father simply said, with some pride and confidence, *Amollo K'Odhiambo* (son of Odhiambo), which is my occasionally chosen literary (media) name. He would resort to the name whenever he thought somebody did not quite know me and was playing with fire! I once overheard him telling someone about another, "*....Ero, otugo gi Amollo K'Odhiambo!*" translated loosely as "... that one is making a mistake playing with Amollo K'Odhiambo!"

For whatever clarity it might give, my own name, as of many others, is spelled with double L. Many others spell theirs with a single L. There is nothing African (Luo) versus colonial (English) about the difference. My explanation is that "Amollo" is a name, while "Amolo" is akin to the Luo phrase "amolo" (I have entered), but elevated by the capital "A!" For me, that is the long and short of it. Let others take their pick!

For a long time after independence, but before devolution, Kenya was divided into eight provinces. Only recently have the provinces been subdivided into 47 counties. Homa Bay County was then Homa Bay District.

During colonial rule, Homa Bay and Kisii Counties were both combined to form a large land mass known as South Nyanza District. Later, with periodic adjustments of administrative units, the same name was retained for the Luo side of the landmass, while the other side became Kisii District. Later still, the new South Nyanza was itself divided into Migori, Rachuonyo and Homa Bay Districts. It was the title 'District' that was converted to 'County,' as the country's administrative units were devolved in line with the new Constitution of the year 2010. The exercise included review and adjustment of boundaries over the whole country.

Kendu Mission Hospital, in the Kendu Bay area of Karachuonyo, is in present-day Homa Bay County. Locally, Kendu Mission Hospital is also known as Gendia Hospital. The Seventh Day Adventist (SDA) missionaries reached and established the Gendia Mission in the year 1906. Indeed, almost the whole area was and is known as Gendia, within which unitary activities fitted with their respective names – Gendia School, Gendia Press, Gendia Chief's Camp (*Doho* Gendia), etc. Kendu Bay itself was a smallish shopping centre at the lake shore, about 2 -3 kilometres away from the school-church complex. It had been built a right within the bay on the lake shore itself. Unlike Gendia Mission, which was perched on a hill barely three kilometres away and was the epicentre of the SDA denomination of the Christian religion and religiosity, Kendu Bay was totally different. It acquired its fame from many secular activities there. It had a charisma of its own. For miles and miles away, almost everybody wanted to be identified with Kendu Bay, as '*Ja*-Kendu' or '*Nyar* Kendu' – directly translated as 'Man from Kendu' or 'Daughter of Kendu,' respectively (the word 'Bay' being presumed and understood!). Otherwise, it was a Moslem township.

I was the fourth child and the first son of my parents – Tukiko Odhiambo Asuke and Zipporah Owiti Odhiambo, daughter of Ocholla (hence her pet name *Ny'Ocholla*). My mother's other given name was Mireri, but nobody used it and it just 'disappeared.' According to my youngest maternal uncle, Jackton Nyakiti, the name Owiti was almost a nickname, branded when she left home in search of the established SDA institutions of Kamagambo and Wikondiek. Gendia was geographically much closer to her father's homestead at Anding'o

Opanga in the Kasaye community of the expansive Nyakach in the then Central Nyanza District, now Kisumu County. However, Gendia did not quite feature in her story of adventure and exploration for spiritual and educational enlightenment.

Mum never made it to Kamagambo. At Wikondiek, she was hosted by a matriarch, Mariam Otonde Ochuodho for her abortive sojourn. There was already notable church activity at Wikondiek itself, so her dream of heading for Kamagambo was effectively shelved, and then abandoned for good! She settled down to church and school and became sufficiently literate in written Dholuo.

It was at Wikondiek that young Tukiko Odhiambo, son of Asuke, met her. There were at least two other suitors, but he won her hand. They wedded on 4th July 1934 according to the SDA church practice. They did not have rings and she did not have or wear shoes! We can only presume that by the time they wedded, they had already been baptized in the church.

Young Odhiambo Asuke had also left his father's homestead to go for education and join the church, within the larger clan at the original locations of Adiedo and Omboga. He was like partially adopted by his youngest paternal uncle, Amollo 'Rarado' Onduru. Because of that closeness between them, when I was born, I was named after this great-uncle of mine as a sign of respect, gratitude, friendship and everlasting memory. The Luo name their children after great and influential people, memorable occasions, time of day, historical events, etc. Names of prominent people were usually picked for naming babies after the death of such personalities. It was unorthodox but understandable that I was named after my granduncle when he was still alive, almost as if my parents feared they might never get another son for that preserved historical family honour! As God would have it, the next three children after me were all boys. My fourth follower was born when Amollo Onduru, my naming benefactor, died in 1956. The new baby was duly named after him, like I was, but this time in harmony with the Luo culture and traditions just referred to above! So, there are two of us Amollos, sons of the same parents, Tukiko and Zipporah, named after the same granduncle.

My parents on 4th July 1934: The wedding that was. Notice the humility of a barefoot bride.

Before or soon after their wedding, my parents moved into the compound of a Sabbath School, a piece of land that had been donated by a few families from the clan, including our immediate Onduru family complex. The very first location of the Sabbath School was some four kilometres away on the land of another family complex in Komwoyo, near Adiedo, but was relocated from there by order of Chief Paulo Owuor. Some 'ruins' of house structures are still traceable today at the earlier site. It was a silent competition between clans wanting such institutions nearer home and part of their family 'ownership.' Even today, family complexes still join hands to build 'their' church or school.

In this case, it also worked out that way for two possible reasons – Ex-Chief Paulo Owuor was very powerful and forceful, and it was all under his jurisdiction; secondly, the people lived like one family, grand children of Owaga Nyaluo, first wife of Rachuonyo (see Chapter 28: *Ancestry and Roots*). The new compound into which my parents moved at Omboga was barely one kilometre away from my grandparents' homestead.

Those days, education was graded differently. The very first classes were A, B and C, before starting Standard I to proceed to II and then III, etc. My father made it to Standard III. Mum made it to C.

Back to the marriage of 4th July 1934. It was not until April 1935 when they were blessed with their first child, my eldest sister. They named her Truphena Ooga after an aunt but later changed her name to Truphena Onyango. She was followed by Phoebe Odero, the very next year, 1936. The birth of my third eldest sister Maritha in 1938 stirred some anxiety in the young family and in the immediate clan.

In those days, three girls in a row, with no boy, was not so blessed: Everybody prayed! Time passed! At last, those prayers were answered with the birth of a baby boy, the storyteller, on 2nd September 1940! That ushered in a non-stop run of three more boys – Jacob Ochieng' (Israel Olonde) in 1943, Abel Ouma (1946) and David Ocholla (1948). Elsa Omollo (Atieno), our fourth sister, came next (1952). Her follower, Akeyo, sadly suffered a cot death in her infancy in August 1954 when two weeks old. Mum and Dad got two more boys in 1956 (Joseph Amollo) and 1958 (John Ochieng').

Although we never celebrated any birthdays with parties, all the births were dutifully recorded. At my own request, my parents gave me the neatly recorded register and I copied the list for myself. That is the only comprehensive record we have today with all the names of my siblings and me! This is detailed at the end of this book, in the table showing the Odhiambo lineage (The same section also has lineages from the sides of both parents respectively).

My parents with my two youngest siblings, Joseph 'Jossy' Amollo (left), and John Ochieng,' circa 1961-2.

Of note was the fact that around this time, our father had joined the teaching profession and was posted to different schools, here and there, within a radius of some twenty-five kilometres. He was the third to be posted at his home school, Omboga, after Gideon Majiwa (future father-in-law of lawyer and FIDA heroine, Joyce Majiwa, as well as the father of one of a handful molecular biologists in Kenya, Professor Felix Ocholla Majiwa, Joyce's husband). The late Ezra Choka Omollo was the second teacher at that school.

Living in the school-church compound with my parents, along with my starting and going to school, was considered part of normal home life to me, even with the lack of dedicated or formal classrooms, or an organized nursery school. The youngest children would just play around and gather under a tree for the one teacher to introduce them to the alphabet and the numbers. By this time, my time, the old grading system of Standard A, B, C, before joining Standard I had been discontinued, actually modified. Fitness to go to school was partly a factor of age-groups and peerage on the one hand, and actual recorded age on the other. On average, it was between eight and ten years. I was eight years old when I started. There were many much-older classmates.

My father himself was teaching some twenty kilometres away from home. His most recent postings were on opposite sides of Oyugis Market Centre: one in Muksero, near Ruga and not far from the boundary with Kisii Location; the latest was Kakelo Ringa Primary School in East Kasipul. In 1950, he took my eldest sister and I to go and live with him there, but he did not admit us into his school, maybe to avoid a conflict of interest. He secured admission for us in a nearby school, some 2-3 kilometres away – Dudi Primary School (later to become Dudi Girls Secondary School, after Kenya's independence). The rest of the family joined us the next year, before his (early) retirement in early 1952. We then returned to Omboga. My eldest sister proceeded to Kamagambo. I re-joined Omboga Primary School. The same year, I sat for the Common Entrance Examination (CEE) and passed, but my father and my teacher at Omboga thought I was still "too young" to join Standard Five at Gendia Intermediate School. Intermediate Schools were the equivalent of today's upper primary schools, covering Standards 5, 6, 7 and 8. After the headmaster at Gendia agreed to admit me there the next year, I stayed in Standard 4 and continued at Omboga.

Gendia Intermediate School was some ten kilometres away from home in Omboga. To get there, we had to cross three rivers, one of which was seasonal. There were no bridges on our route. There were no roads, just footpaths. There was no commercial or 'official' transport, and no dream of school vans and buses! *Boda boda* was a true distant future vocabulary. So was the school lunch programme.

There were four years ahead! Sure enough, I was the youngest of the boys from Kanyaluo (Kanyaluo is today a Ward in Homa Bay County.) We walked, jogged, and ran from 5 a.m. to reach school by 8 a.m. and left school at around 6 p.m., many times at the earliest! In the rainy seasons, we never reached home because of flooded rivers! Back in the clan, my 'senior' school mates would have reached their homes when I still had two kilometres to cover. If we reached by 8 p.m., I would walk the distance alone. If by 9 p.m. and after, I would wait for my Dad at my grandmother Bwogi's house, then we would walk home together. He always came.

My grandmother and friend, Bwogi Ariko Ny'Odhuno (Bwogi Asuke). The background was beautiful red amaranth; her dress was pink.

My younger brother Jacob Ochieng' (left) and I during his school holiday in December 1961. He had visited me in Nairobi.

If it rained heavily then he would not bother because he knew that we would sleep at a home on the other side of River Sare. For River Awach Kibuon, we would avoid the direct route and detour to follow the side with a bridge, so it never blocked us.

During my Standard 8 year, my father procured a bicycle for me for the run from a maternal cousin, the late Peter Akech Obunga. I used it also to lift my younger brother Jacob who had since joined me at Gendia. He inherited it when I finished my intermediate school education.

I sat for my Standard 8 examinations in 1956. That was the last time it would be called the Kenya African Preliminary Examination, or KAPE, after the famous Beecher Report on education in Kenya. Thereafter it was re-named Certificate of Primary Education (CPE). It retained that name for decades to come, even after primary school education was reduced from eight to seven years.

Out of about thirty pupils in our Standard 8 class, only four of us made it from Gendia to join secondary school! Besides myself, there was Humphrey Kamire Ochieng,' Jacob Owino Aroka and Joseph Maena (not Maina) Ochieng.' The four of us were called to join Form One.

Over at the Kisii Government African School (famously, prestigiously and fondly known simply as "GAS"), a full boarding boys' school, student numbers were already straining accommodation space. A new dormitory was created out of the block which had housed the phased-out and relocated teacher training batches.

The existing dormitories had been named after well-known hills in South Nyanza – namely *Ruri, Manga, Sameta* and *Wire.* The new one was now named *Homa,* after Homa Hill. The entire new Form I class was taken there, with one prefect from the Form III class, Mr. Nyariki. That created a block of Form I students under one roof, so to speak! Simultaneously, it shielded us from the 'traditional' bullying of new Form Is (who were referred to as *wageni,* Kiswahili for visitors or *ogeno* in school slang; in short, newcomers to be treated as 'punching bags') from our seniors. By that token, we acquired an identity of our own. Some of us used that to impact on the oldies and the rest of the school. We had been given (and granted, so to speak) an identity and some unique autonomy!

When we graduated to Form II and the new Form Is arrived, we formed ourselves into groups. Starting with us from Karachuonyo, we embraced new arrivals from Gendia and Rachuonyo as a whole and organized makeshift 'tea parties' to welcome them. We protected them from any senior student who might have been inclined to bully them. That practice caught the school by storm and spread like an epidemic. Senior students from other schools and areas now also began to organize their own tea parties and undertook the protection of their own *wageni*. We from Rachuonyo had the advantage that there was a thriving student's welfare body, Rachuonyo Students' Association(RSA). That new 'mass' movement at the school literally and effectively killed the monster of bullying of Form Is, at least as long as our influence lasted after we left!

The rest of my stay at Kisii progressed very smoothly, until Form IV, where we had the famous strike and strike trek, on which I shall elaborate in the coming chapter.

Over the years, I managed to remain among the top five in class performance. My Form III year (1959) was quite eventful! I was appointed the Deputy Captain of the volleyball team, and was elected Secretary of the Bible and Debating Societies of the school. I was also elected Assistant Secretary of the School's Psychology Club.

That year also saw me acquire my first pair of shoes during second term holidays! My father sold his favourite (local) milk cow. He then requested a much younger cousin friend of his from a close clan who had just joined the teaching profession to go with me to the shops in Kisii and help me buy a pair of shoes. That was none other than the late Daniel Gor Omollo, a very polished, popular and respected teacher! He was also a role model for cultural change, because in the nearly the whole location, he was among the first, if not the first, to refuse to obey the mandatory Luo cultural tradition of having his six lower teeth removed!

Before that shopping, I attended class and played games barefooted! Whenever there was a demanding formal occasion, ever so rarely, I would borrow shoes from fellow students.

It was a very sad day for me years later, in 1966, while I was in my third year in medical school way out in Calcutta, when news came that my dear uncle and mentor, Daniel Gor Omollo and his brother Ndege Omollo were among passengers in a boat that had capsized and killed all on board! It was a vessel that used to ferry people between Kendu Bay and Kisumu. The Abudo family also suffered severely as the brothers from that family who drove the boat also perished. Gloom engulfed the whole country. No more boats plied that route again. Only steamers and ships remained.

The two families of Odhiambo Asuke and Gor Omollo had remained close all along. My aunt, Mama Miriam Amilla Gor became my stepmother a few years later when, for her widow remarriage, she and my father got together as man and wife. That made my father a polygamist, albeit an unpredictable one! The usual unavoidable tensions within polygamist homes featured, but did not tear the households too far apart.

All that time, I was still in medical school in Calcutta, India. To date, I have refused to use the phrase "wife inheritance," in preference to the other more befitting human rights-based term **"WIDOW RE-MARRIAGE,"** because I took and still take the stand that widows and widowers have a right to remarry, usually culturally within the family complex and clan. That is distinctly different from demanded liberal "freedom to choose" from anywhere and nowhere for cohabitation, almost always unmindful of existing children! In the cultural setting, the children are absorbed almost automatically into a family setting.

Further, it is the responsibility of the family complex *(anyuola)* on the man's side to take care of the widow. To abandon the widow is not quite "an abomination" to borrow the phrase all the way from Nigeria, but is quite a shameful aberration on the clan. Similarly, a widow who abandons the clan and neighbouring communities for a distant place (outcasts herself; best said in my vernacular as *dhi por*) is also frowned upon and a shame to her own children.

That was then! Today, with ever-growing urbanization, inter-'tribal,' inter-religious, "educated" and "modern" marriages, together with impressionable exposures abroad and overseas, compounded with human rights and gender disorientation, not even our sociologists, psychologists and anthropologists can address this subject coherently for their own families and descendants!

When my stepbrother, David Okiki Odhiambo, wedded in 2010, our father had long died in 2003. I joined my stepmother in church to escort him to the altar at the SDA church in Homa Bay, as the eldest male among us brothers and stepbrothers. My stepmother's household has siblings who use the respective names Gor and Odhiambo without any problem at all!

My eldest sister, Truphena Anyango Benson (she later chose to modify her given Luo name, Onyango), long retired as a teacher, also suffered a very untimely bereavement when her husband – my career choice adviser mentioned previously – was killed in a land feud. She also remarried within his clan. The only difference is that she chose to retain her husband's name, Ochieng,' as the surname for all her children born after remarriage; again, without any problem! Her family (mainly herself and the children) and I kept close all along, with me playing guardian to some extent. When it was time for her firstborn daughter, Margaret Rose Acholla Ochieng,' to wed, she and her fiancé, Dr. Vitalis Pius Abira, decided to wait for me from late 1978 until I returned from Montreal, Canada in 1979, to act as a fully-fledged guardian and be the one to hand her over at their wedding at St Paul's church in Kisumu. It is unfortunate that, even today, our sociologists and anthropologists are still buried in western models and appear to have failed to divorce themselves from those academically borrowed 'taught and examined' models of western religions and cultures!

My eldest brother-in-law, Benson Ochieng' Nyangoro, with my eldest sister Truphena and their children in Kericho in 1961. Their eldest daughter, now Margaret Rose Abira (with baby in her arm), is an 'expatriate' nurse in the UK; their eldest son, George Opala Ochieng' (left), is now an Education Officer.

Back at Kisii, among the students in general (outside the academia and school curriculum, that is), I was elected chairman of the Kanyaluo Students Association and of the larger Rachuonyo Students Association (RSA) respectively. With the latter, we organized various activities during school holidays. These included football matches at and with intermediate schools back home, accompanied with mentoring, guidance and "counselling" talks long before this term became commonplace! We also organised Christmas and other parties! These continued as a tradition in our home lives, during holidays away from school, and kept everyone out of harm's way.

Over time, things changed so much that one does not hear of, or see, such activities anywhere anymore! Only nostalgic 'oldies' would dare go back and attempt such games, but not with unbaked and undigested political undertones or defined but disoriented unproductive and unconstructive political alignments.

2

STRIKE TREK

IT WAS THE BEGINNING of the first term of my fourth and final (Form IV) year at Kisii High School. I approached the Principal, Mr. M. C. Grounds, to request his permission, for the sake of the motivation, inspiration and discipline of students in the school, to create large, hand-written cardboard posters and post them inside the classrooms, on the walls and doors of the corridors of the main classroom block and in other strategic positions in the school. I would get the words for these posters from the pages of *The Student's Companion*, a book by Wilfred D. Best which is well known to this day and which, along with books like Dale Carnegie's *How to Make Friends and Influence People*, were making waves in the school. The posters would include such proverbs and catchphrases as "TIME IS MONEY!" "A STITCH IN TIME SAVES NINE!" and "FORE-WARNED IS FORE-ARMED!" among others.

The three Form IV classes ahead of us at Kisii High had contained smooth, humble and influential mentors, such as Professor Samuel Owino Okong'o, Professor David Oyugi Aseto, the late Caleb Omogi Ong'wena, Momanyi Nyairo, the late Frederick Onyango Ngao (first Vice-Chancellor at Maseno University), Okoth K'Orombo, the late sports genius, Dr. Isaac Modi Aroka (actually an academic, games and sports all-rounder), and the late Dr. Andronico Oduogo Adede, who 'came back' long after leaving us behind at the school to write about our strike (in which he never participated) in a book entitled *The Quadrangle*.

The Principal was positively impressed and happily granted me that permission, instantly. I must have obtained the papers, marker pens, pins and glue from the library or elsewhere within the school. In no time, the posters were everywhere. No one missed them. They were not signed, so obviously they belonged to the school, but everyone knew the source, the writer and the 'distributor.' These three tasks I carried out single-handedly.

At the end of that term, Mr. Grounds went on his home leave for six months. We shuddered at the rumour and thought that he might not return. By that time, the entire Form IV class had been registered for the October-November Cambridge School Certificate examinations.

Come second term, in the first week of May 1960, we returned to school and found Mr. Gillespie, a Physics teacher, as the acting Principal. He had introduced new rules in the school. They were draconian, ruthless and crude, at least to the class of candidates.

Farm time was increased by two hours – not to learn, but to work – and library time was shortened by a similar margin, among other changes. Mr. Gillespie's administrative mannerisms earned him the label 'Boer.' It was now common knowledge that he had faced strikes in at least one other school before coming to Kisii High.

After that week, the entire Form IV class – Streams A and B – staged a boycott. The next morning, the Provincial Education Officer, a Mr. Lake, a former school inspector who was feared by all teachers in the then Nyanza Province, arrived at the school and summoned us to a space in the library.

On this occasion, however, fear was not a factor. Mr. Lake found himself faced by a solid wall of self-disciplined students, which included prefects and the school captain. No one seemed moved by his initial tough talk, and he quickly sensed that.

His body language changed, and then came the hollow words: "I know you are a very good class. In fact, as far as I am concerned, you are as good as you have already passed your final examinations!"

At the end of his talk, only one question came; it was asked by Robert Okello Arunga. That immediately put him on the Gillespie-Lake radar. For the rest of the class, there followed what we would today refer to as a 'go-slow,' the deflated tempo of a demoralized class.

A few days to the end of the first month of that term, an explosive development was precipitated by another teacher, Colonel Lofters, an old, retired war veteran and English Language teacher who once gave me a 100 % score in one essay and 0% in another.

This time, the 'focus group' was the Form III class, which contained the likes of Silas Nyamato, Tobias Ocholla Ogur, Harrison Ouso Ocholla, Michael Okeyo Owuor, the late Thaddeus Okatch, Walter Juma, the late John Arunga and the late Ezra Otieno Ayodo, among others.

As Col. Lofters walked along the veranda that afternoon, headed for a lesson in Form III, he heard the sound of hearty laughter coming from the classroom whose students had not even seen him coming. He immediately assumed they were laughing at him. When he walked in, he singled out and accused Thaddeus Okatch (later deceased in USA) of orchestrating the laughter. Okatch was reported to Mr. Gillespie (with whom Col. Lofters enjoyed some camaraderie) and was summarily dismissed from school.

Aha! They had just asked for it! Enough had finally become enough.

A sombre darkness and silence descended on the school like an unannounced solar eclipse. A spontaneous committee emerged. The Form IV class, which still had an axe to grind with the head teacher, seamlessly took charge of the management of the inevitable strike, along with the lower Form III class. They mobilized the entire school, creating codes of communication and writing and mounting rebellious posters everywhere in the school overnight. By daybreak, the school was awash with chilling 'paperwork.' It had nothing to do with my posters of the previous term, but fingers appeared to have been pre-pointed at me.

Two things are worth noting here. First, the school prefects were later accused of not alerting the teachers of the 'silent' or secret commotion at night. Secondly, I was perceived as the poster-writer, although no finger was pointed directly at me. More openly, the school administration perceived Michael Okeyo (Okatch's bosom friend) as definitely being involved!

The whole day, we herded ourselves on the grass to one slightly raised side of the dining hall, guarded by the entire line-up of school prefects, until Mr. Lake arrived in the evening, at around 5:30 or 6 p.m., barely two weeks after he had visited to speak to the finalists.

The entire school was ordered into the dining hall. Before Mr. Lake walked in, however, benches were quickly rearranged to face any and every direction, without provision for a head or high table or separate space for prefects or teachers. There was to be no chairman or spokesman. The Form I class was thought to be a weak link in that setting and was to be kept entirely in the dark on the nerve-centre control of the strike. Seated on the benches all through, those who would speak before Mr. Lake were to do so with their heads buried between their thighs and legs, mainly to prevent first years and himself from seeing them. Besides, the room also was darkening fast with the approaching sunset!

Mr. Lake eventually walked in alone, without acting headmaster Mr. Gillespie. This time round, the ultimate threat-cum-warning was that there would be no dinner for anybody if we did not stop the boycott. Of course, we could hear and smell the *ugali* being prepared in the kitchen. It was not going to be thrown away. To my recollection, there were no dogs in the school to benefit by default!

He left without making any headway. We ate the *ugali* and the accompaniments of the day with no interference or hindrance.

However, we feared overnight raids and arrests, so *the invisible command post* ordered that there would be no going out for long calls at night. For short calls, buckets were to be kept inside the dormitories.

All dormitory doors were to be locked from the inside. No one was to open any of those doors, if knocked on from outside, on any order of either the police or a teacher, or even on a purported SOS from any student.

Sure enough, the entire school compound was surrounded by 'Johnnies' (today's General Service Unit, or GSU) and regular police for the whole night.

At daybreak, as doors opened, the GSU forces quickly grabbed Kenya's future Ambassador and Permanent Representative to the United Nations, Michael Okeyo Owuor, and locked him inside the headmaster's office. As soon as the 'bushfire' was ablaze by way of signals, errands and words of mouth, an "emancipation squad" forced its way into the "cell." Eventually, before 10 am, Mike was freed! The immediate cost was that one student was badly hurt in the abdomen with a thrust from a police baton.

The whole school gathered on to the games pitch, mainly standing. It was evident that Kisii High School was about to be closed.

Not before some more action, however. Out of nowhere, in the middle of the dubious lull, my name was called.

"Come forward!"

Literally, that very same instance, the crowd swallowed me, and I was told to sit down on the grass, right in the middle of what seemed like a protected spot. I disappeared from view of whoever might come looking for me. There were not going to be any more, not even one, arrests. The calls came a few more times and died out. For as long as it took, I just sat there!

Then, now, everybody was to go home immediately, but nobody moved. Students demanded bus transport. Most of the communication from us was chorused by a global or joint 'spokesmanship.' By that time, some dignified elders (including Chiefs and ex-Chiefs), had entered the school compound and joined the teachers' rank in front of the school block, ostensibly to strike some awe in the students and help in the negotiations. For the students, it was bus transport or nothing. Then came their plea that all buses had in fact left town much earlier for the day, so bus transport was not going to be possible! Finally, the students agreed to be ferried in lorries to their various and respective Chiefs' Camps in the many different directions, including those going beyond Kisumu into present-day Siaya County. The school was soon evacuated. I have absolutely no idea how many lorries were eventually hired by the school!

Now, the roads to Mbita/Rusinga, Mike Okeyo's route, and Karachuonyo to Kendu Bay, my route, were different. We suspected that police would follow the lorry to Mbita and kidnap or arrest Mike Okeyo along the way. We quickly agreed that he would come with us to Karachuonyo and eventually to my parents' home, even though my father was an Assistant Chief and there might be some government requirements of him as 'Provincial Administration.' Mike was to stay with me overnight and leave for Nairobi early in the morning. He would head to Kendu Bay, take a boat from there to Kisumu, and then proceed by train to the capital city. I was to ensure his identity was protected and hidden until he had left the area, headed for the security of his home people in Nairobi.

The points to note here are that Mike Okeyo and Thaddeus Okatch were bosom buddies, that they both hailed from freedom fighter and trade unionist Tom Mboya's place, Rusinga Island, and that in the colonial eye, they were deeply political and had to be watched. It was all happening at the peak of the country's freedom struggle; anybody asking any hard questions was automatically taken to be a politician. Already, one of our best teachers, Samuel Onyango Ayodo, had recently left teaching for politics. Not many of us would join politics anyway, but at our formative stage, we were already wading through a somewhat disruptive last gasp of a self-defeatist colonial paranoia.

At Gendia Chief's Camp, where the lorry-full took us, we found the Chiefs' usual or routine *'baraza'* just about to start. My father, the late

Mzee Tukiko Odhiambo Asuke, was among them. They asked us questions. We simply said we had been given an early half-term holiday. As my father told me later, they never believed us anyway. After all, we were ordered to report there every week!

At our home, I introduced Mike Okeyo to my father by his correct name, but varied his home area to Sae, a place near Kosele, between Karachuonyo and Kasipul in Homa Bay County.

All hell almost broke loose, to my embarrassment! Mzee knew every home that mattered in that area, so whose son was Mike? Did he know so-and-so? Mike did not know the area at all! I had not imagined that Mzee would know people those sides, either! I had cleverly avoided the other side of Oyugis, where he had taught for a long time. He must have seen through us because he did not pursue the discussion further. One question he did not ask was why, if Michael's home was so close, did he not go to his own home, like everyone else, friendship aside!

The next morning, I took Mike on a bicycle to Kendu Bay and waved him off as he got on to the boat to Kisumu and later Nairobi. Up to that point, apart from the baton incident at the school when the Principal's door was being forced open, even with Johnnies surrounding us, we did not experience any more undue police harassment, in notable contrast with today's excited and excitable police responses, which robbed me of my innocent son, James Hillary Ang'awa Ocholla Odhiambo, 'Jordan,' in 1998.

We reported to the Chief's Camp every week; just like a brief 'roll call.' For the next few hours after reporting, a few of us, including classmate Robert Okello Arunga, always gathered at the home of another schoolmate, Samson Oluoch Rota, barely one kilometre away from the Chief's Camp, to chat and to write our memoirs, with special reference to the ongoing strike. I was the custodian of the drafts-cum-minutes. I kept them over the years until the 1990s when my wife accidentally burnt them together with some other waste papers, mistakenly assuming that they were part of the same bunch!

At home, I helped with herding our few goats, sheep and cattle, carrying my books and notes along with me and reading under the shade of trees. Remember, I was a registered candidate for the Form IV Cambridge University examinations later in the year, quite aside from the strike.

Sometime in July 1960, we heard that a few of us were being looked for. I packed my books and pens and went to Kericho, to hide at my eldest sister and brother-in-law's place. Before the end of the third week there, in early August 1960, I received an official message that I was required to appear at the school with my father. I immediately returned home. Mzee and I each rode a bicycle as we headed together to the school. It was more than 30 kilometres of riding, but we reached in reasonable time, well before 9 am.

We had heard that the school would soon open, but when we got there, there were no students. A panel made up of three teachers interviewed me in the presence of my father. They were Mr. Gillespie, acting Headmaster and Physics teacher; a Biology teacher, Mr. Brunden and a Geography teacher, Mr. Hannington Mtula.

"We have information that you led the strike," Mr. Gillespie began. "Is that not true?"

"No, Sir!" I responded.

"We have evidence that you were the one who did!" he insisted.

"Who saw me?" I asked.

"Two Form-I students," he told me.

"Are they here? Did you invite them, so that they can confirm to my father that I did?"

"We shall call them and invite you back. Meanwhile, you can wait at home."

Not a single thing was put to or before my father, either as a report about me as their student, or regarding my part in the strike. Instead, Mr. Mtula called my father aside and chatted with him for a few minutes, and off we went.

I could sense that something was not right with my father. Outside the school gate, he stopped, fuming.

"Who the hell is that man?" he asked. "What does he think he is? Does he think I am a child he can play with? Are those the types of teachers in your school? I am not surprised that you people went on strike! Like your friend from the island, you should not have hidden anything from me! I was not going to abandon you at all! I am sorry, but I did not like what I saw today. And that man? Stupid!"

We went back home to await Mr. Gillespie's promise of what was supposed to be an engineered confrontation with the Form I students. Meanwhile, the school was soon reopened, and everybody was called back, except a few of us:

Form III:
1. Michael Okeyo Owuor (deceased 2012).
2. Tobias Ocholla Ogur (deceased 2020).
3. Thaddeus Okatch, expelled a day before the strike.

Form IV:
1. Haggai Abong'o K'Oyier, School Captain.
2. Joseph Maena (not Maina) Ochieng,' School Prefect.
3. Yours truly, Peter Amollo Odhiambo, erroneously assumed to be the (only) writer of the strike posters!

Of the lot, the School Captain and the School Prefect were expelled because of their 'disloyalty!' As appointed leaders, they should have displayed some responsibility by staying on the side of the teachers and raising the alarm on what they saw, heard and knew!

Time was flying. The examination dates were approaching. About two weeks to the exams, the three of us in Form IV reasoned that since we had registered for the exams, we should be allowed to sit for them without necessarily re-joining the class. Departing from Karachuonyo together, which was at least some 30 kilometres away, we set off on bicycles to check our registration status. Upon entering Kisii town and meeting people here and there, we got wind that Mr. Grounds was back. Oh, what elation, excitement and confidence we gained for our mission! I rode into the school a completely different person. I cannot clearly remember the fate of my two classmates that day, other than that they were not allowed back to school or class for the reasons quoted above, but they were allowed to do the exams, and that they both made it through with impressively strong Second Division passes.

On my part, I appeared before Mr. Grounds by just knocking the door and being allowed in. He was seated on his chair. But Mr. Gillespie was also there, seated at a corner of the office, facing the door!

"Peter, where have you been? What happened to you?" Mr. Grounds asked me.

"Why did you not come back?" Mr. Gillespie asked. "We asked you to come back."

"No, Sir! I was last here with my father, at your request. You told us that you would yourself call me back and produce the two Form I students who would prove that they saw me lead the strike. You never did! I just came back myself now to check on my exam registration, and I am happy to see my Principal back!"

"What happened to your bursary?" Mr. Grounds asked.

" 'They' withdrew it, Sir!" I replied.

He immediately grabbed a piece of paper and began to scribble a note. At that point, it seemed as if Mr. Gillespie did not exist in his horizon!

He looked at me and said:

"Take this letter to the District Education Board office. I want to see you here, with your box, tomorrow!"

The day after I returned, Mr. Grounds called me to his office and lamented that all the career application forms that the school had received for the year were finished. Only one was left, from East African Railways and Harbours (EAR&H). "Just complete it and give it back to me." I did and literally forgot about it as we headed for the examinations.

I joined the class for the next few days, did the exams and left with everybody when the school closed on 4th December 1960. On or around 14th December 1960, I received a letter from EAR&H, inviting me to an interview at the Railway Training School in Nairobi for the 'Trainee Clerk, Grade II' position. It was the first letter received by any student in my class that year.

The interviews lasted one full week, with English, Maths and General Knowledge papers, as well as games and athletics.

Was I blessed by the strike, or Mr. Grounds? I received an invitation from the Railway Training School (now Institute) to join the "The Railways!" That was the outcome of the only career form I had filled upon rejoining the school two weeks to the Cambridge certificate exams! I was the first member of my Kisii High School Form IV class of 1960 to proceed to Nairobi, where I had never been, for training and work. I would now be the guide of my classmates, who came in later, from January 1961, on job and career hunts. A few of us regrouped and were able to fit into the urban jungle. By that time, Mike Okeyo had long left Nairobi for the USA.

1959: Form III Open Day play. I acted as *The Prodigal Son*. I am seated centre-right.

As a Form III student at Kisii High School in 1959: Donning my first pair of shoes and stockings, bought in August 1959 during the 2nd term holidays with money from the sale of Father's favourite cow.

Kanyaluo students in 1960 at Kisii High School. I am seated in the centre.

Rachuonyo Students' Association (Kisii Branch), 1960. Chairman: Mr. Peter Amollo Odhiambo. Vice Chairman: Mr. Humphrey K. Ochieng.' Secretary: Mr. Jeckoniah Ogeda. Vice Secretary: Mr. Andrew Muga. Treasurer: Mr. Ezra Otieno Ayodo.

World "Roll Call" demonstrated at Kisii High School, 1960. President: Harrison Ouso Ocholla. General Secretary: Silas Nyamato. Vice Secretary: Chumo.

Form IV school debate, 5th March 1960 (I am seated far right). Motion: "That War is the Only Way of Settling Disputes." I opposed, and won.

Form IV school debate, 5th March 1960. Motion: "That War is the Only Way of Settling Disputes." I opposed, and won.

Strike Trek: 1st June 1960. From left to right: Mr. Daniel Mbeche Obado, Mr. Harrison Ouso Ocholla, Mr. Michael Okeyo Owuor, Mr. Jeckoniah Owiso Atang'a, Mr. Peter Amollo Odhiambo and Mr. Enos Ochieng' Obado.

3

BIRD IN HAND: A DATE WITH HIPPOCRATES OF COS

I WAS BLESSED to be selected as a Trainee Clerk, Grade IIB at the Railway School interview. Grade IIA was reserved for Asians, while Grade I was the preserve of the Whites. On this occasion for this course or training, only two of us were taken; the other one was an Asian boy from Nakuru (and, therefore, a Trainee Clerk Grade IIA). Remember this was before "Independence," in 1960-61.

When the Cambridge Certificate Examination results were announced in February 1961, I had received a First Division pass while he (my new-found Asian colleague) had gotten Division II. I appealed on these grounds for a promotion to either Grade I or Grade IIA. This was done literally automatically, to Grade IIA. By this time, the racial apartheid-type stratification had already been discredited in Kenya, despite there being, just recently, signs of escalation of racial segregation.

Soon, I was called to Mang'u High School for the Arts subjects at what was then called the "A-Level" leading to an Arts degree. When I turned that down and preferred science subjects, I was told to wait for the following academic year to be considered along with the new school leavers at that time. So, I continued to work-train with the EAR&H at their headquarters in Nairobi, in the Department of the Chief Mechanical Engineer (Mechanical), or simply CME(Mechanical).

That gave me time to window-shop and weigh other options: Ibadan in Nigeria; Leicester in the United Kingdom; Ottawa in Canada (via the Tom Mboya airlift – also known as the Kennedy airlift – which was organized by Tom Mboya and saw hundreds of East Africans gain scholarships to study in the United States of America); and India as well, through the Indian Council for Cultural Relations (ICCR) scholarship at the Indian High Commission in Nairobi, in that order.

For Leicester, the money required was way beyond the ordinary Kenyan family! I had applied to Ibadan directly myself and the money part was not clear. For ordinary school fees, a family would sell a bull and pay, year after year through high school. For this one the only options to hope for were a scholarship or other sponsorship. Either of these was conspicuously scarce! The remaining option, which was already practised in many cases was community support through mobilization and fundraising, literally like today's harambee funds drives. The difference was that the word "Harambee!" was yet to be adopted for such locally inspired mutual support. Such gatherings in many places were popularly called "TEA PARTIES." The word Harambee was already in use here and there, but its adoption as a rallying lingo came after Kenya's 'Independence,' and was popularised as national rallying mechanism by Mzee Jomo Kenyatta and Tom Mboya, and duly incorporated into the national emblem!

It is said that the word "Harambee!" was first coined and used by a community leader in Nyakach, now in Kisumu County, called Kere. Fortunately, in my larger clan of Kanyaluo, the first tea party had been held in support of a very promising and popular total orphan by the name David Oyugi Aseto in 1958/9, who soon after went to the United States of America through the historically famous Tom Mboya airlifts. The environment was fully enabling. The community was strategically well-exposed! My parents, the immediate clan and the entire community organized and held the tea party for me on 27th August 1961 under the iconic and symbolic fig trees of Omboga Schools.

The response was overwhelming, with contributions in cash and kind. Those who did not reach their self-set targets continued for many days after that date! A total of KSh. 3500/- was realized! That was good money in 1961, to say the least! I could never thank my people enough, even today! It made and still makes me very happy, ever grateful, and proud to be called **"Amollo Wuod Omboga"** (Amollo, the son of Omboga, my birthplace)!

The small exercise book in which all contributions were recorded at the tea party for my fundraiser is still with me (intact) to this day. My prayer is that my family will continue to keep it after I have gone, as a souvenir, not just for myself, but as a symbol of community goodwill and strength, whenever people join hands and work together! May God bless Kanyaluo! May He bless Kenya, Africa and the world!

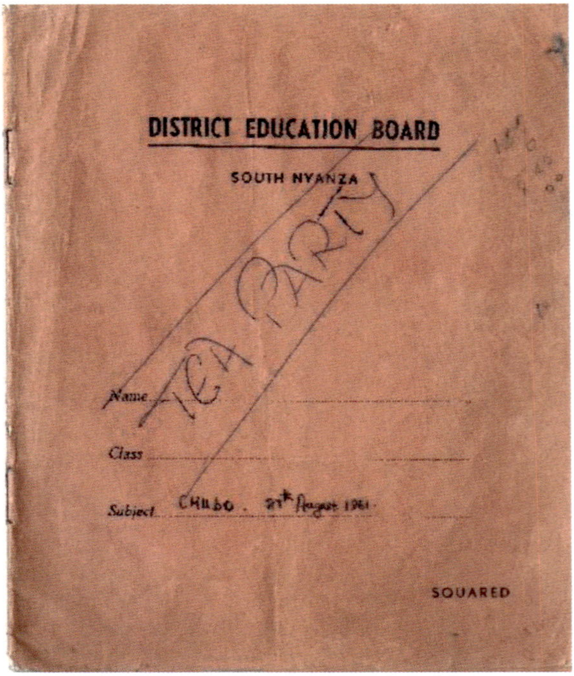

What we call 'harambee' fundraisers today were known then as tea parties. This was the second one in Kanyaluo in the 1950s and 60s. The first one was organized for the late Prof. David Oyugi Aseto. Other get-togethers, including Christmas gatherings, were also referred to as tea parties.

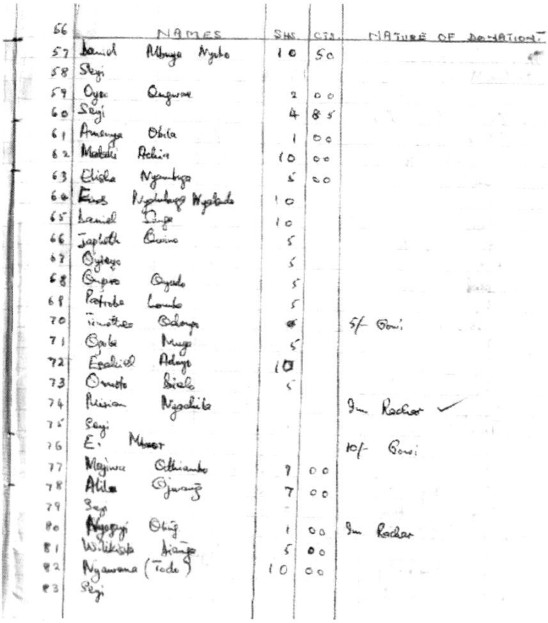

What goodwill! The generosity of these kind souls who gathered together to support my education will never be forgotten by both myself and my people!

By mid-1961, the airlift to North America was the most promising for me and many other fellow youngsters. But it was never to be. There cropped up a confusion of names for the would-be plane- loads of applicants, some listed twice in what seemed like competing organizations. It later emerged that some other politicians envied the late national politician Tom Mboya's success and wanted to organize their own airlifts for their own political mileage. They made their own lists of desperate but hopeful applicants who tried to grab any chance that presented itself and ended up double-listing. That much-anticipated flight of September 1961 flight was aborted. But the admitting institutions undertook to take us in during the next round, which was to be in 1962. For many, including myself, that meant the next academic year.

I now had yet more time to shop around while waiting for September-October 1962. First, I went back to my former bosses at the EAR&H headquarters. They knew my plans to become a medical doctor; they had seen me fundraise for that and had participated in the exercise. I explained to them the latest turn of events and requested that I be reinstated for a period of approximately one year, to September 1962, when I would fly off! I had a very good record with them, and I was not surprised when they readily took me back.

In early 1962, the Indian High Commission in Nairobi announced scholarship offers by the Government of the Republic of India for Kenyan school leavers for further studies in various institutions of higher learning in India. I applied and the interview was held somewhere in March-April 1962 for the July intake. The Indian Council for Cultural Relations (ICCR)'s scholarship was an annual event, mainly for Third-World countries, Africa included.

My application was not just a 'by-the-way.' I was intentional about mopping up every opportunity that presented itself while I waited for the flight to Ottawa, Canada. It would not matter so much if I did not succeed, but it chanced that I was selected to go over there to study Medicine. The venue for the interview was the Indian High Commission offices at Jeevan Bharati House on present-day Harambee Avenue, where it still graces the Nairobi skyline.

The panel that interviewed me for that ICCR scholarship included the late Hon. Taita arap Towett. He asked me why I did not want to go and study the 'humanities.' I was almost taken aback by the term 'humanities,' which was new to me, especially as an area of study, but I managed to give a simplistic answer that I could probably give again any day at any other interview – that with medicine, I had the liberty and the opportunity of serving humanity directly through medicine itself, without missing the chance to incorporate the celebrated

Humanities as an area of study, but even more so as an area of service!

In my whole life, I have lived exactly that kind of life – a lot of 'medicine' and a good mix of 'humanities.' Inevitably, the latter kept very close to my main training in health and medicine in general.

I shared my success at the interview with my seniors at work as soon as I received communication from the Indian High Commission a few days later. I had a lot of goodwill from the entire office of the Chief Mechanical Engineer (Mechanical) and later, once again, from the entire office of the Senior Mechanical Engineer (Works) – SME(Works), where I now worked. This was in spite of the fact that I would now be leaving the job and the country much earlier than September.

Why, with the promise of a flight to Canada in store?

With Kenya's independence within sight, the struggle for "self-rule" (a stage before full independence), had gained a lot of momentum. Unfortunately, there were still strong undercurrents of the existing rivalries in the airlift campaigns. One could not predict what might happen come that September. It was a new competition against Tom Mboya, who had initiated and championed the programme all along! Some political alignments were shaping up fast. With regard to India, here indeed was a bird in hand.

I was admitted into the Hindu College of the University of Delhi for Pre-Medicine, which would take two years and lead to admission for Medicine proper in a dedicated Medical College. This first phase was equivalent to the "A-Level" (Advanced Level) in the Cambridge University curriculum used in East Africa. I opted to grab the bird in hand and then watch how September arrangements would unfold. I planned to leave India later, anyway, cross the Atlantic Ocean, and then proceed to Canada.

It was time to bid everyone goodbye as I headed for my studies. I started with Ong'eche, my home, to bid farewell to my parents and relatives, definitely including my grandmother and friend, Bwogi Ariko

Ny'Odhuno! From there, I mounted my old bicycle to ride over to Homa Bay, nearly 30 kilometres away, to bid farewell to my senior old school friend, Mr. James Nyakira Adongo (now deceased). It was he who introduced me to his brother-in-law, Mr. George Nyawade, who was working in Mombasa at the time and would host me there before I boarded the steamship that was to ferry me over and across the Indian Ocean to Bombay (now Mumbai).

I made a separate special trip to Kericho to bid farewell to my brother-in-law and sister's family. Back in Nairobi, I had uncles, cousins and friends bid me goodbye. A few of them managed to reach the Railway Station to actually see me board the train to Mombasa, the sea-exit port.

I left Nairobi on the evening of 19th June 1962 and reached Mombasa the next morning. As I finalized my travel arrangements, I met two fellow students who were going to India for further studies on the same ICCR scholarships: Mr. Wael Maliza from Tanganyika and a Ugandan whom I never met again after we parted in Bombay. The Tanzanian was off to study Pre-Medicine, like me, in the same University of Delhi but at a different College: Delhi College at Ajmeri Gate. The Ugandan was going for a course in Commerce in another city.

We were booked in third class on the steamship MV *Kampala* and headed for Bombay via the Seychelles. My accommodation was a bunker several steps below the deck. My fellow scholars and I only met a few times, but we bonded well as fellow travellers. After about six days, the steamship docked for six hours at Mahé on the shores of the Seychelles. This was fast, in those days. It was going to take us nine days to get to Bombay, as opposed to the usual 12 days hitherto. é

We came off the ship and strolled around the town, but the time factor seemed to bear on people for fear of missing the ship, should one return late from the walk-around. I have a snap of the main mosque-like temple within the vicinity of our uncharted adventure. After the six-hour layover, we set off for Bombay. It took us a total of those nine days to reach the Bombay Harbour.

We did not wait long in Bombay. We boarded a train to Delhi that same evening for a smooth, nine-hour rumble to the capital city, Old Delhi. Again, we were in third class, but the train was much more comfortable than the steamship. We realized later that train travellers preferred a third class booking because of the comfort, which was much better than the massively crowded second class.

It was around midday when we arrived and boarded a taxi to take us to the colleges. Mine, Hindu College, was nearer along the way and I was dropped off first.

It looked quite neat. The hostels were behind the classroom block. My first impression, with the name "Hindu" and its respectable appearance, was that there was something positively original here! That was a good start – the first impression! But this was summertime, with killer heat waves. I cannot forget the 'flame' that hit my face through the taxi window as we were driven to the colleges.

As mentioned earlier, before joining a medical school, I would need to study Pre-Medicine for two years. It was exactly like East Africa's "A-Level" study in the sciences. The course included English, Mathematics, Physics, Biology and Chemistry. At Hindu College, I found other African students, but I was the only African at the time admitted for a preparatory programme for Medicine.

Mr. Maliza had proceeded to Delhi College at Ajmeri Gate for the same course. There, he found two Kenyans who were already on the same programme. One of them, Gideon Barak Agembo Okelo, had just completed and passed the Pre-Medicine examination and was already admitted to Calcutta Medical College in West Bengal State. Willie Mwaura had one more year to go. Maliza, like me, was starting the first of our two years of the same course of Pre-Medicine.

It caught my attention that Gideon Okelo had managed to condense the whole course into one year and had passed. That must have taken a lot of focus, hard work and determination. It taught me that it was doable. I instinctively applied to be permitted to join the second year class at Hindu College. I was pleased to no end when I was granted that chance, and I took the challenge in stride. It made me Willie Mwaura's year-mate in the sister College. In June-July 1963, I presented myself for Part II Pre-Med examinations. Thank God I passed!

However, for more than six months, I continued to nurse the thought of crossing the Atlantic Ocean to go to Canada. It took the determination and persuasive power of the then President of the African Students Association (ASA – India), Mr. Kintu Musoke from Uganda, who was doing his master's degree, to get me to drop the idea.

In mid-1963, all three of us – Gideon, Willie and I – found ourselves in the same University and the same Medical College in Calcutta (now Kolkata), the Calcutta Medical College of Calcutta University, whose mouthful of a name has since been changed to the Medical College and Hospital, Kolkata. Gideon was one year ahead of us, but Willie and I now sat in the same class, and did so for the ensuing five years, until 1968.

My initial culture shock had long melted away. The ice was long broken. I was now fast becoming a *nusu*-Bengali. In my fourth year at the College, I wrote an article in the College magazine entitled *Namuskar and a Lump of Ice*, in which I described the metamorphosis from a foreign student to a welcome struggler with the local language and culture! *Namuskar* (sometimes spelt *Namaskar* or *Namushkar)* is the Bengali word for the respectful first greeting, said with a person's palms held or pressed together in front of them, fingers pointing upwards – "Hallo!" "Good morning!" "*Jambo*!" The article was very well received at the college.

In class, I counted distinction passes in Human Anatomy in second year, and Preventive and Social Medicine (PSM) in my fourth year. In the terminology of the institution, these were labelled 'Honours Calls.'

However few, those who earned this score would then go *for a real and separate, competitive examination at* which one got a chance, as it were, to prove and confirm one's distinction by re-scoring a distinction grade!

Bidding farewell to Humphrey Kamire Ochieng' (left), in 1961. He was the first of our high school classmates to leave the country. He went to the UK for further training with the Forestry Department.

TOP: Bidding farewell to friends and relatives in Kericho. I am standing far right; Benson Ochieng, my brother-in-law, is second right.

LEFT: With the late Mr. James Nyakira Adongo, who introduced me to his brother-in-law in Mombasa, George Nyawade.

Homa Bay, 1962. Farewell to Mr. James Nyakira Adongo. In the background is the landmark hill, Got Asego.

Relatives and friends bid me farewell at the Nairobi Railway Station after boarding.

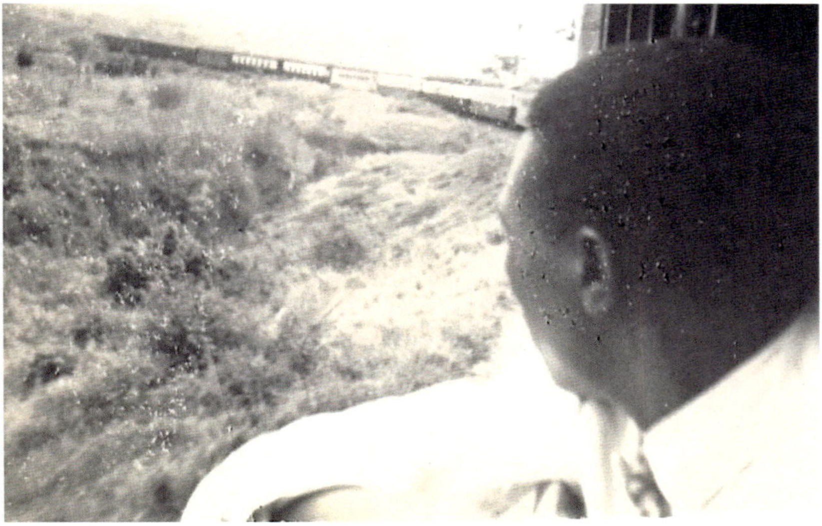

TOP: On the train to Mombasa.

LEFT: With George Nyawade (left), brother-in-law to James Nyakira Adongo. He was my host in Mombasa.

22nd June 1962, Mombasa: Lunch with George Nyawade and his friend.

22nd June 1962. Walking along Kilindini Road in Mombasa before meeting fellow travellers.

Three students on their way to India: I am in the centre, flanked by a Mr. Wael Maliza from Tanzania and a Ugandan whose name I cannot recall.

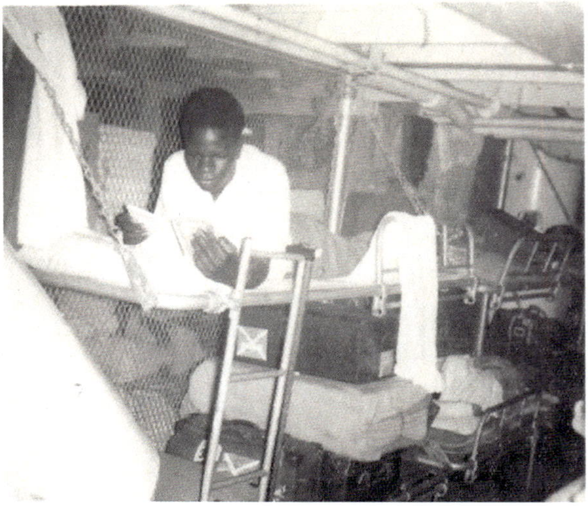

In a bunker aboard the *SS Kampala*. We left Mombasa on 24th June 1962 and docked in Bombay on 2nd July 1962.

The Mahé skyline. This was captured during a walkabout when the ship had docked at the Seychelles for 6 hours.

The Hindu College hostel front entrance.

The Pre-Medicine years: Dissecting a frog in my room.

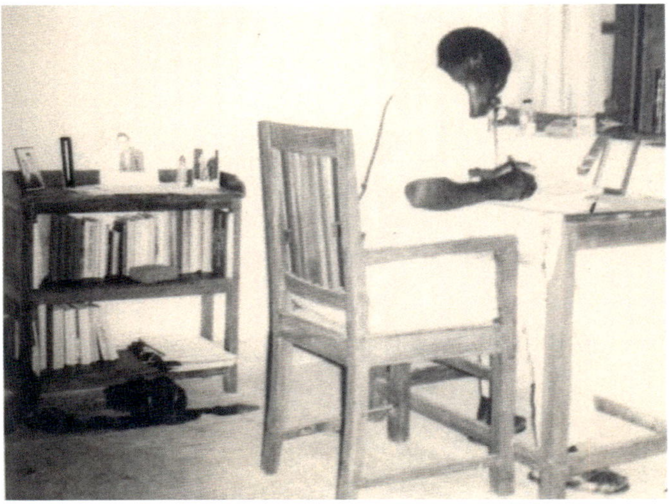

The Pre-Medicine years: Studying in my room at the Hindu College hostel.

4

ICE TO BREAK AND A SKILL TO SHARPEN

CULTURAL BARRIERS no longer mattered. There was no going back. Some rugged edges and ends reared their heads but were taken care of.

Among the foreign students, the indigenous African students stood out (aside from the African students of South Asian origin) and continued as a distinct group.

By far, the majority of the African students in India at that time were on the famous ICCR scholarships. They came from different English-speaking countries. The scholarship gave them a distinct identity, but they were also encouraged to work together in matters beyond academics, especially for their social welfare. Politics of the African continent seemed an inevitable and prominent corollary, in fact more than a corollary!

When I arrived in India in 1962, the African Students Association (ASA-India), into which I was inducted by its President, Mr. Kintu Musoke during my early days at Hindu College, was a thriving student body. Its activities were limited to itself as opposed to relating internally to the different colleges and universities where its members studied. Nevertheless, there were city-based branches of the Association in the different regions where members lived. ASA-India headquarters were either in Delhi/New Delhi or in the city where its President was based for studies. At the time, Kintu Musoke was himself a master's scholar at Delhi University.

Because the strong wave of liberation on the African continent was still ongoing, with one country after another gaining independence around that time, there was more than a mere touch of politics in the

Association. We felt very much a part of the entire process, the history and the obligation. Simply stated, we shared a lot of the inspirations, sacrifices, commitment and determination amongst ourselves and with individual African countries. We were, I believe, the most organized diaspora of Pan-Africanism at the time.

Recall my simplistic reply to the late Taita Arap Towett's question from the interview panel – that in a course like Medicine, there was science, medicine and the humanities, all wrapped up in one! Think about it: Indeed, I was right! Or was I?

The eventual dynamic was that I was able to be involved in all three (medicine, science and the humanities), within the realm of student activities curricular, co-curricular and extra-curricular with notable political literacy, but with a calculated avoidance of career politics, especially as it unfolded on the African continent.

There were only about 300 African students scattered all over India at that time, literally all of whom were on the ICCR Scholarships. There was a smaller number of South Asian-origin students from Africa, especially from East Africa. Nearly all of them were self-sponsored. The two groups did not interact in any substantial way, officially or otherwise; there was even an undeclared tension between them.

I was elected the ASA Secretary-General in my fourth year at the medical school (1967), and then President in my final year of undergraduate medical education in 1968. Prior to that, while in my third year of medical school, I had been elected Secretary-General of a subsidiary, the Kenya African Students Association (KASA – India), with [future Professor] Samson Kegengo Ongeri, also in medical school but 1400 kilometres away, as my President. The KASA election took place at a general conference held in Bombay, where Prof. Ongeri, who would soon return to Kenya, was spending his final year at the Grant Medical College, Bombay.

At the ASA, we agitated for the release of Nelson Mandela through a publication we called the *South African Tribune*, of which I was the first and the last editor. ASA's regular annual publication was called *African Youth*. We had, in our own way, joined the war against apartheid and published the *South African Tribune* to pile additional pressure on the vile system from our own 'front.'

Under my watch, we continued our annual conferences and liaised a great deal with embassies and high commissions of African countries which already had offices in India, particularly Tanzania, Egypt and later Kenya.

In one memorable incident, we became locked in a near-confrontation with our hosts, the Indian Government itself. A Mr. Kamal Choudhry, an Indian teacher based in Uganda who doubled as an artist, had staged an art exhibition of his paintings in an art gallery in Calcutta. The exhibition was about Africans and their culture.

There was a sizeable number of African students in Calcutta. We all found the paintings and drawings to be derogatory. We submitted our protests via direct verbal consultations with the authorities as well as in writing. These protests were spearheaded by the Calcutta branch of ASA-India, chaired by Mr. Gideon Barak Agembo Okelo. The branch secretary was a student from Southern Rhodesia (present-day Zimbabwe). Although I was president of ASA-India as a whole, locally in Calcutta I was simply a member of the branch.

All our appeals and protests fell on deaf ears.

The members of the ASA-India Calcutta branch eventually marched to the gallery and destroyed *all* the paintings on exhibition. I joined this local group in my capacity as a branch member.

Police were called in, intervened and bundled most of us to the police station. But one of us escaped and we worried about his whereabouts and safety. After evading the police swoop, he hurriedly rang the African Consulate in Calcutta for their intervention. It was the Egyptian Consular Attaché who came and rescued us.

A couple of months later, some of us received invitations from the Ministry of Education in New Delhi to go and discuss 'matters related to the ICCR scholarships.' From Calcutta, three of us were invited: myself, Gideon Okelo (branch chairman), and the branch secretary from S. Rhodesia. The letters were personalized, without addressing our ASA-India offices. My all-India ASA Secretary-General was based in Poona. When I checked with him, I found out that he had not been invited, but I told him to join me in New Delhi anyway. I also alerted our New Delhi-based Liaison Officer to join me. I had smelt a rat!

Without knowing who else might have been invited from the other cities, I told everyone else to let me go with just the latter two. But whereas the Calcutta branch chairman agreed to stay back, his secretary refused; he felt that having been recognized and honoured by none other than the Ministry of Education of the Indian Republic, he had a right to be there, and I had no right to – and could not and would not – stop him. At that point, I told him that I had no problem with him enjoying the trip, but he would be on his own. I would deal with all ASA-India issues myself, assisted only by the colleagues I had mobilized. He would only be in attendance to complete his joyride and not utter a word, because it was a matter that went beyond a single branch.

We arrived in New Delhi separately and I quickly consulted with the Secretary-General and Liaison Officer. We were unable to so much as guess the reason for the selective invitations. But of course, to me, the rat was still smelling.

Within the sprawling and complex ministerial-government block, we were conducted through several long corridors, up and into a large boardroom with a long oval table. On one side of that table there were seated a number of people. We were welcomed to sit on the opposite side. Every one of them was introduced to us as tea was served.

They were Ministers and representatives of Education, Home Affairs and Security, Foreign Affairs and I think Finance, and others.

The agenda was then tabled by the Home Affairs chief – BANG!

"We invited you here because of the episode in Calcutta where some paintings were destroyed."

A palpable, pin-drop silence fell in and on the room like a cloak. Out of the corner of my eye, I saw my Rhodesian joyrider shrink and freeze. He remained in a trance to the end. The meeting was far from a prestigious recognition to enjoy, as he had assumed. If he did not shed a drop of sweat, his body language spoke it all. The matter never came up later for any discussion between us. There were enough lessons learnt and I was content to leave it at that.

As we all sat there silently, we were told off and threatened with cancellation of scholarships and deportation in a proper government dress-down.

I pushed my tea away and did the rest of the talking from our side of the table. I said that in the spirit of the cultural relations between India and Africa that had formed the foundation of the friendship between the two, *and* the scholarships, the Calcutta paintings were in such terribly bad taste that they threatened the partnership and friendship between the African continent and the Asian subcontinent. The peaceful protests by our Calcutta branch had fallen on deaf ears, I informed the government officials. The officials at the gallery and the state offices of the West Bengal government had ignored our Calcutta branch appeals and pleas. I spoke on behalf of all African students in India, I continued, and I had first-hand knowledge of the episode, because, coincidentally, I was a member of the Calcutta branch itself.

Then came the ultimatum from their end: **"Please ensure that none of your members *ever* do such a thing again."**

"Yes, Sir, I shall do that," I responded, "and I can give my word, on behalf of all of us, that we shall not do it again, ***provided,*** with all due respect, that you also make sure that the likes of Choudhry ***do not* ever again** insult the African continent and her people. Without that assurance, my undertaking is null and void!"

Without further serious discussion, the meeting ended with loose-ended niceties. My rebel branch secretary from Zimbabwe never uttered a word until his branch term of office expired.

I detail this here because from high school, through college and to date, for whatever reason, people always thought that I would leave medicine and join politics. Those who have tried to genuinely understand me know that I was never going to join career politics. Whatever else I have done outside medicine has been more of social involvement in the environment in which I live and work, than beyond. Career politics is polluted and complicated by ill-understood, unproductive and counter-productive power dynamics, many times to the detriment of the people and of the entire African continent. The other reason for detailing that story is the nascent power play and unbridled self-serving disunity among African leaders who are literally hell-bent on dismembering the continent from both within and without; and how early this seed germinates in our generations at very youthful ages!

It must, however, be noted that being professional in a seemingly non-political field does not – and should never – be misconstrued to mean that one must be apolitical, both socially and historically.

I participated in several additional extra-cum-co-curricular activities prior to and after KASA and ASA.

Having long abandoned the idea of returning home to proceed to North America or crossing the Atlantic Ocean from the Orient, thanks to Kintu Musoke's intervention and persuasion, I had continued to keep in touch with events back home in Kenya. I subscribed to a new, highly intellectual publication, the *East Africa Journal*, edited by the late Odinge Odera and others before and after him, including Professor Bethwell Allan Ogot.

In 1964, the journal organized an essay competition on the theme of *East Africa's Greatest Problem* for senior high school (A-Level) students and above. I had just completed my Pre-Medicine course in mid-1963 and thought I qualified to enter into the competition.

This was during the immediate post-Independence period in East Africa. Just like today, the period was coloured with buzz words, such as the "reconstruction of Africa" and its individual countries and the elimination of problems like poverty, disease and ignorance, chorused loudly, like Sabbath and Sunday School lessons combined!

The winner of the essay contest, the late (then yet to be) history Professor Elisha Atieno Odhiambo, approached his essay from that angle.

My approach was different. My thesis was that East Africa's greatest problem was the state of mind – the attitude – of the people towards issues that mattered for reconstruction, development and prosperity.

We were already exhibiting signs of a class society. There was a cheap, self-acclaimed mentality akin to the much hyped "been-to" attitude in West Africa. Having observed the Indian caste system, I reasoned that however educated or wealthy one was, his or her state of mind mattered more. We were just emerging from the sensitivities of *Mzungu*'s "divide and rule" and we needed to be together in our mental frames: our perceptions, perspectives, attitudes and commitment.

I did not know how many we were, but it seemed that there had been many entrants. I was awarded fourth place in the competition and was mentioned among the top ten. I bet this problem still persists today, with highly educated, often destitute people, say professionals, lamely mingling with, or overwhelmed and over-shadowed by millionaires and billionaires!

Several years later, there also came an ICCR-sponsored essay contest for all African students about Indo-African relations. At that time, I was doing my internship at Calcutta Medical College. I took part and won second place, after a Nigerian journalist studying elsewhere. That took the Nigerian in Delhi and me from Calcutta to the capital, New Delhi, to receive the awards. Mine was a briefcase, which I really cherished!

In New Delhi, I was hosted by the Kenyan High Commissioner to India, H.E. Leo Odero and his family. It was my first time to ever appear on television. The Nigerian seemed at ease and unruffled. But it was something great for me – a medical doctor rubbing shoulders with 'a man of letters,' above many others who took part in that essay contest.

To briefly mention other activities:

1. In my second year, I wrote an article for the East African Journal, which was published as a letter to the editor, entitled *Is Witchcraft Psychiatry?*
2. In our third year, I was elected a class representative in the Students' Union. In the same year, I took part in - and won - a college debate in memory of a brilliant medical doctor, Dr. Avijit Guha, who was an alumnus and had died young. My prize consisted of the 1962 edition of the two volumes of *Pye's Surgical Handicrafts*, which I cherish to date. Some of my later senior students simplistically thought it was outdated, because of the year it was first published, 1890. But that was the 1962 edition. It is still in print, being edited and updated! This is a telling indictment on our perception and attitudes, even toward poverty, disease and ignorance – especially ignorance! The book is packed with fundamental basics and principles of the 'practice of surgery,' which is an examinable paper in many, if not all, medical schools! In the very middle of this digital era, that is, at the contemporary time of this writing, one of my former students, now a Professor and an administrator, eager to condemn the book to oblivion upon seeing my reference, ***googled*** **"Pye's Surgical Handicrafts"** and found a very recent edition of the same book, still in print as I write, and being updated as so-called "*modern surgery*" marches on! I said nothing, because I noticed his attitude was not that positive or progressive for surgical education, practice, evolution and progression, not to talk of innovation, where basics are not just mandatory, but critical! There are variants and variations of ignorance! Obviously, he had not read *all* the books, in spite of his access to the computer and the digital world.

3. I took part in other debates, including inter-college, inter-university, intra-city, and all-India inter-university debates, which I also won. Some motions were typically Indian, e.g. 'That migration should be liberalized,' 'That Hindi should be the national language of India,' etc.
4. I was co-opted briefly into the main Students' Union of the College.
5. I wrote yet another paper entitled "*Science, Leisure and Common Sense*," for the students' magazine. In this one, I highlighted the inevitable, almost natural process of simplification and routinization of inventions and innovations in human life for implementation and applications. I think that it still makes quite some sense!

Outside the academic institutions, towards the end of my stay in India, I was invited to participate in a debate organized by a body called **"Friends' Forum."** I obliged!

Sometime in the first half of 1969, an organization known as *Experiment in International Living* (which I later found also existed in Kenya when I returned home), invited foreign students to a get-together where there would be cross-cultural interactions. I was among the few African students who were invited. I was, by that time, very much at home with the people and the place! Little did I know, this would turn out to be the beginning of a new chapter in my life!

With Ambassador Manuel Stolik at the Cuban Embassy on 26th July 1962. This was the very first reception I attended, only three weeks after arriving in India.

1964: The 13th Annual Conference of ASA-India in Delhi. We are introduced to the guest of honour, the Vice President of India, at the inauguration. At the time I was the chairman of the Calcutta branch of ASA-India (I am standing second left).

The 13th Annual Conference of ASA-India in Delhi; the inauguration on 26th December 1964. I am seated far left.

ASA-India, 1967: I am flanked by Vice President, Mr.Chidobel Omeh (right), from Nigeria and Secretary Lutaya Kamya from Uganda.

With Vice President Omeh (right).

Calcutta University Institute

CERTIFICATE OF HONOUR

This is to Certify that Sri Peter Amolla Odhiambo

representing Calcutta Medical College in the

Annual Inter-Collegiate Debate Competition for the

Session 1966-67 secured position as follows :

SUBJECT	POSITION
English	first

President
Section.

Under Secretary
Section.

Hony. Dy. Secretary
Calcutta University Institute.

President
Calcutta University Institute.

Hony. Secretary
Calcutta University Institute

The certificate, now with frayed edges, awarded after one of my debates in India.

TOP AND BOTTOM: 1966: Commemorating my first debate in India, which I won. I received a trophy and two textbooks, *Pye's Surgical Handicrafts* Volumes I and II.

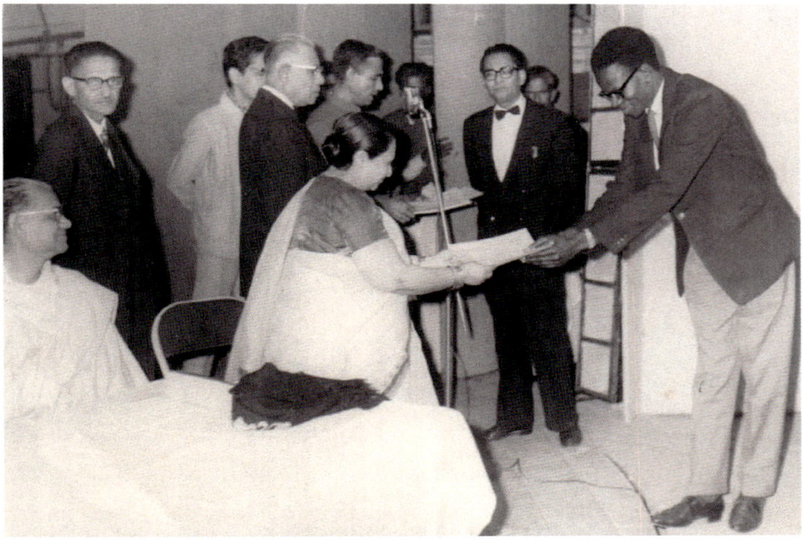

1967: The All-Indian Inter-University Debate at Jadavpur University. I represented both Calcutta Medical College and the University of Calcutta.

1969: Speaking at a Friends Forum gathering.

5

"KWAHERI YA KUONANA!" EXIT INDIA: HOME AGAIN

AT THE COCKTAIL reception hosted by *Experiment in International Living*, there was an elderly lady who became very interested in me after learning at introductions that I was a newly qualified medical doctor from the prestigious **'Great Medical College of the East,'** which, having been founded in 1835, was more than 130 years old at the time.

Her name was Mrs. Basu, and she knew several of my teachers at the Medical College Hospital (MCH). She asked who among them I considered my favourite, as well as who I thought was the best. She became even more interested when I gave the obvious answer – Dr. Pasupati Bose, Chairman of Anatomy, referred to by everybody as P. Bose, as few knew his first name.

"You must come home and meet my husband!" She exclaimed. He was a heart surgeon at the Calcutta Post-graduate SSKM Hospital. He was India's first heart surgeon, and would be very happy to see me. I later learnt that he had a contemporary in Bombay. I honoured her request and followed her directions to their home at around 5 p.m. a couple of days later. I had to wait, however, as he was delayed at the hospital.

When Professor Ajit Kumar Basu finally arrived after 6 p.m. (tall and elegant, betraying no sign of fatigue from the operating theatre), he told me that he had just performed a porta-caval anastomosis for portal hypertension. Anatomy was still ringing in my head! After my questions and comments, which included a tour of that anatomy, surgical anatomy and surgical technique, he said, to my surprised pleasure: "Why don't you come and work with me? We can work out a stipend for your upkeep, now that your (ICCR) scholarship is over!" This was around June/July 1969. I had just completed my internship at the MCH, which was a six-month rotating internship. My undergraduate course, for which I received the MBBS degree, had ended in December 1968.

So, I did. He was highly respected and feared almost in equal measure, and I became his new kid on the block.

He assisted me to register for the awesome Master of Surgery degree of India at the Calcutta University. He also obtained for me a small research grant from the Hoechst medical company to undertake a clinical trial on their new intravenous plasma volume expander, *Haemaccel*. I completed the first part of the study about the assessment of blood loss during surgical operations and published it in the *Postgraduate Hospital Bulletin*. I proceeded to complete the main clinical trial and prepared a paper for presentation at an all-India conference in Bombay.

Prof. Ajit Kumar Basu

With Mrs. A.K.Basu in February 1992 when I paid her a visit (her two sons were not at home - one was in the US, the other was out of the house). I was in India at the time for the All-India Thoracic and Cardiovascular Conference in Calcutta which was held at the Birla Heart Institute. Prof. Basu had passed away some years prior (1986).

In my discussion in that second paper, having seen the need for intravascular plasma volume support and expansion, I proposed that the oxygen-carrying capacity of the red blood corpuscles could also be boosted if we found a way of carrying and delivering oxygen to the hypovolaemic intra-vascular compartment at the same time. The chemical that easily came to my mind was potassium tetrachloride, which has a high affinity for oxygen. Highly toxic (as it is), or not, the rest would be a matter of science and clinical trials. I did not get to present that paper, because the date clashed with my booked departure from India.

To everybody's surprise, I left India rather abruptly, without doing Part I of the MS (Master of Surgery) degree programme and, sadly, without attending the Bombay conference.

Kenya's first High Commissioner to India was the charismatic and ever cheerful diplomat, H. E. Leo Odero. He had visited Calcutta to check on his people (Kenyans) there, and had accommodated me in New Delhi when I went to receive my prize for the essay contest. In his own assessment, he thought that I was a potential, if not ready-made, brain-drain! I seemed very comfortable, what with an untouchable patron and sponsor, not even to talk of my foster-mother, among the many friends, individuals and families! He reckoned that I might not return home that soon. The solution was to intervene in the short run rather than face me later. He hatched out a strategy, flew down to Calcutta and gave me "government orders" that I was wanted back home immediately. Coincidentally, my parents were ailing a little too frequently. That, more than the orders, made me decide to return home.

I had told him that it did not make sense to me because when I felt patriotic and had wanted to return home and do part of my internship in Kenya, the Ministry of Health at first agreed, but soon wrote to say that I should not return until and unless I completed all of my internship in India. With professional and career opportunities knocking, even just sitting there at my door, I told myself that they were not in any overwhelming need for medical manpower. So, I said once again to myself: "*Maliza kwanza!*" meaning "Complete the present task first!"

The other part was that H.E. Leo Odero was a very nice person; a gentleman 'par excellence.' As High Commissioner, he had looked after us Kenyans in India very well. I could not let him down, particularly since his voice 'represented' that of the government.

And so it was that I bid Calcutta goodbye to "go back to Kenya, my country..." as David Amunga had proclaimed in his *Goodbye to America* song, even though he himself had not by then visited, let alone studied or worked, there!

The Banerjees (family friends) were silently devastated; so was the budding author Biplab (founder of *Celluloid* magazine, a publication parallel to our *South African Tribune*), and the promoters of the last minute debate from "Friends Forum," Alpana Gupta (later Ghosh) and Ratna Sen.

Biplab Bhusan Basu, the last friend to bid me farewell from Calcutta on 24th February 1971. Surprisingly, we did not reconnect! At the time, he had ventured into producing a Bengali and English publication called *Celluloid*.

I **flew back** to Nairobi on 28th February 1971, eight years and eight months after I had **sailed off** on the *SS Kampala* from Mombasa to Bombay, and then journeyed further on to Delhi and to Kolkata ('new' spelling for Calcutta). But my unstoppable path to heart surgery had just begun.

With prior communication, I was posted to the Kenyatta National Hospital (KNH) for six months for an 'orientational internship' in internal medicine before registration by the Medical Practitioners and Dentists Board of Kenya as a Medical Officer. It was partly a requirement, but even more so, I requested it in order to orientate and domesticate myself through internal medicine only. I had done two years of surgery already and there was no reason to repeat a surgical internship. The Ministry of Health understood, recognized and approved my case.

Come September 1971, I was posted to Murang'a District Hospital. I did not have to negotiate. It was normal posting, the way I took it. The surgeon there, the late Dr. (later Professor) Jeshrani had just left to complete his post-graduate surgical training at the Makerere Medical School. So, I suddenly became both a Medical Officer and a District Surgeon of sorts. The Medical Officer of Health at the time, Dr. Popat, felt very relieved by my arrival, which would enable him to pay more attention to his administrative duties. Soon enough, he also left to go into private practice. I remained alone!

Because of some political pressure and a gross shortage of doctors across the country, the Ministry of Health rushed to Murang'a to transfer and deploy me elsewhere, not knowing that there was only one doctor (myself) at the hospital at the time. Mr. Simon Shitemi (a Deputy Secretary at Afya House), arrived and found me working alone, but somehow coping, in spite of a bout of common cold! He let me be and proceeded with his 'hunting safari' to Kerugoya. I heard him tell that story a few times later.

My first operation in Murang'a was a caesarean section, which I had not done before. I was, however, familiar with the pelvis and abdomen. The medical assistants and theatre nurses, who had seen generations of doctors come and go, and knew something of good surgical operations, literally marvelled at my unintimidated handling of the procedure. I would perform other bigger operations during the next nine months of my stint at Murang'a, including a lumbar sympathectomy for Buerger's disease in a smoker with blocked leg arteries, headed for amputation but saved by that operation. The Nairobi surgical stalwart, Mr. Roy Miller, wondered who this Odhiambo was, who was "doing more than he knows." It was a very special operation that general surgeons found daunting. In the ensuing years, with the development of scientific basis of vascular surgery, this procedure was relegated to a distant background and literally abandoned; but not before the newly contracted vascular surgeon and new Chairman of the University Department of Surgery at KNH, Mr. P. Dhall and I later argued in my postgraduate class about its merits and circumstantial indications for the procedure 'out there' in parts of the country lacking in 'surgical luxuries,' let alone surgical capacity. I had learnt something about **"limb salvage!"** I applied the know-how. My Murang'a theatre team, just like the overall hospital nursing team, was great – we bonded well, we worked hard, and we helped a great deal.

Murang'a became almost like my second home; even my mother came to visit me there, travelling well over 500 kilometres! On the side, I chaired a committee that we had formed in town to fundraise for the proposed Ramogi Institute of Advanced Technology (RIAT). Who could ever have guessed or predicted that I would one day be appointed Chairman of the Board of Governors, more than four decades later, in 2014, even as George Ojijo and his band put it down in song and music for posterity!

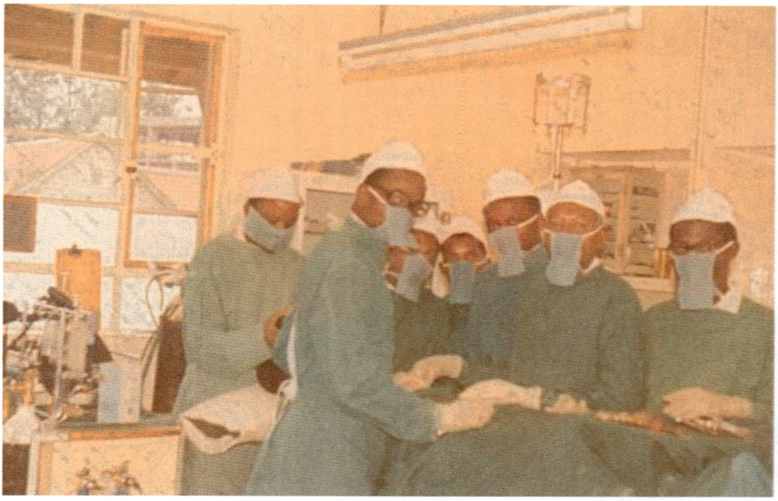

With a surgical team at Murang'a (I am second left): Operating under a tube light.

With the team after the operation. I am standing third right.

With a team at Murang'a. I am standing far left.

Soon, it was time for me to complete my general surgical training and then go full blast for heart surgery. Surgical training in Kenya at the time meant local exposure and then proceeding to the United Kingdom for examinations at any one of the Royal Colleges of Surgeons in England, Scotland or Ireland. The successful surgeon would then become a Fellow of the Royal Colleges of Surgeons, or FRCS.

The next natural step for me was to be selected for that pathway, return to KNH and join a postgraduate batch, earmarked for further overseas training and qualification.

At that very time, the Medical School of the University of Nairobi had embarked on initial steps to start a post-graduate medical training as an essential and integral programme for development and advancement of surgery and other disciplines locally. At the KNH, there was already a batch of doctors lined up for the overseas trip, but the University of Nairobi programme at the Faculty of Medicine (as the School of Medicine was known then) was also being fast-tracked. That batch of doctors ended up being the first class of the local programme, dubbed Master of Medicine (M. Med.), which became the generic degree in the major disciplines of internal medicine, surgery, obstetrics and gynaecology, paediatrics, pathology and public (community) health. They were destined to be degrees and not fellowships or other diplomas like the fellowships of the Royal Colleges of the United Kingdom (England, Edinburgh, Glasgow and Northern Ireland).

My batch was the second class in the academic year 1972-73. There were fifteen of us. At the Part I exam the following year, 1973, only three of us passed! In no time, one (Dr. Kapasi) left for Canada to pursue the rest of his surgical training and work out there. The second one, Dr. (now Professor) Joseph Samuel Oliech left on his own arrangements for further surgical training in Britain. That left me alone as the only student in the second 'batch' class!

On the grounds that I had already had a good amount of surgical exposure before, I pleaded with the Faculty Medicine, through the

Department of Surgery, to permit me to skip that year and join the first batch class of three doctors! They were Doctors Gerishom Mudanya Sande, Benjamin S. Mbindyo and Peter Ochola Abila, all deceased in different years since then. Thankfully, I was allowed to join them. I now belonged to the first batch of four in the M.Med. (Surgery) Part II Class. We did the examinations in August 1975. All of us passed. I received a second prize from Ciba-Geigy, one of the collaborating pharmaceutical firms.

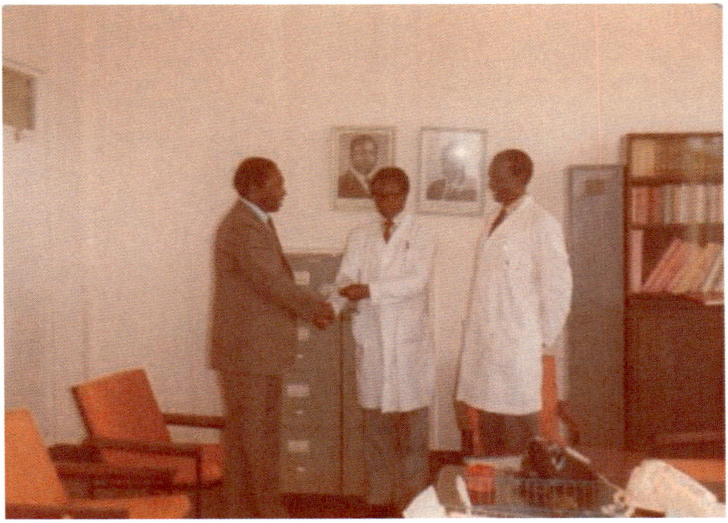

1975: Receiving the second place Ciba-Geigy prize for my M.Med (Surg.) degree, Nairobi. The late Dr. Peter Ocholla Abila won the first place prize. After this I branched off into thoracic and cardiovascular surgery (actually, it was more like a return to the specialty I had started in Calcutta).

6

HUNTING FOR THE CANCER BUG

THE GREEKS HAD SAID IT – "The eyes do not see what the mind does not know."

But here we wanted to see what we did not know! Working in Kisumu and being keen to 'see' (observe and document), Dr. Nazir Ahmed had made it seem like cancer of the oesophagus (gullet) was a disease affecting the lake region dwellers only, the 'fish-eaters.' He documented what he came across very well and published his papers in the East African Medical Journal.[1] Although he did not as much as state it, he created the impression that this was a disease of the Luos, particularly, but also the Luhyas, the two main communities residing in Western Kenya around Lake Victoria. To many subsequent 'secondary' (second-hand) observers, it must have seemed like the disease came from inside the Lake itself. How misleading! Nazir Ahmed's papers were published mostly in the 1960s.

Time passed.

I was sitting at my Dean's desk in the early 1990s when, it being known that I was a thoracic and cardiovascular surgeon, a young man walked in with a Ph.D. thesis proposal. The main objective was to find out what was wrong with the lake people, particularly the Luos! Obviously, he (my visitor) had not read our paper, which I shall describe shortly. He was from the Kenya Medical Research Institute (KEMRI). I sat him down and we talked. I walked him through some of the relevant issues and possibilities. We critiqued Nazir Ahmed, and I drew his attention to our research paper from the medical school.

I never heard of either the student or the proposal again. If it was for science, he would have gone on anyway. But even prior to the discussion, you tasted something sour from one community to another, due for sanitization by 'science' – or pseudoscience!

Not long after that, there came reports in lay newspapers that a 'new disease,' a form of cancer, had been 'discovered' in Tenwek, an area found approximately two hours from the lake shores and located in present-day Bomet County. Could scientists and doctors please go and find out what the problem was with Tenwek and Bomet! I came across the reports, one of them by a senior medical lecturer, Professor Kihumbu Thairu, and submitted my comments. These were also published in the same newspapers.

Shortly thereafter, in the middle of my rounds at Ward 4B at KNH, a KEMRI dental surgeon and researcher walked in, accompanied by another individual.

The doctor and I knew each other well from prior interaction. He had come to recruit me to go and do research with them in Tenwek. It was my service ward round with only a few postgraduates on call, not a teaching ward round with many students and team members. I requested him to join me on the round, but saved his time by selecting and stopping only at beds with oesophageal cancer patients. I would see the rest later, including open heart patients.

Out of 36 beds, pushed by demand from an original 32 bed capacity, we counted ten patients with cancer of the oesophagus. They came from different parts of the country. I knew them, but as I introduced my science and research visitor, I asked each one to tell us by themselves where they came from. When we finished, my good friend, Dr. Mwaniki, was almost nonplussed. It must have been over a cup of tea before I saw the other patients in the ward (to complete the ward round), that I told him that what he had seen was the case with *Kenya.* It was bound to explode; it was not an exclusive monopoly of Tenwek. What had happened was that Tenwek had just created an awareness, aided by oral narrative (word of mouth) from clan to clan and from town to town over a wide area, which had woken up both its catchment of patients as well as members of the print media. More people went to Tenwek from far and wide because of the news, rather than that there was necessarily more disease or any new type of cancer in the area! The role the media played in elucidating matters on this development at the time was wanting. For researchers, these anecdotes highlight the basic principle and fact that, before embarking on (any) research, the **research question** must be ***appropriate!***

There was also a possibility of a true increase, not just statistically, but in real terms biologically, say pathologically; however, no epidemiological survey had been undertaken to affirm the case.

Today I see people who ignored – and initially fought – my clarion call against tobacco; nay, colluded with the tobacco industry behind my back, and got big rewards, all the while eloquently 'wowing' everybody by extoling the virtues of and the urgent need for cancer treatment institutes. They trampled over prevention, playing make-believe with frantic efforts for an elusive cure! Why does it sometimes look like it is fashionable to declare being a victim of cancer in languages and terminologies that betray no intention to heed counsel? There must be another bug around. Wrong priorities? Greed? Dangerous (stupid) lifestyles? Politics? Causing cancer! Think of those three: Disease. Hunger. Poverty. Which one? Cancer is not like HIV/AIDS, for which one can go public after getting help from antiretroviral treatment and live a relatively normal life, as a necessary in-built counsel.

Whatever the cause, beware!

Decades before today, 2023, the political class and members of the health profession slept when 'foreign powers' dumped radioactive substances in the north-eastern area of Kenya!

In 1975-76, the late Professors Ambrose Eric Onyango Wasunna and David Gatei received research funding from the World Health Organization (WHO) to look into the causes of cancer of the oesophagus (or gullet) – often loosely referred to as 'cancer of the throat' – specifically the kind that blocks swallowing because of the involvement or affection of the gullet itself, not the voice box, tonsils or other purely throat tissues. It is a 'new' growth (neoplasm) in the walls of the gullet (oesophagus) at different levels of its length – upper part, middle part or lower segment, divided anatomically and clinically into thirds: 'Upper,' 'Middle' and 'Lower.'

At the clinical level, one of the main problems is that patients consult doctors late - so, first of all, ***awareness*** is crucial so that they have early access to care. If, within a week - at most one month - you are compelled to escort food with water in order to swallow it, please run to the doctor. If he or she speaks of allergies or some such simple and simplistic diagnosis, you have read this book, draw the doctor's attention to this paragraph and request a referral to a chest (thoracic) surgeon or oncologist (cancer specialist).

Next to awareness is ***prevention*** - whether aware or unaware of the cause of this cancer, going along with the doctor's advice, as a search, research and investigation, often confirms the cause of the swallowing problem, although not the actual cause of the cancer itself. That helps in the treatment.

The two professors took the path of a search for the cause. They recruited two others: Dr. Donald Ochieng Orinda, a medical biochemist, and myself. I had by that time settled into the specialty that dealt with the chest (lungs, oesophagus, etc) as well as the heart and blood vessels (arteries and veins).

Our team of four decided and planned to cover as much of the country as possible by, if you will, large-scale 'sampling.' Prof. Wasunna went to the Mount Kenya region, Prof. Gatei went to the Coast, as Dr. Orinda and I went to Western Kenya (Western Province and Nyanza). Word went round and even a lady doctor from abroad, Dr. Elizabeth Rose from Transkei in South Africa, came and joined one of our trips to the Lake Victoria region.

What had been 'known' or thought was that this disease had not been encountered in human beings in the Rift Valley for a long time. 'Only' cattle had been found in the recent past by veterinarians to suffer from this form of cancer!

Dr. (later Professor) Donald Orinda and I made three trips to Western Kenya, covering parts of the then Western Province and then Siaya District. (We also visited Nyanza Provincial Hospital, present-day Jaramogi Oginga Odinga Memorial Teaching and Referral Hospital). We spoke to families, especially those recently bereaved of elderly relatives. We took samples of grain (both clean and rotten); we reached the banks of River Yala both upstream and downstream as far as we could and drew both water and vegetation. We did the same for River Nyando but this time not far away from the main road. We did not go south of the lake gulf because of limited funding.

Samples from the Coast and Mount Kenya were taken along with ours from 'Western' to the Government Chemist laboratory in Nairobi.

Then we checked parts of the country where more patients were coming from as a result of increased awareness. There was an actual observable increase in the number of patients. They came from all over Kenya, including North-Eastern Province and the Rift Valley. Demographics did not influence the scattered origins of **the new trek to KNH**. A similar trend must have been at play in the hands of Dr. Nazir Ahmed in and around Kisumu, those many years before! KEMRI, Tenwek and the media were not discovering a 'new disease' in the decade that followed![2]

From the point of view of research, science and clinical experience, it is unfortunate that we never had any more Nazir Ahmeds to talk of virtually in all specialties, except for one team, the late Prof. Jeckoniah Ndinya-Achola and a Professor Plummer from Canada who researched HIV/AIDS within Majengo Estate in Nairobi! We, the professionals, are partly to blame; the over-politicized environment in the not-too-distant past which did not enable science to grow is equally at fault.

Even as we innovate, discovery by (just) 'finding,' like the Greeks (because the mind is prepared and surroundings fertile), and 'finding out' (through strategic and structured scientific methodology) are almost the exception, if not too scarce, in our midst!

For cancer of the oesophagus, two points emerged from our research:

1. The disease is a scourge of the whole country, and is not limited to just Western Kenya.
2. We still do not have concrete evidence of the cause of the scourge, but when your doctor shouts "Thief!" in medicine, even in medical terms, for public awareness, primary health care, public health and lifestyle dangers, it means tobacco, alcohol, bad ("junk") diet, radioactive and other pollutions, or other known carcinogens.

Beware and take ***very good care!***

Run for your Life!

Do your part to help science, medicine, the doctor, your neighbour and yourself!

1. Ahmed N. Geographical Incidence of Oesophageal Cancer in West Kenya. *East African Medical Journal.* 1966 Jul;43(7):235–248.

2. Gatei DG, Odhiambo PA, Orinda DA, Muruka FJ, Wasunna A. Retrospective Study of Carcinoma of the Esophagus in Kenya. *Cancer Research.* 1978;38(2):303–307.

Collecting water samples

At the bridge over River Yala. Dr.(now Prof.) Donald Ochieng' Orinda, myself and UoN driver George.

A roadside home near Mbale, in what is now Vihiga County. Any crop contamination?

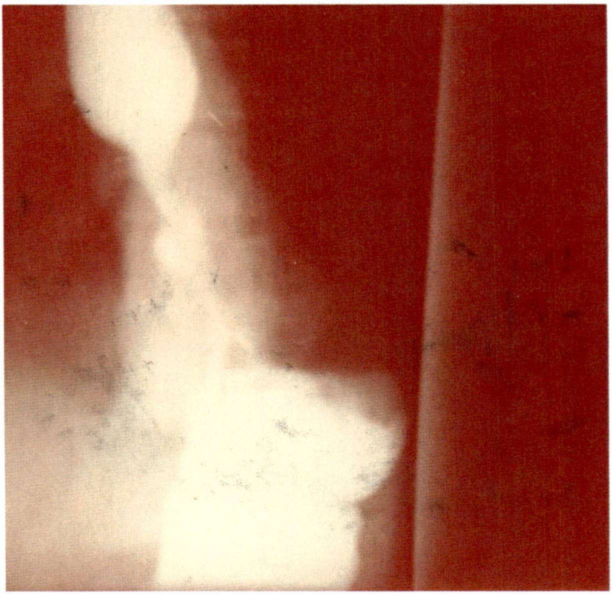

A barium swallow of a 45 year-old patient at Nyanza Provincial Hospital (now the Jaramogi Oginga Odinga Memorial Teaching and Referral Hospital).

7
STARTING A FAMILY

I MARRIED MORE THAN ONCE. Ordinarily that is called polygamy. But if it is not consciously and deliberately planned, then it is not the traditional polygamy which is based on and perpetuated by culture. Nor is it the 'come we stay' of modern youth and non-youth! It is also not what David Maillu called the 'serial polygamy' of Western (Euro-American) communities.

As an introductory passing but crucial remark, I must start by saying that I was not going to marry anyone while my mother still lived in an old temporary house. Not because of any complex, just that she deserved better. My four younger brothers agreed with me that we had to build a permanent house for our mother before pursuing any other personal undertakings. Our youngest two brothers were still in primary school. It would take us more than two years.

As the eldest son of the home, I had to marry and 'open the way' for Jacob and Abel as soon as I could. My 'delay' almost became an issue, but I did not bother making a fuss when they both went ahead and married in modified customary ways ahead of me. Our father took it all in his stride and let things roll on under his close watch, with but a token effort to harmonize strict cultural norms and somewhat liberal Christian spiritual cleansing – pray over it and go! My turn finally came, with a formal, but also modified, interdenominational church wedding, after the completion of both Mum's house and my postgraduate studies in general surgery at the University of Nairobi. Our other houses followed, starting with my second 'home-hut,' or *Simba* in Dholuo, quite distinct from the Kiswahili word for lion.

I met Florence Atala Ule Adoko (Ugandan) in September 1974 at the Mwadui Hospital of the Williamson Diamonds complex in Shinyanga, Northern Tanzania. She was a final-year medical student doing her elective term at that hospital. I had gone to relieve the consultant surgeon in charge of the hospital, the late Mr. Ben Obonyo, FRCS, an Acholi from Northern Uganda. He had been a lecturer in the Department of Surgery, University of Nairobi, but had resigned and taken a job with the Williamson Diamond Mines Hospital. He was due to take leave and needed a surgeon to relieve him. He was very good friends with Dr. (soon to be Professor) Edwin Knight from Jamaica, a cardiothoracic surgeon who at that time was Chairman of the Department of Surgery in Nairobi. There were four of us about to start our final year in the Master of Medicine (M. Med) in the Surgery programme. He asked me to help because there was one issue or another with the other fellow surgical trainees.

I went to Mwadui for the month. Sometime in 1975, I was accompanied by a cousin and friend of mine, Harrison Ouso Ocholla, who covered East and Central Africa with his job at M/S Black and Decker company, to visit Florence's family. He travelled around East Africa quite a bit for work, so it was easy for him to accompany me. To save costs, we timed the trip to overlap with job obligations he had in Dar-es-Salaam. He flew down a day or two ahead of me.

Florence lived with her eldest brother, Naphlim Akena Adoko. Because of their close familial connection to Milton Obote, who had been deposed by Idi Amin, they had fled Uganda (Mr. Akena Adoko himself had been Uganda's first Attorney General. He was, with his cousin, the ousted former President Milton Obote, one of Idi Amin's prime targets for elimination, along with many other marked Ugandans). They were in Mwadui as refugees, courtesy of Tanzanian hospitality through their then President, Julius Nyerere. It was to Naphlim Akena, as the present head of the family, that we had to pay the cultural visitation to and ask for the hand of his youngest sister marriage. Their father, ex-Paramount Chief Yakobo Adoko, was still alive back home in Uganda. We met many of her people that evening at a reception specifically put together for us, the in-laws-to-be.

That done, she continued and completed her medical degree at the end of 1975. The first medical degree known as MBChB in Kenya and Uganda is designated as MD in Tanzania. She applied for an internship at KNH, was accepted, and completed it in 1976. We planned a simple wedding for later that year. In the meantime, an opportunity presented itself for me to go for further specialization training in Britain on a scholarship from the Bowater Corporation, based in London, starting at the end of September 1976.

Tight as time was, we wedded at the Holy Family Basilica on 1st September 1976. She was fairly a more orthodox Catholic than I was a devout or rigid Seventh Day Adventist. It was an inter-denominational wedding without any ripples!

When I left for Britain on 30th September 1976, she remained with my two younger brothers, who were in primary school in Nairobi and were staying with me. Tension cropped up when she left them in the University house alone and went back to stay with her brother in Dar-es-Salaam. I struggled, with the help of my sponsors, to communicate with the University to allow them to stay in the house a little longer, while I arranged for them to stay with my other siblings and relatives within Nairobi. The University was very understanding, while the sponsors went full throttle to facilitate my would-be 'online' communications with those at home, absorbing the bills of my many international telephone calls! Upset and distressed as I was in the midst of very intense training in open heart surgery, I declared aloud (on the phone of course), that when I returned home after my training, in Britain, I would make arrangements to marry afresh! Then I took a very deep breath to refocus and settled back into my mission abroad!

On 24th December 1976, she landed in London, unannounced, to join me. On that very day, every year, everything out there in Britain comes to a standstill because of Christmas! I had to rush before the shops closed for me to get anything edible at all for the ensuing days. Thank God I was able to get some groceries to tide us through the next two days up to 27th December, when businesses would be back, even if not to normal levels.

I spent six months at Guy's Hospital for my training in cardiac and general thoracic surgery. Unfortunately, it was around that time that I misplaced my wedding ring in the changing room of the operating theatres. I never found it! Perhaps it was a metaphor for a second wedding to theatre. I never went for another.

The next six months were dedicated to vascular surgery at Charing Cross Hospital, also in London. That marked the end of my scholarship, but then there came an advertisement for a "Senior Registrar" post in Cardiff, Wales. My teacher, Mr. Alan Yates (FRCS) of Guy's Hospital, assisted with refereeing my application. Mr. Ian Gillespie of the University Hospital of Wales took me on, this time to focus on general thoracic surgery and some of the other two sub-specialties, cardiac and peripheral vascular surgery. That meant spending time nearer the Welsh coal mines at the Llandough (pronounced '*Landock*') Hospital while being able to join the University Hospital of Wales in the city centre of Cardiff for shift duties and calls.

Florence and I went through all that time together as I resisted any more distractions. In Kenya, my two brothers were somewhat settled, though one had had to go back home to Karachuonyo, Homa Bay District. When I returned to Kenya in mid-December 1978, they returned to stay with me and completed their secondary school education.

Towards the end of my contract with the University Hospital of Wales, my Departmental Chairman in Nairobi, Prof. Ambrose Wasunna, informed me of yet another opening. There was an opportunity to gain even more training and experience at the McGill University in Montreal, Canada – could I go? Florence returned home in February 1978 as I waited to cross the Atlantic ocean after the expiry of my contract in Cardiff.

I left for Montreal in June 1978 and stayed there until December 1978, this time as a visiting lecturer from the University of Nairobi. I returned home on 16th December 1978. Earlier in that same year, there had come a lot of politics surrounding the issue of open heart surgery in Kenya. This is in my other book, *The History of Heart Surgery in Kenya.*

By July 1979, as I moved to start *MEDICOM – The African Journal of Hospital and Scientific Medicine*, tension cropped up once more in my marriage. This was just before the birth of our first son, Michael. Florence moved out to stay with her sister, Esther - who was also based in Nairobi and was working with the East African Examination Council - until Michael was born that September. She returned with him to the house after he was born.

In mid-1980, we officially and legally separated. My parents and uncles came to help, but nothing worked. We remained separated until 1985.

In 1982, I met a young student of nursing at the Kenya Medical Training College (KMTC) School of Nursing, which is on the same KNH campus as the School of Medicine: another Florence. We followed all relevant cultural formalities and went to Eldoret (where her father had a bookshop) for introductions. All went well until our friendship was recognized by both families, especially after completing her Kenya Registered Nurse (KRN) course.

Another two or so years passed. In late 1984, the senior Florence responded to *Wazee's* pleas. That added new emotions in the equation, but the younger Florence and I had already had a baby girl in June of 1985. So now I had two spouses. Not like polygamy in the traditional African cultural setting, but yet also not quite an urban polygamous arrangement. I remained conscious of my fatherly responsibilities and was 'Dad' to my children!

As always, when the barrier of monogamy is broken there may be no other barriers. That is what happened. The very first lady in whom I was interested in 1972, and with whom I had had a baby boy, featured. Then, soon thereafter, at the funeral of my younger brother, David Ocholla Asuke in January 1989, an old friend of mine from my Murang'a days (and a former neighbour of his at the KNH staff quarters), Penina Apiyo Ochola, attended the funeral prayers in Nairobi. There followed small communications, which centred first around the boy we had had in 1974, and then gradually and eventually extended into connections with families on both sides.

The younger Florence was soon dramatically persuaded by some members of her family to leave the marriage and move to the United States of America. She eventually did, in mid-1989, and lives there to date. Our two daughters (another was born in 1986) now reside in Kenya, having gone there much later after completing their high school education in Kenya. Once in USA, they joined and completed their university education. She facilitated their permanent residency permit (commonly and officially known as the 'Green Card'). They opted to return home after a decade to 'help build their home and country.'

The very first lady I was introduced to by a would-be go-between in 1972 could not return to me but we remain civil friends. She had given me a very handsome son, Lowry. Her own subsequent marriage ended after nearly two decades of turbulence, but she was able to complete her university education at the master's level while she continued as a very successful international civil servant, at first with UNICEF in Nairobi and then UNEP, spanning Nairobi, Bujumbura, and New York. In the aftermath of her retirement, she started a private school (an "academy" as such schools are popularly and fondly known around), and continues to run her school peacefully and successfully in her corner of the Republic of Kenya, helping nurture solid future Kenyan citizens!

With the remaining two spouses, I live in Homa Bay and Kisumu Counties, respectively. Home 'proper,' my rural ancestral home where

I would be buried, is in Homa Bay, zeroed down to Ong'eche-2, in Omboga, Kanyaluo Ward of Homa Bay County. I am married and married again (not re-married), but I am not a consummate polygamist in the traditional sense, or by plan. In a sense, the 'overlaps' were inescapable!

When I moved in with Penina Apiyo Ochola, Mama Jim, it was like a given part of the equation, even though it happened more than two decades after we had met in Murang'a!

A health worker of international repute, Penina, originally a fully-trained registered nurse and registered midwife, continues as a well-grounded public health expert with a master's degree from Harvard. She was at the forefront of shaping the health policies of both Namibia and South Africa when they were newly independent, through UNICEF, AMREF and Plan International. She also made an impact in Tanzania when she worked with Family Health International of USAID.

For all my three marriages, there were no traditional 'go-betweens' (*jagam* sing. or *jo-gam* plur. in Dholuo) to preside over the rites and consummations. The usual practice is that the celebrated 'go-between' is the one who identifies a young man and a young woman and their respective families and introduces them to one another, literally overseeing the process as a friendly 'broker' up to the conclusion of the ceremonies. Thereafter he or she continues and remains like a 'stand-by' lifelong counsellor. All three, however, were ladies I met in the 'line of duty' in my workplaces!

Of all 'my' three ceremonies, only the first one combined all cultural requirements with a proper (but interdenominational) church wedding. That further made it special because, as I have said above, Florence Atala Ule Adoko is a Catholic, while I am a Seventh Day Adventist (SDA). On my part, I saw one God and agreed that we be solemnized at the Holy Family Basilica, a well-known Catholic church, in Nairobi. But I did not change my denomination. She did not change hers either. With her, I share two children, Michael, mentioned before, and a daughter, Loi (named both after her mother, Imat Loi, and my own mother, Zipporah), born in 1989. Florence is now a retired consultant paediatrician and neonatologist in Nairobi.

For all the three occasions, the cultural steps were largely fulfilled, through from "Visitation," "Negotiation," "Payments," (of 'Consent' and Dowry), to the final stage of [bride] "Transfer" or handing over, and, for lack of a better word, "Bride Migration" to the new groom's home. With the help of a very dependable uncle, Mzee Johnson Ng'oma Aneya, younger brothers, close cousins and friends, I personally visited markets in the neighbourhoods, bought, escorted and delivered cattle respectively to Lira in Uganda, Usenge in Imbo (Siaya County, Kenya) and Onding' in Gem, also within Siaya County. My father made sure that I did no less!

Perhaps our contemporary sociologists may provide plausible insights into the changed and changing social and cultural dynamics of the community as a whole, and in the light of 'mixed' (inter-community, inter- or cross-religion and inter-racial) marriages, which are bound to increase in our midst, very much in spite of David Maillu's book entitled *Our Kind of Polygamy*.

Never Baptized

On at least three occasions, I failed to be baptized in my church, the Seventh Day Adventist church. The very first time was when I was in Form II, in High School, in August 1958. For reasons I cannot remember, the date was changed and a new date for baptism reached when I was already back at school. Other dates came when I was not able to attend any baptismal preparations, both in Nairobi and at home in Omboga.

The very last time was back home out there at Omboga. I had expected the outcome. My direct approach to the Presiding Pastor at

Omboga happened when I was already entangled in marriage. The Pastor must have convened a committee of his church elders and said "No!"

To date, I go to church just as me, for me. Thinking back, I can say I never purposed any of my extra marriages. I could see then that the Bible, a given church doctrine and, additionally, an individual's direct spiritual pathway for relationship with God could be different entities. The last might be the most difficult to appreciate or comprehend for ardent churchgoers and hardcore denominational faithfuls, because there is a key, if not fundamental, part played by one's own church. Nevertheless, when one sees the goings-on in different churches perpetrated and perpetuated by human (or earthly) dynamics, then one might opt more for direct communion and communication with God, especially where these cannot be effected according to the doctrine and practice of a given denomination.

Wedding day. 1st September 1976.

1982: My mother, Mama Zipporah, enjoys a laugh with my son, Michael, as the maid looks on.

With the younger Florence and our daughter, Paula, in 1985.

1988: With Florence and my daughters Paula and Olivia.

My sons Michael (left) and the late Jim (right).

Four of my children. L-R: Lowry, Paula, Olivia and Michael during one of many family photo shoots.

With Penina and Jim before going out to dinner.

With Penina.

At home in Kileleshwa with Dr. Florence Odhiambo and Lowry, Michael, Paula and Olivia.

Family photo studio session: With Dr. Florence, Michael, Paula, Olivia and Loi.

With Dr. Florence at our home in Kanyaluo.

With my son, Michael (centre) and an uncle, Mzee Johnson Aneya, who housed me when I first arrived in Nairobi. Beyond River Nile to the left is the vast expanse of Karuna Forest.

2014: With Loi and Lowry at the première of the movie *Veve*, in which Lowry played a leading role.

With Penina at Nelson Mandela's house in Johannesburg, South Africa.

My father, Mzee Tukiko, acting as foreman during construction at my Ong'eche-2 home.

My mother (right) with the younger Florence's mother, Juliana, before Florence's relocation to the US.

Returning from Lira, Northern Uganda, via Kampala: My cousin, Paul Singa, atop the region-traversing ('trans-region') "Matatu" at the Mabera Forest Reserve – for the sake of memory only!

Flanked by my father, (right foreground) and my every supporting uncle, Naaman Singa Amollo (I was named after his father); they were blessing the first floor of my home in Ong'eche while it was undergoing construction.

With the younger Florence when I visited the US in 1992 to represent PASCAR at the convocation of the American College of Cardiology.

8

BOWATER CORPORATION AND BOWATER BENEVOLENCE

EVEN AS A BUSINESS, the name "BOWATER BENEVOLENCE" might have been more befitting for the company! That aside, it was a company with several business and manufacturing interests in East Africa, with a focus on the cotton industry.

When they offered a scholarship to Kenya's Ministry of Health in early 1976, the ministry forwarded the offer to the medical school of the University of Nairobi. It was a wonderful opportunity for us surgeons, but my contemporaries did not seem interested for one reason or another. On my part, it fitted in beautifully, like a hand in a glove! It was a golden opportunity to pick up thoracic and cardiovascular surgical specialization where I had left it in Kolkata in February 1971.

Here I am today, and I cannot thank Bowater Corporation enough! After declaring my interest, I found myself the lucky beneficiary of their scholarship!

Mr. Denis Rees, the Bowater Corporation Chief Executive Officer, was in charge of my scholarship at Guys, Charing Cross and Cardiff Hospitals. I am pictured in the photos below with him and others, including Prof. Harding Raines, Mr. Alan Yates, a fellow trainee from S. Korea, and other Bowater representatives, led by Frederick James Erroll, 1st Baron Erroll of Hale. The lady in the picture (seated at the dinner table) is Mrs. Elizabeth Braithwaite, the Public Relations Officer.

Llandough Hospital, South Wales (Sept. 1977 – June 1978). Consultant in charge: Mr. Hugh Harley (seated left), Ward E-5.

Charing Cross Hospital, 1977. With Mr. Roger Greenhalgh, vascular surgeon in charge, and a trainee from Southern Rhodesia (now Zimbabwe).

In London at Lillian Penson Hall. We ccoked our own meals. Here, Florence sits with Dr. (later Prof.) Henry S. Adala (left) and another individual.

Lillian Penson Hall, University of London. The late Dr. Pius Achola, Dr. Adala(centre) and Florence.

9

PIONEER TIMES, PLUS

AT THE VERY LEAST, I am happy and proud to have rubbed shoulders with some of the pioneers in the health profession in this country and abroad.

My induction into heart surgery (1969-70) came in handy. I joined the Cardiothoracic Surgical Unit at KNH in January 1976 for completion of my specialization the same time I joined the University of Nairobi as a lecturer. I had passed through the same Unit in July, August and September of 1974 for my postgraduate surgical training rotation, which I completed and passed in August 1975. Between August and December 1975, I was deployed to relieve the Neurosurgery Unit. My joining the University of Nairobi superseded my post-M.Med (Surg.) posting to Kakamega Provincial General Hospital. I could not go immediately. In August, I consulted with the Chief Surgeon, Mr. Roy Miller, to permit me to sort out a family commitment up to November 1975 and then I would go.

My two youngest brothers, who were staying with me and schooling in Nairobi, were due to do their Certificate of Primary Education examinations that October/November. He said "Yes!" to me, verbally. However, when he went to the Ministry of Health headquarters to effect postings of newly qualified surgeons, he reported that I had "told him" that I was very happy to go to Kakamega *immediately*! No word about my constraints with the guardianship of my brothers and their impending examinations! I was posted there "with immediate effect!"

I could not take the lie in the midst of pretended integrity. I stayed put, resigned from the Ministry of Health and successfully applied for a lecturer's post at the Medical School, University of Nairobi, with effect from 1st January 1976. He got wind of my resignation and must have tried some trickery with both the Ministry of Health and the University. On 2nd January 1976, he strolled into the corridors of the Department of Surgery (quite a walk), and was shocked to see me in a white coat in the corridors of *that* department, the Faculty of Medicine at the University of Nairobi. It seemed like he was tracking me down: he was not a member of the department, nor did he have reason to be there that early! By that time, he had already upset Professor Ambrose Wasunna, chairman of the Department of Surgery, by asserting audibly, if not loudly, that it was not yet time in Kenya to bother about any research! That was before I had joined the University as a lecturer, but we were good pioneer 'old boys,' and interacted freely within the department. I had been interviewed and recommended by Professor Wasunna and a WHO representative to do part-time research at and with the Welcome Trust at the KNH-based Welcome Laboratories. That assertion of Mr. Miller seemed to have upset the Professor very much! Now my whole stint with the Ministry of Health was over. In the end it meant foregoing the benefits of my five years' service in that Ministry!

Just as I moved back into heart surgery from 2nd January 1976, each one of my classmates spread out into other specialties after their brief Provincial postings: Gerishom Sande took to Neurosurgery, Ben Mbindyo went to Orthopaedics and Trauma, as Peter Ochola Abila was posted to the Kenyatta National Hospital and embarked on Paediatric Surgery. All of us soon ended up at the Medical School. Gerishom Sande had been posted to Nakuru and actually went. Then he got a job in the same department as me. After the agreed duration in Nakuru, he requested Mr. Miller that he be released from there to take up his new appointment when the Chief Surgeon visited Nakuru on his rounds. To his surprise, upon Mr. Miller's return to Afya House, the Chief Surgeon praised him and reported to the Ministry that he was very happy in Nakuru and was happy to continue there! Mr. (later Professor) Sande used my formula and resigned immediately and came over to the Medical School; in his case, he eventually got his benefits transferred from the Ministry of Health over to the Ministry of Education and the University of Nairobi.

Mr. (also later Professor) Benjamin Mbindyo had been posted to Machakos Provincial Hospital. After a very short stint, he was posted to Nyeri Provincial Hospital, as if to relieve somebody. When he got wind of another impending transfer soon thereafter, he also resigned in a huff and joined the University. Mr. Peter Abila who had stayed at KNH with the Ministry of Health all along also crossed over to the University and paired off into Paediatric surgery with Mr. (later Professor) Julius Kyambi who had trained in Germany.

The ripples that came in the wake of local specialization and super-specialization lasted slightly more than one decade. It seemed to pose a challenge to the much older and long-established general surgeons, not just in Kenya, but the region, as it attracted more and more of the younger generation of doctors, especially surgeons. Thus, sub-specialties in the medical profession among Kenyans emerged and quickly entrenched themselves.

Our senior peers, especially the expatriates, had also entrenched themselves as unofficial-cum-official advisors to the Governments of the whole of the Eastern Africa Region. They held a lot of sway in the Ministries of Health!

They soon came up with the monster cadre dubbed the **"District Surgeon."** Those of us who knew and could see the trickeries involved exposed the whole affair and it did not take off! But the diehards never gave up! They bought less than a decade and returned with a shortcut sweet-named "Fellowship of the College of Surgeons of Eastern, Central and Southern Africa (COSECSA)" backed with significant financial sponsorship; however, that one is yet to truly gel, academically, professionally and regulatorily! It has created a contingent of surgeons who doublespeak, almost unashamedly!

By all considerations, the threat to general surgery was real. Before some of us embarked on an attempt to redeem it, some very senior doctors approached it from a completely different angle. In their historically warped view of general surgery, they felt that it was time to simplify surgery to a level where even a paramedic would be able to go through a makeshift system of training, and be graduated as a surgeon, without as much as a plausible surgical curriculum or modicum of basic medical sciences, like Anatomy, Physiology and Pathology: just template surgical textbooks and some familiarity with the surgical scalpel. The concept and approach was to regularize the system with the sweetener that large numbers of doctors would be produced to offset the ever-looming gap in doctor-patient ratios. It was set far away from the other possible sweetener that it would be run as a crash programme, until, say, when "things improved." Which "things" they were referring to was a big question. Was it standards of training, or some semblance of a better doctor-patient ratio? As the proponents hoodwinked the governments of the region, this course was soon made to compete with the M.Med programme!

This improvised contraption of medical education at the delicate level of surgical services was sold to governments, institutions and doctors with the seemingly realistic categorization of **'District Surgeon,'** coming in through strong personalities in the Association of Surgeons in East Africa (ASEA). The corollary was that one did not need more detailed training beyond the barest minimum at the district, as if there were no bigger surgical issues at that level! The allure of donor funding money was palpable in what was rationalized and sanitized as what the doctor would order for good boy third world (and third class countries). I addressed this matter in my (invited) inaugural lecture of the Surgical Society of Kenya (SSK) on 6th September 1991, under the heading ***Could There Be, and Should There Be, Kenyan Surgery?***

It more or less threw the newly formed Surgical Society of Kenya (SSK) of 1991 off balance for more than five years, pitting the culpable against the critical and progressive into a cold war that has hardly died out even now as we call the spade a spade! The first elected General Secretary took office and quickly shut off that office for several years, until a fresh re-grouping woke him up, even to a point of seeking a higher office and seemingly, yes, seemingly, playing game.

Opening ceremony of the first SSK conference at the Aga Khan Hospital with Hon. Mwai Kibaki as guest of honour.

First AGM of the Surgical Society of Kenya. Founder Chairman Mr. Michael Wilson Warambo is seated in the centre. I was his Vice Chairman. I soon acted as Secretary and later as Treasurer after the passing of Mr. Hasmukh Harilal Kamdar.

After the death of the Founder Treasurer of the SSK, the indefatigable Hasmukh Kamdar (MS, FRCS, FACS), we had strategized with the Founder Chairman, Mr. Michael Wilson Warambo, FRCS, to revive SSK. I was acting as the Treasurer in the late Kamdar's place, in addition to my being the foundation Vice-Chairman. The Chairman asked me to step in and handle the office of the Secretary-General who had been missing in action for a good part of the decade. Accordingly, I wrote a circular to an *ad hoc* surgical group. It was then that the Secretary-General woke up! A scorched-earth campaign followed, and it saw a new line-up take shape, with the outgoing Secretary-General emerging as Chairman. Something very African had reared its head here, noticeably at the behest of survivalist expatriates, and not-so-hidden self-interest! I was 'offered' the post of Treasurer in the emerging formation, but I declined. Mr. Warambo was not amused and sure enough not interested!

The vocabulary that I just learnt as I proof-read this book is instantly relevant; it is reportedly used by outsiders to sum up and mitigate their would-be frustration: **"This is Africa"** (or simply, TIA)!

I deem this digression to be relevant because of my part in it all. The very first clarion call came from Mr. Warambo, FRCS, who mobilized the entire surgical fraternity in Kenya. A number of us joined him and SSK was born and registered. When it held its maiden elections, Mr. Warambo was duly and unanimously elected the first Chairman* of the Surgical Society of Kenya. I was elected Vice Chairman. In due course, after a committee resolution to create an SSK logo, I presented a sketch, complete with the wording, which was eventually discussed at committee level. A final version was given to Dr. (now Professor) Stephen Oduor Ogendo for production of a computerized graphic of the same, as it is today. That forms part and parcel of the history of SSK!

*There can only be *one* first one!

Without pretending to be an artist, I must complete the story by adding that I had some experience in logo designs when I conceptually and in pencil designed the logos of the Kenya Cardiac Society (KCS) which Hillary Ojiambo, myself and others founded, and then that of the 'Heart and Lung Centre,' my creation. I also used the logo of the Egyptian Cardiac Society as inspiration for the Pan-African Society of Cardiology (PASCAR) logo. I still have the pencil sketch and original colour separations of the KCS logo.

Noting that SSK is an umbrella surgical body, and that general surgery is a most needed universal specialty, I dare say that SSK has not nurtured general surgery to its rightful level. Instead, it has tended to accommodate shortcuts in an increasingly and progressively technological environment. The College of Surgeons of East, Central and Southern Africa (COSECSA) is the ultimate institutionalized maceration of general surgery in this region – all, it would seem, for the love of money!

Like Mr. Warambo, there had been another pioneer, exactly one decade earlier. Professor Hillary Peter Witts Ojiambo (or just "HP" – 'Horse Power!') convened the first meeting of the heart team in Nairobi in late 1980. By early 1981, the Kenya Cardiac Society was registered in time and readiness to attend and participate in the inaugural congress of the Pan-African Society of Cardiology **(PASCAR)** – *la Société Pan-Africaine de Cardiologie* **(SOPAC)**.These were visions translated and put into realizable and realized practice (not "Me too, Boss!"), and they remain etched in gold!**

At the first post-registration meeting, I was elected KCS's first (pioneer and founder) Chairman. That gave me the mandate, responsibility and humble pleasure to lead a strong Kenyan delegation

**The common challenge is the disheartening trend of those who inherit an institution, even after fighting for it, only to helplessly and hopelessly find themselves presiding over total disinheritance and collapse of an entire edifice under their very noses, often times due to incompetence or greed or both! KCS seems to have passed through such a phase too.

to Badagry, Lagos State, Nigeria, to attend and help inaugurate PASCAR. The first Scientific Conference of PASCAR was also held on that same occasion.

Lagos, 1981. Kenyan PASCAR delegates. From left to right: Prof. Mutuma Mugambi, Dr. Heywood Asesso, Dr. Wanene and myself.

Lagos, 1981. PASCAR delegates. From left to right: K.C. Patel, S.K. Shah, myself and Prof. Mutuma Mugambi.

Lagos, 1981. PASCAR delegates. From left to right: Prof. Ambrose A.E.O Wasunna, gastrointestinal surgeon and chairman of the department of surgery, UoN; Dr. Carlyle, cardiologist at the University Teaching Hospital, Lusaka; Prof. Hillary Peter Witts Ojiambo, cardiologist, and myself.

With the African continent organizationally divided into five regions – Northern (or Mediterranean), Eastern, Central, Western and Southern – there was to be one President and four Vice-Presidents; that is, four Vice-Presidents less one from where the President hailed.

Professor Papa Koate of Dakar, Senegal, was unanimously elected first Founder and Pioneer President. Our own Professor Hilary Ojiambo took the position of the Vice-President for the Eastern Region. That period also saw a strong wave and clamour on the African continent and in the International Society and Federation of Cardiology (ISFC), the forerunner of the World Heart Federation (WHF), to address issues of prevention and care of heart diseases and heart health, including heart surgery.

The Lagos meeting was to be followed by a continent-wide conference to address *Cardiology in the Tropics*. The year 1983 had been declared by WHO as "Year of Tropical Cardiology," soon duly amended to **"Cardiology in the Tropics."**

Kenya, in the Eastern Region, bid and won the hosting contest, beating the Mediterranean Region, specifically Algeria. We hosted the first Continental Conference of Cardiology in the Tropics in 1983. I was honoured to be the Chief Host in my capacity as Chairman of KCS. It was an unqualified success, fully recognized by the then Minister for Health, the late Hon. Dr. Mukasa Mango, on behalf of the Government of the Republic of Kenya. He was the guest of honour at the opening ceremony.

PASCAR's constitution spelt out that its own official conferences were to be held at intervals of four years. With the first one having been held in Lagos in 1981, and Kenya having hosted the special sessions on cardiology in the tropics in April 1983, and with other activities beyond our own borders, KCS did not hold its own dedicated inaugural and any subsequent annual conferences until 1984 at the Norfolk Hotel, Nairobi. After all our exposure up to that point, our conferences instantly became regional and international by catchment and volume of attendance. Attending delegates came from Nigeria, Uganda, Tanzania, India and elsewhere. As it were, and 'until further notice,' the rest became history.

Continental Congress on Cardiology in the Tropics, hosted by KCS. Seated next to me is the guest of honour Dr. Mukhasa Mango (centre) and Prof. Papa Koate (left), then president of PASCAR.

Pioneer committee members at the first KCS conference in 1984. From left to right: Dr. Surya Kant Shah, Assistant Secretary; Dr. Heywood Asesso, Vice Chair; Dr. William (Bill) Lore, Secretary; Dr. P.A. Odhiambo (myself), chairman; Dr. Alan Kisia, Treasurer and Dr. Hasmukh Harilal Kamdar, Committee Member.

Delegates at the first KCS conference held in 1984 at the Norfolk Hotel. Dr. Alan Kisia, anaesthetist, is far left standing next to Dr. Peter Okanga, a cardiologist. I am standing far right.

Delegates at the first KCS conference held in 1984 at the Norfolk Hotel. From left to right: Dr. Peter Okanga, Dr. (later Prof.) Arthur Obel, myself and Dr. John Kariuki who had recently returned from further training in Milwaukee, WI.

The dinner portion of the first KCS conference held in 1984 at the Norfolk Hotel. The dinner dance was graced by Prof. Japheth Mati, then the Dean of the Faculty of Medicine at UoN (he is seated to my right).

The dinner portion of the first KCS conference held in 1984 at the Norfolk Hotel. With my good friend and colleague, Dr. Hasmukh Harilal Kamdar, who never shied away from any work. It was he who ran the cardiac surgical unit throughout my deanship while every one of our trainees was abroad. Totally self-driven! Unfortunately, he died in his sleep the night he had performed a chest operation at a private hospital in Nairobi. As if by premonition, I had asked him if I could join him to help with the surgery, but he had said he was O.K! Later, I overheard that his wife, a gynaecologist, complained that I had been overworking him!

It now fell upon the Egyptian Cardiac Society to host the designated second congress of PASCAR in 1985. Once again, Kenya sent a very strong delegation to Cairo, Egypt, in 1985, under the leadership of both Vice-President Professor Hillary Ojiambo and myself.

Coincidentally, that was also during my second term as Chairman of KCS. Our own elections in KCS were to be held every two years. It chanced that I held that office for an additional **third** term, before handing over to Dr. Heywood Ochieng' Asesso, a Consultant Paediatrician and Paediatric Cardiologist, in 1987. Here was a fantastic family of professionals, with absolutely no politics.

The 2nd Congress of the Pan-African Society of Cardiology held in Cairo in 1985: I am seated with Prof. Papa Koate to my right and Prof. Gabriel Anabwani to my left.

The 2nd Congress of the Pan-African Society of Cardiology held in Cairo in 1985: The overwhelming support showed by Nigeria for Kenya (read KCS) and myself ensured that the reputably strong Egyptian contender for the PASCAR post of Secretary-General lost to me by a very wide margin! With me here at the elections during dinner are Dr. Ogunyemi (right), my senior at Calcutta Medical College, and a close friend, Dr. Ike.

The 2nd Congress of the Pan-African Society of Cardiology held in Cairo in 1985: At the Cairo Marriott. Left to right: Prof. Bill Lore, myself, Prof. Gabriel Anabwani and Prof. Hillary P. Ojiambo.

The 2nd Congress of the Pan-African Society of Cardiology held in Cairo in 1985: Waving from atop a camel at the pyramids in Cairo.

During the elections in Cairo, I was surprised by the overwhelming support I received from the rest of the continent for the position of Secretary-General for the ensuing four years. I do not remember seeking a nomination, but the continent somehow got my name on the ballot. It was as good as a unanimous election. There was an Egyptian surgeon in very good standing there for that post (it was just the two of us) who lost with a wide margin! Down memory lane, I am sorry that I cannot be sure of the name – it could have been Professor Hassouna Saba, also a cardiac surgeon! It was a very humbling occasion for me and, of course, a great pride for Kenya!

During my tenure as Secretary-General of PASCAR i.e., before the close of the nineteen-eighties, I made a point of calling on the Director of Health of the OAU (Organization for African Unity), now the African Union (AU), Dr. Amin Hanna Salama, at the OAU's headquarters in Addis Ababa, to drum up support for our campaign against the grossly neglected **non-communicable diseases** (NCDs), notably heart disease and heart health. He lamented to me that nobody ***would*** listen to him! He had attempted to put some perspective on the continent's most lethal infectious scourges, especially malaria and yellow fever, which were killing millions around the continent, but received no meaningful response from the member states of the gigantic organization! Talking to them about **"non-communicable diseases" was bound to be a taller order!** By that time, his contract had expired, and he soon went back to Egypt. His assistant, a doctor from Zambia, did not seem to have any clue what I was talking about! This was during the period when, as Secretary General, I would transit through Addis Ababa on my way to Dakar, Senegal, to join the Senegalese Society of Cardiology to help organize the third PASCAR Congress that was slated for March of 1989. The only reliable airline on the continent at the time was the Ethiopian Airways, which always touched base in Addis Ababa.

At the Cairo conference, Professor Hussein Badawi of Alexandria, a renowned and respected cardiologist and himself a heart attack survivor, had been unanimously elected PASCAR's second President. It was a befitting tribute to the hosts, Egypt, and the Egyptian Cardiac Society. The next eight years literally confirmed that, even though South Africa (the home of Christiaan Bernard of the first human heart transplant fame) was still locked out because of apartheid, the specialties of cardiology and cardiac surgery had taken root elsewhere on the African continent, despite the challenges posed by limited resources. Regular open heart operations were being performed in Egypt, Abidjan, Côte d'Ivoire (Ivory Coast) and Nairobi, even though Nairobi suffered a two-year lull between October 1993 and December 1995, because of outdated and broken-down machines and depleted supplies.

My election in Cairo was one good reason why I stepped down as Chair of KCS. The other was the KCS Constitution itself. I was not going to seek re-election anyway. KCS and its membership had long come of age.

My new challenge was to mobilize and keep the continent together and vibrant. Those were the days when, in order to travel from one African country to another, one had to pass through one European capital or another, depending on the airline, and then connect to another part of Africa. Fortunately, as mentioned earlier, we had Ethiopian Airlines. I used it to travel continent-wide, connecting via Addis Ababa instead of Europe. The airline covered the continent very well. I shuttled back and forth to Senegal to consult with the local organizing committee for the 3rd PASCAR Congress, which was slated for Dakar, the home of the Founder President of PASCAR, Professor Papa Koate, in March 1989.

That same month, we held another landmark congress. For the upcoming elections, I had my candidate for the office of the new President and openly campaigned for him, my friend Professor Walinjom Muna from Cameroon (now deceased).

I arrived in Dakar for the congress one day earlier; before I was assured of a quorum, I quickly proposed that we convene an *ad hoc* group called the *Council of Elders* to quietly chart the way forward for the continent. I was summarily told off by both the first and second Presidents – the true Elders of PASCAR – who said in unison that they did not like the term, and that it was not in the Constitution.

Lo and behold, at elections, they essentially exercised their authority as a two-man Council of Elders! They had it all planned! They got both their say and their way!

At the session of elections, when our outgoing President, Professor Hussein Badawi was no longer an official and every delegate seated was ready to vote, he very promptly took, literally hijacked, the floor and lectured the Congress on how hard and how passionately I had worked. He then pronounced (as opposed to nominated or proposed for seconding) that there was not going to be anybody else to take that post, but me, his outgoing Secretary General! He even spelt out a formula for office successions in future – that the office of the Secretary-General should be the stepping rank to the Presidency.

The hall responded in style – there was a palpable sigh of relief. My attempt to avoid that office by fronting someone else flopped instantly! And what an embarrassment for me – did I betray Wali Muna by proposing him and then 'robbing' him of the post? However, the small mitigation was that he became my Secretary-General! The proposed road to the Presidency via Secretary-General was adopted unanimously. In another four years he was bound to be PASCAR's fourth President.

Somehow, it was decided that there would be a PASCAR congress within the ensuing two years without elections to keep scientific and professional dialogue alive. It was earmarked for Addis Ababa, Ethiopia. Unfortunately, a few months before the appointed date, there were really loud rumbles of war in Ethiopia, which eventually ended in the overthrow of President Mengistu Haile Mariam.

Our Chief Host in Addis Ababa, Dr. Belay Abegaz, who was an army doctor and an excellent cardiologist, kept assuring us that the worst was yet to come (he must have known something) and that we should just go there and hold our congress without concern, because the "real thing" would come long after the congress.

On my part, as PASCAR President, I was not going to "herd" Africa's best into a war zone. I was not going to expose Africa's cream to the continent's other communicable and infectious disease of coups. I called off the Congress and moved it to our usual fourth year (1993) to Yaoundé, Cameroon, the home of my Secretary-General, the next year. I know and feel inside me that my very good friend, Belay, never forgave me!

At last, I now had the chance and pleasure to crown my erstwhile candidate and hand over to him the golden chain of office! But very soon after his election, my memories inevitably, even regrettably, swung back to the days of my abortive Council of Elders, at which I was to propose an advance line up for the new officials. Those memories, of course, caught up with the *de facto* self-appointed 'Council of Two Elders.' They were indeed very sad memories for me, especially having been at the helm of PASCAR affairs for eight years.

The last time that golden chain of office was seen was when I passed it over Walinjom Muna's head on to his neck in Yaoundé in front of cameras, in April 1993. Whatever they knew, those two old men! Whatever they had seen! I had regrettably ignored the rumour that the late Professor Koate and Professor Muna never saw eye to eye! The *Mzee* of Cardiology in Africa never approved of the 'derailed' ways of my friend!

PASCAR weakened very fast thereafter. My frustrating thought was whether it might be true that ***the African professional had the same genes as the African politician!*** It took many years for it to be revived to any plausible level.

TOP: The 3rd Congress of the Pan-African Society of Cardiology held in Dakar, Senegal, in 1989. I am seated far right.

LEFT: At the 3rd Congress of the Pan-African Society of Cardiology held in Dakar, Senegal, in 1989.

The 3rd Congress of the Pan-African Society of Cardiology held in Dakar, Senegal, in 1989: I am third from right, standing next to Prof. Hussein Badawi and Prof. Papa Koate.

The 3rd Congress of the Pan-African Society of Cardiology held in Dakar, Senegal, in 1989: Boat ride to Gorée island, off the coast of Senegal. I am far right. To my immediate right is my PASCAR successor, Walinjom Muna.

The 3rd Congress of the Pan-African Society of Cardiology held in Dakar, Senegal, in 1989: PASCAR delegates at Gorée island, the former slave trade outpost off the coast of Senegal. I am top right.

The 3rd Congress of the Pan-African Society of Cardiology held in Dakar, Senegal, in 1989: With Brigadier Dr. Belay Abegaz (right).

The 3rd Congress of the Pan-African Society of Cardiology held in Dakar, Senegal, in 1989: At Gorée island.

The 3rd Congress of the Pan-African Society of Cardiology held in Dakar, Senegal, in 1989: The chain of office passes to me. I am flanked by two past presidents, Prof. Papa Koate (left) and Prof. Hussein Badawi.

One year before those 1993 PASCAR elections, the year 1992, had been very eventful for me! The first week of February that year saw me attend the all-India conference of their gigantic Cardiovascular and Thoracic Society at the Birla Heart Institute in Calcutta. Back home, in my absence on the 14th, I was elected the 10th Dean of the University School of Medicine. Earlier on, before these two events, I had been invited by the American College of Cardiology and I represented PASCAR and the African continent at the convocation of that College in Dallas, Texas in March,1992.

The 1992 convocation of the American College of Cardiology. I represented PASCAR as its president.

With my new engagements as Dean, the surgical heart team got even more depleted (several of our up and coming specialists were still training abroad). I had to join Mr. Kamdar ever so frequently in theatre for general thoracic and peripheral vascular work. Until late 1995, open heart surgery slowed down to a standstill, but I had to be there when facilities were rehabilitated enough, by November-December 1995.

The Kenya Cardiac Society joined the Kenyatta National Hospital Heart Team to hold the first heart walk to raise funds for the purchase of consumables for the surgical unit and operating theatres. That is when the phrase "Heart-To-Heart Walk" was coined, specifically referring to and proposing a gift from a healthy heart to a sick heart. The phrase was derived from the early 1980s Kenya Broadcasting Channel (KBC) TV series *Hart to Hart* whose main characters were Jonathan and Jennifer Hart. The cross-over from "Hart" to "Heart" (my coinage) was automatic, to say the least. Accordingly, I stuck the label "HEART-TO-HEART" both in front and at the back of the hat I wore during that first heart walk in June 1985, to signify healthy hearts walking to save sick hearts, as we in the Kenya Cardiac Society and as the KNH Heart Team walked to raise funds for the Heart Unit at the KNH. The Patron of KCS, H.E. (Rtd) President Daniel Arap Moi subsequently rallied Kenyans until a total of two million Kenya shillings was raised. All that was during round one of my (Founder) Chairmanship of the Kenya Cardiac Society. As history would have it, I was re-cycled into that seat by election at the Annual General and Scientific Conference in June 1996.

All the same, the decade immediately following also saw KCS, once a front-liner in Africa, grind to a near stand-still.

I did my two terms of Deanship and then opted out, although the Vice-Chancellor of the time was somewhat reluctant to rush to authorize elections for the next Dean. He finally agreed three months later when I pleaded that I needed to join my colleagues in both the Heart Team and KCS (to be there as the facilities were improving), so as to reactivate open heart surgery at KNH and in the country, as well as to save KCS from weakening further! Besides, the media had been checking in with the KNH CEO, Professor Julius Meme (now deceased) as to when open heart surgery would resume.

We held elections for a new Dean on 31st May 1996. By 30th June 1996, I found myself re-elected, or recycled, as Chairman of KCS. Our specialty trainees who extended their training overseas started trickling back, and we have not looked back since, even as I hung my boots. The team is solidly in place! The KNH Heart Unit now has a team of well-trained heart, chest and vascular specialists who can fit anywhere in the world! Their only possible limitation is the sheer psychology of 'third-worldliness' and the realities on the ground concerning equipment and supplies.

As my pen rolls now (2023), both PASCAR and KCS are firmly on their feet and are marching on. Kenya has held the PASCAR position of Vice-President the most number of times, with Professor Elijah Nyainda Ogola currently serving as president as I write this.

For me, administratively, I am now a retired general – but not before I took the KCS flag to Tobacco Control in general and the Tobacco Control Board in particular, when we hatched and demonstrated the **Submarine Formula**.

All indications in the tobacco control world showed that the press was gagged. Was it by the tobacco industry? At what cost? Could we compete with them? Would we dare compete? Good for us! If the press always highlighted our words and activities, that industry would, in return, fight us directly and indirectly through selected corridors of power in the country. For sure it appeared that the press had slowed somewhat. With the media to some such extent gagged against publishing and disseminating information about tobacco and its dangers, we adopted a "double gagging" strategy. With us not bothering about the press anymore, that would amount to 'gagging' them by not informing them of our activities. And that is what we did, in spite of their espionage and bribery! We swore to never stop working. We took charge of our own public participation; we ensured we invited the tobacco industry for face to face discussions, to forestall their backdoor machinations. We toured the country widely and satisfied the requirements for public participation, including taking photographs with the official representatives of the tobacco industry. Their subsequent complaints and denials that we did not do any public participation were, therefore, childish and inconsequential!

In time we would choose the moment of publication and publicity, without that industry itself knowing, but even they would have been part of that process, anyway!

Our 'home-made' strategic obscurity was, therefore, like taking a boat under water and working from there – always by the rules, including public participation – only to emerge at another water point far ahead, to complete and declare a job done in broad, if not broader daylight, ready to face any consequences and repercussions, if any, or the enemy.

The tobacco industry sued us and lost their case in the High Court; they went to the Appeal Court and failed, and still dared to climb the ladder to the Supreme Court. In the end, they still lost the case before the end of 2019! Bravo(!) to the entire anti-tobacco fraternity! To you, I say (in the 'new chapter' of freedom struggle: "Aluta Continua!" Although they had to pass the Tobacco Control Act, the politicians remained behind, literally by choice of suicidal myopia, bereft of any historical insight and prominently displaying global political illiteracy! With tears in my eyes, that always reminds me of "strongman" African ancestors who pocketed beads and perishable ornaments and released (read *traded*) their able-bodied men as **slaves,** themselves remaining untouchable locally but utterly stupid in history, and historically, metamorphosing into the cursed gene of perpetual dependency!

Meanwhile, Kenyans do not need heart diseases, cancers, and related scourges, as the main menus for their health. Soon, healthcare professionals and the healthy-minded populace will have to fight local executives, alcohol, drug abuse and tobacco business, as well as the homes of men and women who promote and persist with promotion of abusable drugs, alcohol and tobacco, both directly and indirectly, even by default! There will be no need to re-invent the wheel: the laws are in place!

10

SNOW IN NEW YORK, STORM IN DETROIT: AN AMBULANCE, ONE PATIENT AND ONE DOCTOR

IN EARLY 1982, a white expatriate American lady (whose name I withhold, and simply refer to as Lady ABC), who was a schoolteacher at the Jacaranda School for the Disabled in Nairobi, was referred to me with lung cancer. A heavy smoker, she underwent resection of a part (the lower lobe) of her left lung. One year later in late February 1983, she was re-admitted with widespread metastases. She soon expressed the wish to go back and die in her own country, the United States of America (USA). Her Consultant Physician, Dr. Samuel Mwinzi and I had no problem with that.

Because she was too weak to travel alone, it was necessary to arrange for an escort to accompany her. Her husband could not come over from the USA for her. That meant an escort from Kenya – in fact, directly from the hospital, because she would need some nursing care along the way. Her Kenyan 'husband' would not manage that kind of care and had no 'locus standi' to arrive in America! Because it was a surgical case, even the physician had his limitations. None of her ward nurses agreed to escort her. That left me alone, her surgeon! Her reaction to that whole scenario showed that even her confidence was reassured!

Come March 12, 1983, all preparations and arrangements were complete. We set off in the evening for the John F. Kennedy Airport (JFK) in New York aboard the now-defunct Pan American World Airways, often simply referred to as Pan-Am.

Four seats at the rear of the passenger cabin had been collapsed, or flattened, to create room for her mattress and beddings. From the hospital ward, I carried a bedpan, nappies, bucket, gloves and tissues. She already had urinary catheter in place. I did have to worry about the availability of water; the entire crew had been briefed adequately. On board and throughout the flight, they were very kind and ready to help in whatever way possible; very professional! Even after connecting from New York later, I had no problem inflight.

My patient was a High Dependency Unit (HDU) candidate and, any time, might have required fully fledged ICU-level care. Fortunately, she could talk. That kept me abreast of whatever she felt or wanted at her subjective and symptomatic levels. I was armed with a hard-cover exercise notebook for moment-by-moment documentation of her condition and actions taken.

After a routine landing for what was supposed to be a brief stop-over at the Monrovia airport, we were informed via intercom that there was going to be a four-hour delay right there in Monrovia. No one was to leave the plane. Thank God it was not because of my patient, but I was concerned about the long delay; anything could have happened to her while waiting under those strained conditions! She might even have needed oxygen.

The reason for the delay was that John F. Kennedy (JFK) airport was four feet under a thick carpet of snow. They needed those four hours to **clear the runway for us**. Precisely because of my patient, the runway, and only the runway, was being cleared.

After a little over four hours, we were permitted to take off from Monrovia. It is instructive to note that New York was not Lady ABC's home destination. We were to connect to the Detroit airport and then take an ambulance, complete with an American movie-style paramedic squad, to Ann Arbor, Michigan.

We landed at JFK in the afternoon. The runway was cleared just enough for our landing. Although it was not actively snowing at the time, no other plane was landing or taking off from New York. In fact, before touching down, our plane circled at least four times over the City of New York to deplete aviation fuel in the aeroplane's tank in case of what I may call a 'snow-crash landing' and flame burst! At last, we landed safely!

My patient and I were taken to a 'neutral' corner of the arrival lounge. Other passengers sat or sprawled all around. I hoped that we would be cleared to proceed to Detroit the next day, but even that destination was inaccessible because of both snow and a storm.

I requested that the two of us (patient and doctor) be taken to the base hospital at the airport; but that could not be done immediately, because the hospital was outside the inner airport complex, and there was still snow everywhere. The road itself also had to be cleared of snow for the ambulance to negotiate its way there. We were not moved until the next day beyond 4 p.m., arriving at around 6 p.m.

I was beginning to feel relieved, because I was now on American soil, outside the airport, and would soon hand the patient over to local professional colleagues, the American doctors at the base hospital. Unfortunately, that was not to be - at least not in the way I had anticipated it.

There was no doctor within the hospital premises at the time. Called by the nurses, they declined to come. The reason was that the patient had not "quite" arrived on US soil; therefore, they could not and would not attend to, or take over, such a patient!

That was worse than being alone with the patient on the plane and at the airport lounge as doctor and nurse in one count! There was dire need of resources for basic hygiene, intravenous fluids and drugs!

I decided to mobilize the few nurses on duty in the ward. The context of my appeal was that for any patient, doctors and nurses always cooperated and collaborated, whatever the circumstances. Could they join me for the sake of Lady ABC? They did, and very keenly too! I was very grateful! That left the weather challenge.

By daybreak, the weather report was that there was a storm heading in the direction of Detroit. With that, we could not leave the hospital just yet; but it was understood and planned that as soon as the storm cleared, we would leave immediately, however short the notice! Thank God, I did not have to spend another night at the hospital with the patient!

By mid-afternoon, it was reported that the storm had swerved away from the Detroit skyline. On the ground, the snow was still thick; that included the road to the airport! Clearing a strip (like one lane) of that road for the ambulance to take us to the airport took some time. We left well after 5 p.m., but it was a short trip and there was constant communication with the Detroit airport, Lady ABC's husband and the paramedics.

When we arrived, her husband and the paramedics were on hand to meet us and take us to Ann Arbor. The husband greeted his wife and they talked briefly, but time was of the essence. The paramedics took charge with the usual agility – oxygen by mask, fixing a new intravenous line, and starting a fast intravenous infusion. In no time, we were on our way to the Ann Arbor hospital aboard the ambulance with a convoy that included her husband in his own car.

At the hospital, I handed over to the doctor on duty. The 'staff' (consultant) on call was an orthopaedic surgeon, he was called and came soon enough thereafter.

Once that much freed, I was guided into the admissions room to present her details, including her passport for registration. Her husband would sort out her immigration issues. I also presented my passport for necessary formalities.

We were barely half-way into the formalities when a paramedic rushed into the room and directly and appealingly addressed me with the report that the patient had collapsed. I rushed back to the bedside and found everybody standing still, as if a final event had taken place!

I was enraged! The paramedics appeared almost equally disappointed with the inactivity! They had done their part but did not belong to that location and could not push their initiatives much further, so it seemed, especially when the doctors and nurses had received the patient. I castigated everybody for **just standing there**, as if they had no stake in the hospital or the patient! I started a vigorous external cardiac massage. My orders flowed with corresponding rhythm – sodium bicarbonate, calcium gluconate, adrenaline, endo-tracheal intubation and ventilator support. **Nobody, but nobody, was going to *give up* on my patient under any circumstances!**

The paramedics were the first to swing into action, helping me with cardiac massage, alternately. We managed to bring back the heart, but the brain was gone!

By that time, by token of the resumption of heartbeat, the place itself seemed resuscitated! Everybody rallied themselves **back to some semblance of patient care and support**. There was even an inkling of 'textbook display.' But there was a nasty after-taste in my own mouth! I found myself cursing, literally! 'To hell with American medicine and American ethics!'

I spent the night at a very tall campus hotel owned and run by the students.

The next morning, the husband reached me and confirmed that there was still no neurological response from Lady ABC, but that she was otherwise stable on support! He said something about her being a 'human vegetable' and wondered how long he would himself keep her going or afford prolonged care! I was not keen on that line of conversation. I did 'hear' him, but I did not respond! It was time enough for me to be paid and return home to Kenya!

Only four things followed:

I. My payment – The husband of Lady ABC refused to take responsibility. He said that the lady was "married" in Kenya and someone else should take responsibility for my payment. On his part, he took me to the university bookshop on the campus nearby to buy me a book of my choice! The variety was not impressive; the budget ceiling was low! I opted for a smallish book – *A Dictionary of Symptoms*. That was it!

II. I learnt that one of the thoracic surgeons at the hospital was scheduled to perform an operation that bears his name, "Mark Orringer's ***Trans-hiatal Esophagectomy,"*** for cancer of the oesophagus. It was a golden opportunity to meet the man and watch him perform the operation himself. Necessary formalities were sorted out for me to be able to enter the operating room. I deliberately deferred my return flight by that one day. He had been duly notified about a visitor to be in attendance in the operating room. Whatever the luck, he did not go to theatre that morning for that case. His Resident performed the good old Ivor-Lewis two-stage operation. Things were still tasting bad in my mouth!

III. My foster host showed me around the nearby part of the city, reaching up to the Ann Arbor National Aeronautics and Space Administration (NASA) Centre, or some such, seen from outside the fence!

IV. My flight back to Nairobi, Kenya – At least, 'Mr. ABC' sorted that one out! I returned home in one piece. To this day, I have never heard back from Lady ABC's Nairobi husband, nor have I had the time to look for him.

On or around the fifth day after my departure from Ann Arbor, Lady ABC's "American husband" telephoned me to inform me that she had died.

My professional part was more than complete. My encounter with fellow professionals was a huge mirage. The 'Land of Opportunity' and *top-noise* human rights advocacy (or maybe arrogance), bid me farewell. I left behind my physical and professional sweat as my "foreign aid donation" to America with my head held high, straight above my shoulders. I felt an indelible pride in what I taught and practised! I remembered the awesome adage and stance from the Orient – 'Simple living and high thinking' – even if you say it in reverse! Cheers West Bengal! Cheers India!

The two photos above depict my earlier encounter with snow at Llandough Hospital in South Wales, UK, in October, 1978 when it snowed there after decades of little to no snow. For me, the two snow-cum-patient encounters, complete with ambulances, are enduring memories.

11

FROM TRIPOLI TO LUSAKA

TRIPOLI

DR. EL SAYED, a cardiothoracic surgeon, was a long-time friend of my teacher and mentor, Mr. Alan Yates, FRCS, of Guy's Hospital, London. I had trained there in 1976-77; Dr. El Sayed had been there some years before me.

He now intended to spearhead more of his specialty in Tripoli, Libya. His base was Tajoura Hospital. He was himself a Palestinian, working in Libya as an expatriate. There were a few other Palestinians working at the hospital at the time; perhaps the critical mass that sustained the hospital.

He organized a regional cardiac conference in Tripoli in early 1980 to be attended and patronized by none other than Mr. Alan Yates. I was invited to attend. However, our communication went only as far as confirmation of my attendance.

When I arrived in Tripoli via Rome airport the day before the scheduled conference, I was received very well at the hospital, but there was no sign of a conference!

I was soon informed that Dr. El Sayed had been taken ill and was at Guy's Hospital in London suffering from terminal cancer of the colon (large intestines). Accordingly, there was no conference!

The alternative for me was to turn round and fly back to Nairobi, but there were two stumbling blocks! The main one was that there was no immediate flight to Nairobi – for sure not back through Rome again and not direct from Tripoli to Nairobi! Sudan airline flew direct, but not daily! I opted to change my ticket and wait for its next flight.

I was now a guest of the hospital! I was given a conducted tour. What 'wishful jealousy!' Literally everything was new: equipment meant for the operating theatre and the Intensive Care Unit (ICU). I smelt money everywhere, with no risk of any shortage, plural or singular. The ICU space was for now a store, packed full of equipment. All that remained was human resource, planning and implementation! But it was not my horse to ride! I just wished it was!

Then came the bang! In the new-born unit of the hospital, an echocardiogram had just shown that the cause of the cardiac tamponade (compression of the heart) in a new-born was a large pericardial tumour, distinctly separate from the thymus. Could I assist by operating on the tiny human being to decompress and relieve the heart? Obviously, I said "Yes," but I did not want to do what some foreign doctors did in my country, by involving themselves with elective (non-emergency) procedures without even temporary registration certificates from the local regulatory body! I insisted on a temporary medical permit or license for myself, as well as for the profession and the system. With a 'crack and a crash' approach, partly dictated by myself, this was done within a day.

At operation, I found what looked like an embryonal tumour. I managed to resect it, and gave strict instructions for the specimen to be taken for histology. Unfortunately, the baby died in the ICU two days later! The tissue specimen was never taken to the pathology laboratory!

I stayed in Tripoli for a total of five days. Without submitting any invoice, I was paid handsomely for the operation. Then I was taken for a tour to a nearby town on the western side of Tripoli with historical sites and ruins dating back to the years around 4 A.D. There was some precaution not to go Benghazi on the eastern side, because of the threats of the Iraq-Iran war, almost as if it was likely to spill over any time! My hosts, who included a number of Palestinian doctors working at Tajoura Hospital, were marvellous! But because of the 'drums of war,' I was never tempted to return there for a job!

Eventually, I flew back to Nairobi on my rescheduled flight aboard Sudan Airlines, without undue hold up in Khartoum. I landed safely in Nairobi that afternoon.

More than one year later, in November 1981, we ourselves invited the Guy's Hospital heart team, led by none other than Mr. Alan Yates himself to Kenyatta National Hospital (KNH) for a two week mission of open heart operations. Together with them, we performed fourteen (14) operations; we lost two ... The full story is in another chapter of this autobiography.

Tripoli, 1980. With the hospital surgical team. A good number of them were from Palestine. With the rumbling drums of the Iran-Iraq war, they were busy preparing to return home before the outbreak of full war!

LUSAKA

By 1986, I was already Secretary General of the Pan-African Society of Cardiology (PASCAR). I was also still the chairman of the Kenya Cardiac Society (KCS). Professor Hillary Ojiambo (then Vice President for the Eastern Africa Region of PASCAR) and I were invited by the Zambian Cardiac Society to attend their conference of that year.

We arrived in Lusaka one day ahead of the conference and were warmly received by Dr. Robert Carlyle, Chief of Cardiology at University Teaching Hospital (UTH), Lusaka, Zambia. The Vice President for the Southern Region of PASCAR, Dr. J.K. Manuwele, an army colonel, joined us later at the conference.

Dr. Carlyle took us around parts of the campus. I also wanted to say 'Hi!' to fellow surgeons in their Department of Surgery, where I knew the Chairperson, Professor Anne Bailey, with whom I had sat on the Council of the Association of Surgeons of East Africa (ASEA).

Upon our arrival at Professor Bailey's office in the Department of Surgery, the excitement was palpable!

"Hey, Peter, you are here! Very lucky for us! We have a lady with an abdominal aortic aneurysm in the ward. You must help us operate on her!"

I told her that both Professor Ojiambo and I were there for the cardiology meeting. She would have to negotiate with our chief host, Dr. Carlyle, first! The deal was sealed! Then the nitty gritties!

What special equipment and instruments did they have in the operating theatre? Was there a good ICU and good general nursing care?

In theatre, the nurse in charge showed me around. The available operating instruments were mostly for general surgery, but were usable for a vascular procedure, even for the repair of an abdominal aortic aneurysm. There were some vascular grafts, both tubular and bifurcated, with not much choice of size. All were knitted, not woven. There were no tapes of any description for vascular control!

Searching around, even the medical companies in town did not have any semblance of the same! So, the nursing sister and I went 'downtown' and bought curtain ribbons for due sterilization in the theatre sterile surgical unit (TSSU) in advance for use in the morning.

Once again, like in Tripoli, I insisted on informing the Ministry of Health for clearance as well as a temporary registration. This was done with another 'crack and crash' formula. To date, I still believe that any undue shortcuts, politicized and otherwise, are small, almost invisible, variables that contribute to deterioration of a healthcare system. We had allowed the preceding two days for all these and other necessary preparations They matter as parts of the basics that ensure, at all levels, a safe operation: clinically, ethically, technically, professionally, legally, psychologically and socially!

Professor Ojiambo and I were to fly out the next day, Saturday, at 2 p.m., so the operation was to start at 7 a.m. Hillary would attend the whole morning session of the conference in the meantime.

A very good general surgeon from Uganda (the senior registrar at UTH) and I arrived at around 6:30 a.m., in good time for the procedure, but waited rather long for Professor Bailey, who had said she would be in theatre with me. I had assumed she would be the one assisting me.

There was now great risk of the operation clashing with my flight time the longer we waited! She was chairperson of the department; perhaps she had passed through her office on her way to theatre and gotten held up. We decided to start so that I may leave after escorting the patient to the recovery room, awake and stable.

She arrived when we were deep inside the abdomen, already dissecting the 'neck' of the aneurysm for 'proximal control.' She pulled out a notebook, took a pen and requested me to give her a running commentary about the actual procedure as she took notes.

The operation went very well! Just before midday, I had closed the abdomen and left my very able assistant to close the skin.

As I walked into the meeting hall to signal Hillary about our airport time, everybody wore a curious face! I assured them that all was well. On our way out, I checked on the patient, who was stable and awake!

Professor Ojiambo had actually changed his flight time from 5 p.m. to 2p.m. so that we could fly back together. We landed in Nairobi safely. I followed up on "my" patient through Professor Bailey. She left hospital within a week, and stayed well at follow up clinic attendances for five years. Professor Bailey had taken up her case quite passionately, if not personally. She sent me updates regularly. In the end the patient died in a road traffic accident out there!

Although I missed parts of the conference, I had attended the opening ceremony, where the female Minister for Health was the guest of honour.

In my speech as PASCAR Secretary General and Chairman of the Kenya Cardiac Society, I offered assistance from Kenya to help start heart surgery in Zambia. I followed up with a direct discussion with the Minister after the ceremony, plus a hand-written letter to commit us further. She later sent a team to Kenya, who landed on the KNH side of the Campus, looking for me. There had not been any prior communication to me from Lusaka, through any office or individual about a forthcoming delegation or the date of their arrival. Strangely enough, they were not directed to me, the university administration at the College of Health Sciences, the School of Medicine, or the Department of Surgery which were all on the same Campus! People in KNH offices and corridors are reported to have feigned ignorance about me! They offered no assistance to the visiting team. I never got to know how many visitors had come from Zambia.

I got this story much later. That the Zambians came was a fact. One may opt to dismiss the rest of the KNH part as hearsay. However, as far as I can recall, the Zambians never returned to Kenya for anything!

On my part, I was doing it for PASCAR and for the continent; indeed, also for Zambia-Kenya relations. Kenya's (and African) hidden or camouflaged, and curiously individualized selfishness is one sophisticated conduit to sanitized mass denial that will continue to bedevil many national and even continental dreams of development. Today, many words flow with unmatched eloquence and diplomacy, even make-believe authority! God help us on this **darkened and self-darkening continent** called Africa.

12

OVERCOMING A NIGHTMARE

IN 1989, Dr. Naphtali Agata, then Director of Kenyatta National Hospital, wrote me a four-line letter saying that he had appointed me Chairman of the Division of Surgery, 'full-stop!'

His communication struck me as being too simplistic, if not casual! The Division of Surgery was like two institutions in one. It included and combined surgical teams from KNH, together with heads of relevant sections, like Surgical Ward Nurses, Operating Theatre Nurses, Intensive Care Unit (ICU) Nurses, Medical Technologists, and other supporting departments, on the one hand, and surgical teams from the School (then called Faculty) of Medicine, University of Nairobi, mainly surgeons in the various surgical specialties, on the other. Anaesthesia was a different division, with a corresponding combination of teams; so were Internal Medicine, Obstetrics and Gynaecology, and Paediatrics and Child Health, respectively.

The success of surgical services in a given hospital is the hallmark of the image of that hospital, like the dressing on a shopwindow. So, the Division of Surgery at the KNH was the heartbeat of the place! Any appointment to that position warranted stringent terms of reference and a clear job description. One did not need to go to the Kenya Institute of Administration (now School of Government), to appreciate that! It was part and parcel of the dynamics of hospital management and the health profession at large.

Rather than complain about the 'simplicity' of the letter of appointment, I turned it upside-down, or overleaf if you wish, and saw a clean slate, a whole page, onto which I could write. And write I did! I spelt out my own terms of reference in my acceptance reply letter to the Director. Duly re-phrased, I spelt out the terms of reference for the office of any future Chairman of Division of Surgery at KNH, now and always. They would be the terms of reference for that office, but many institutions have problems with continuity for institutional traditions, and KNH was one such, and is so even today!

I delivered a copy of the appointment letter to the Chairman of the academic Department of Surgery, Professor Julius Kyambi, by hand and engaged him in a small strategic discussion, with mock light touch.

I pledged my loyalty to him as my academic Chairman and reminded him that I was also now his Chairman at the service level! The bottom line for me was that we needed to work together to change the face of surgery and surgical discipline in and at the hospital as a whole, starting with time control and time management. We agreed that surgical operations in theatre should start at 8 o'clock sharp. That meant arriving at the theatre latest at 7:45 a.m.; but, up to that point, that was between just the two of us, '*chairing each other!*' Would the anaesthetists play game and join us in that dream? How about nurses, technologists and the body of surgeons themselves? We were destined to work together anyway. It was now our solemn duty to sell, facilitate and effect!

As agreed between us, I invited my contemporary corresponding Chair of the Division of Anaesthesia, Dr. Calisto Omondi for a meeting within the next few days, after briefing him about my new (job) appointment and our agreement with the Chairman of the University Department of Surgery.

When the three of us met, it was smooth sailing. What remained was to sell the agreement to the workforce of the two service Divisions. It was the lead agenda at my first meeting with members of the Division of Surgery, which necessarily included the University lecturers. On the other side, Dr. Omondi easily mobilized the rank and file of the anaesthesiologists. I further roped in the nursing teams through their immediate charges.

It could not have gone any better. It was like KNH was being re-born. Morale was high; you could smell and hear the breath of commitment in the air of the corridors of the place! One would call it new-found and total ownership of the Division of Surgery! There was no need for the whistle of any referee for work to start! The workplace was the operating theatres; the time was 8am, and there were twelve operating rooms – including Theatre 2 on standby for emergencies! The outpatient clinics were going to be easier to streamline.

After several weeks, it was evident that the honeymoon was on a countdown to a huge disappointment for and disillusionment of many. As the Consultants, Registrars/Senior House Officers (SHOs), nurses, technicians and support staff trooped into the theatre complex, they huddled into groups waiting for theatre and supplies to be ready for them to start work! There was a glaring shortage of supplies and consumables! The available equipment was in truly bad shape! I persisted with my briefs to the administrative authorities.

Soon (but not so soon, since this state of affairs had existed for some time), Afya House, the Ministry of Health base, woke up to the reality of this colossal waste of time and human resources. To my horror, their inspiration, not to talk of vision, was that foreigners, especially *wazungu*, were the answer (read 'panacea') to our institutional decadence! Some international lobby group must have gotten wind and hints about this and quickly cashed in! The Ministry saw it as a managerial problem, not an issue of infrastructure, equipment and supplies; far from it, not even an issue of staff morale, welfare or motivation, leave alone remuneration! So, with thinly veiled flamboyance, they proceeded to spend colossal amounts of short cash on foreigners without batting an eyelid! No local deserved as much, leave alone a chance to try! At another level, one could not help but observe that terminologies like 'collaboration' and 'exchange' were merely politically sanitized dialect!

That scenario at KNH matured into a contract with the International Hospital Group (IHG). Three individuals from IHG soon descended on KNH and gave themselves the domineering titles of Chief Executive Director (CED), Finance Director (FD), and Director of Nursing Services (DNS).

Given all possible benefits of doubt, and granted the equivalent of a 'probation period,' they seemed to effect no change, even as more time passed. I was still the Chairman of the Division of Surgery. We met repeatedly to review issues and developments. The quorums were always over 90 percent. I was sent, repeatedly, by the Division to the CED, Mr. Bob Wilcox, with observations, petitions, requests, recommendations and goodwill messages that the entire rank and file of the Division of Surgery was ready to work. It became my deliberate and proactive routine that after every meeting of the Division, I would go and brief him. I would also consult with him just before the meetings, so that I would report the latest news and situations, as comments and messages from the Chair. After every one of those briefs and errands from the Division to the CED, I generated minutes in the form of follow up letters, summarising our discussion for the record in our files (his and mine).

There was so much *not happening* that I had no option but to request him politely to come and brief the Division and answer questions himself. I invited the other two Divisions who also used and still use the operating theatres, namely the Division of Anaesthesia and the Division of Obstetrics and Gynaecology as well as the relevant key nursing teams (Wards, Theatres, ICU, Outpatient clinics).

On the material occasion, the venue, Lecture Theatre II of the School of Medicine, was packed beyond capacity. The meeting almost ended in disarray when Mr. Wilcox could not respond satisfactorily to the entire surgical work force gathered in front of him! Please note that in that audience were Kenya's top specialists stationed at the two institutions (UoN and KNH).

More-or-less immediately after that meeting, two things happened:

I. A four-page letter, typed in single space on foolscap (not A4) paper, was written by the Finance Director to a friend of a friend in Southeast Asia. He gave it to his office Secretary at KNH to type, which she did. She also did something else – she photocopied both the hand-written piece and the typed text, and then shared them fairly widely around the hospital, because she found phrases and statements about Kenyan health professionals, if not Africans at large, which were disturbingly derogatory and unacceptable!

II. The Division decided to send a delegation to the then Minister for Health, the late Hon. Jeremiah Nyagah. They formed a committee composed of members of the affected Divisions to prepare a memorandum-cum-petition document with which to seek audience with the Minister, hand it in to him and deliberate on pertinent issues and a way forward. That committee was headed by Dr. Khama Rogo from the Division of Obstetrics and Gynaecology. (By that time, I had become Dean of the School of Medicine and was nearing the end of my term as Chairman of Division of Surgery). I had done my part to champion perspectives in surgery and surgical services at KNH at the time.

The following were the members of the **Khama Rogo Committee,** "on behalf of all Consultants, Divisions and workers at the Kenyatta National Hospital":

1. Dr. Khama Odera Rogo (Obstetrics and Gynaecology),
2. Prof. Peter Amollo Odhiambo (Surgery),
3. Prof. Julius Muasya Kyambi (Surgery).

4. Prof. Shadrack Booker Oduor Ojwang' (Obstetrics and Gynaecology),
5. Prof. David Ndetei (Psychiatry),
6. Dr. John K. Kariuki (Surgery),
7. Dr. Gerald Njoroge (Anaesthesia),
8. Dr. James Nyikal (Paediatrics); later Director of Medical Services, Permanent (Principal) Secretary in Ministry of Health and then Member of Parliament for Seme Constituency.
9. Dr. (now Prof.) Elijah Nyainda Ogola (Internal Medicine), and
10. Mr. (now Prof.) Pankaj Jani (Surgery).

As Head of Surgery at the time, as Dean of the School of Medicine and as last-minute replacement of Dr. Rogo, who had just travelled out of the country, the committee appointed me to head the delegations to both Afya House and State House, as well as act as its spokesperson. It is important that I narrate essential aspects of the story.

For the 'long letter' by the Finance Director, suffice it to quote the sections to which many people reacted, as typed. A photocopy of the hand-written version in my possession is almost illegible – it was a photocopy from a photocopy!

> *...Completed first six months out here with such excitement and controversy. We were received with mixed blessings, with most staff hoping that we will change the place, particularly the environment and the way things are done (or not done) whilst a smaller group has been very much against us, using every opportunity to disrupt (us) and protect their vested interests. By being here for six months we have surprised many, learned a great deal and know what we have to do to sort out. An incident with the surgeons triggers off a concerted press campaign with leaks coming from the hospital nearly every day. This started in February and continued for three to four weeks. What was*

printed as facts was of course usually absolute nonsense, twisted and manipulated to cause trouble for us, the hospital and the government. Many reporters had no qualification or experience to comment on health matters and continue to this day to get their articles wrong.

Somebody gave the press a copy of the contract between the Ministry of Health and our group and seeing just three of us here divided the value by three and printed what they thought were our exorbitant salaries. No thought was given to profit, overheads, visits, consultancy services, UK liabilities for three of us and research, lobbying and exchanges to either our hospital with a UK training hospital for skills development both here and in England. It shows you how stupid and naïve staff and the press can be. Our contract is about 50% cheaper than a contract for the same services would be with a USA, German or Japanese group, whilst of course our experience more closely relates to the Kenyan system due to our historical associations. The Ministry advised us to stay quiet rather than seek legal redress, which in Kenya is not as easy as UK. I'm not sure that this is right; however, we followed this advice.

Just recently one of our Medical Advisors visited us to review the scene and offer advice on how to become more effective and improve clinical practices and standards. He held a press conference on his departure and was badly misquoted by one reporter. The reporter in question simply has no knowledge of healthcare and confused himself and printed rubbish. We must correct this in the coming days, but it's an absolute insult to our advisor, arguably the number one Anaesthetist in the World, admired and respected globally. That he should be subjected to gutter press is a sorry comment on Kenya. I guess the volatile political situation has excited everyone to the point that truth is concealed by forceful ideas and perhaps we should be forgiving...

We have an enormous task ahead, trying to get managers and supervisors to accept responsibility and solve problems... The theatres and bed management are a pathetic joke, and one wonders how these so-called professionals can sleep at night. A ten year old could do better...

Below is the full statement, put together by the Khama Rogo Committee, that was delivered by the entire committee physically to the Minister for Health and the Government, with copies officially distributed as shown therein:

WE THE UNDERSIGNED, BEING REGISTERED MEDICAL CONSULTANTS AT THE KENYATTA NATIONAL HOSPITAL REITERATE THE FOLLOWING:

Background:

Services at the KNH have been deteriorating rapidly from the mid-1980s. Several reports have been written and recommendations submitted to the government with intentions of improving services at the institution. Common to all reports is the outlining of shortages of funds and less than effective management.

Since last year a contract was signed between the KNH Management Board and the International Hospital Group (IHG) in the hope that the presence of foreigners would help the situation. We had no prior knowledge of this contract nor were we privy to its details. In November, a group of three expatriates arrived at the hospital, namely a Chief Executive Director, a Finance Director and a Director of Nursing Services.

We were to learn later, through the press, of the exorbitant fees that the presence of the three expatriates was to cost our hospital during the period of the contract.

More recently we came to learn that such fees were not only for salaries but included such unqualifiable non-specific expenses like 'profits, overheads, visits, consulting services, UK liabilities for the three and research, lobbying and exchanges to link our hospital with a UK training hospital for skills development both here and in England'.

It is noteworthy that the contract is to be paid for solely by the KNH from whatever meagre funds it can raise from the treasury. No 'Aid' or 'Grant' is involved.

For the last six months (a good proportion of the total duration of the contract), all of us have remained expectant, hoping that this expensively hired team would bring magical improvement. No improvement has taken place, instead the services have deteriorated further as the meagre hospital resources have had to be shared out to service the contract. The new administrative team has also openly stated severally that without funds, nobody should expect any improvement.

In mid-May, as part of the tasking contract, a Sir Gordon Robson visited Nairobi to 'advise' the team. Within hours of his visit and following adequate briefing from the IHG team he was addressing a press conference and blaming the hospital's woes on lack of 'credentials' of staff, especially the clinical ones.

One week after the well-publicized press conference, no apology or retraction had come from the hospital management or Sir Robson. This led to a meeting of Consultants on Tuesday 25.05.92 in Lecture Theatre 2 where the Chief Executive was invited and challenged to elaborate on the visit, the unfortunate comments and stand of the hospital (read IHG).

Following that meeting the doctors passed a vote of 'no-confidence' in the hired management and appointed a small committee to deliberate and put forward these views. The committee quickly drafted a memorandum copied to the Minister of Health, the Permanent Secretary, the Chairman of the Medical Practitioners and Dentists'

Board, the Chairman of the Kenya Medical Association and the Vice-Chancellor of the University of Nairobi. The memorandum outlined the issues at hand and invited them to meet the doctors on Wednesday, at 2 p.m.

Also mentioned were excerpts from a letter written by a member of the IHG with racist, derogatory overtones, sent to associates abroad. It is the contention of the doctors here that the contents of the letter are very much in line with Sir Gordon Robson's comments and are a genuine reflection of the contempt with which we local personnel are held by the IHG.

Resolutions:

In view of the above we resolve the following:

1. *Immediate dismissal and cancellation of the unacceptable contract between our hospital and the IHG. We shall give up to 14 days for the necessary documentation and movement to be completed.*
2. *The immediate appointment of a new Kenyan management team to take over the running of the hospital. We shall expect to be fully involved in the process of such an appointment as it is our belief that it must not only be done on merit but should be given to qualified Kenyans with exemplary track records in management and who must be adequately remunerated.*
3. *At the end of 14 days, should the IHG team still be in office, we shall cease to recognize their authority, and proceed to organize an interim parallel administrative machinery with the express mandate of returning this institution to its former glory, for the benefit of the taxpayer to whom we are accountable and to all Kenyans who have a fundamental human right to health services.*
4. *In view of the grave remarks attributed to Sir Gordon, which have tarnished our reputations as specialists in various*

fields of medicine both locally and internationally and that of our hospital, we find it our most painful duty to take legal action against Sir Gordon, the IHG, whom he represented, and the Chief Executive Director of the Kenyatta National Hospital through the Medical Protection Society (UK) through whom most of us are legally represented.

5. In the 14 days mentioned above our committee is given the mandate to go to all lengths to explain our position to all relevant authorities and the Kenyan public whose interests should be no less than ours, which is the restoration of Kenyatta National Hospital.

Signed: (Names, given above).
Committee on behalf of all consultants and workers at Kenyatta National Hospital."

Armed with the memorandum, we sought and secured an appointment with the Minister for Health. He did not make us wait for too long! He was very patient and keen to hear us. No doubt he also expected us to listen to him, considering the high profile and magnitude of the contract with IHG. The talks thickened somewhat! Then came the high voltage 'circuit breaker,' from me:

"Honourable Minister, Sir, we Health Professionals sometimes feel that we should agitate for Kenya to also invite some *EXPATRIATE POLITICIANS* to 'help' the country!"

That rattled the Mzee who was known to be calm, patient, methodical, respectable balanced and dignified, almost throughout his administrative, managerial and political careers. He instantly grasped the message of politicians blinking inadvertently, and welcoming back colonialism through the window! His response was a resounding "No!" as a fundamental principle and stance of post-freedom struggle and existing (political) "independence!" That was more or less the end of the meeting, but not our case and memorandum! He had grasped the magnitude of the problem and ruled that he would take us to State House to present the case to the President. We left the meeting with a brighter light at the end of that tunnel. To some of us, comprehending politics and the political environment need not, should not, necessarily, catapult one into career politics with its murky culture, but nobody should play with your rights, or anybody else's rights for that matter!

At State House, he gave us a very good introduction to the President, presented our case (it was neither for us, nor against us - just the facts as they were), and quickly gave us the floor. The mutual respect between the two *Wazee* was palpable! Personally, I felt we were on safe ground and in good hands, even though we were missing our far more eloquent spokesperson, Dr. Khama Rogo!

The President understood us even faster than his Minister had. Our introductory remarks were that collaborating nations had known levels of diplomacy, respect, decorum and communication; that Kenya was no longer anybody's colony, and that recent events relating to the contract with International Hospital Group (IHG) had literally trashed all that, even though the contract in question was with a trading company and not another foreign national government. Of course, individual members of our delegation on both occasions participated in the deliberations.

The President immediately pronounced the formation of a commission to look into the matter, determine the merits of the case and spell out ways and means of revoking the contract with IHG.

To complete the membership of the Commission, the President directed that there had to be added the Attorney General, the Director of Personnel and the Ministry of Health as the office of the Director of Medical Services. Some of us dubbed it the "Divorce Committee"!

The prescription was complete: only to dispense!

The long and short of it was that the contract was ultimately revoked. Our own recommendation was that since the IHG team at

KNH were in breach of the letter and spirit of the contract, occasioning its premature termination, they did not deserve any compensation which might have been based on the terms and conditions of the contract. However, we did not follow up on the fine details which were now wholly in the hands of the Ministry of Health and the Government.

Back at the KNH, we were soon to celebrate the appointment of **Professor Julius Meme** (since deceased) who had just returned from a short programme at Harvard University, USA. His appointment as the new Chief Executive Director was a big plus for us. He was not only a member of my Faculty, but also among the first batch of **sixteen pioneer medical students** to qualify in 1972 from the same institution that he was now to chaperone. It was like we pushed Kenya's independence that far forward! Dr. Khama Rogo was now back. The two of us proceeded to congratulate Professor Meme and took him to the hospital's senior staff canteen (we deliberately chose an eatery within the hospital) to celebrate!

I have detailed this part of my institutional involvement and experience as a case study for all my readers. It was a real nightmare against my dreams for strengthening an institution in a resource-scarce environment. As a case study, it also carries a triad, which is disastrous for this country:

a. Neglect of professionals, professional aspirations and lukewarm commitment (even without talking of vision) to real and sacrificial issues of development;

b. Total political disorientation with thinly veiled relics of colonial mind-sets, and

c. Environmental lethargy and disharmony. Besides, many **appointed** administrators instinctively opted for the trodden path of "how the government works, or operates," rather than be brave enough to generate, innovate and 'patronize' new, even if not so visionary, ideas!

These three co-exist uneasily to plant and stamp the 'witchcraft' of under-development and persisting mesmerisation by anything foreign onto the country and its people. This will carry on until and unless we re-group, re-plan and re-dedicate ourselves for the future of our children and the children of our children, especially if we truly do not want to hear of or see any more slavery (even today, slavery and camouflaged slave trade still dare to rear their ugly heads!).

One must lament the case of leaders and politicians who talk forcefully, like high school debaters, who, while very creative, remain largely if not wholly fictional!

13

A BULLET NAMED 'ASTHMA' AND GENERAL CHINA

WAS IT OR WAS IT NOT "Bronchial asthma?" It was virtually a chance diagnosis.

The patient had presented with breathing problems. A chest x-ray was done and there it was. A bullet-shaped foreign body showed itself at the central part of the upper chest, behind the upper limit of the breastbone, a part referred to in medical anatomical terminology as the *thoracic inlet*, located just below the root of the neck.

Indeed, it was a bullet! The patient remembered that he had been shot by colonial forces at the start of the *Mau Mau* war in 1952. He had survived the shot and literally forgot about it until the present moment, 36 years later, when I asked if he had ever been shot in the past. **The patient was, of course, after all, the freedom fighter par excellence, Waruhiu Itote, better known as "General China."**

All attention was now automatically diverted to the bullet. The inevitable assumption was that this bullet was to blame for the symptoms. Without any more questions, he was referred to the thoracic and cardiovascular surgical unit. The family, including his wife and his daughter, Mary, who was a pharmacist at the same KNH, opted for his admission into the Amenity ward.

In a standard operation that splits the breastbone (sternum) in the middle (sternotomy), a large sharp bullet was located, dissected out and removed from the root of the neck. It was rusty all around its surface. There was fibrotic scar tissue all around it on the patient's body tissue side!

Special care was taken for the safe custody of the bullet. It was ceremoniously handed over to the hospital administration, not so much for legal, military or ballistic reasons, but mainly because it had been retrieved from a hero (*shujaa*) of Kenya's war for independence. The bullet alone was a gem of Kenya's history more than a relic of military confrontation between ruler and ruled.

The patient made an uneventful recovery with good healing of the sternotomy wound. His symptoms had abated. He was duly discharged. His follow-up as an outpatient was more routine than related to any new or recurrent symptoms, with somewhat lengthy intervals and mainly through feedback from Mary. He did not himself return for clinical review. More than a decade passed by. I did not hear of his death until long after the event. Symptoms similar to those that brought him to the hospital in 1988 had recurred!

More years passed. Then the family came forward to hand over the bullet to the headquarters of the National Museums of Kenya. On their request and invitation, I accompanied Mary and her stepmother for that ceremony at the Museums complex on Museum Hill.

"UHURU!!!!" May he continue to rest in peace!

The infamous 'asthma'-causing bullet.

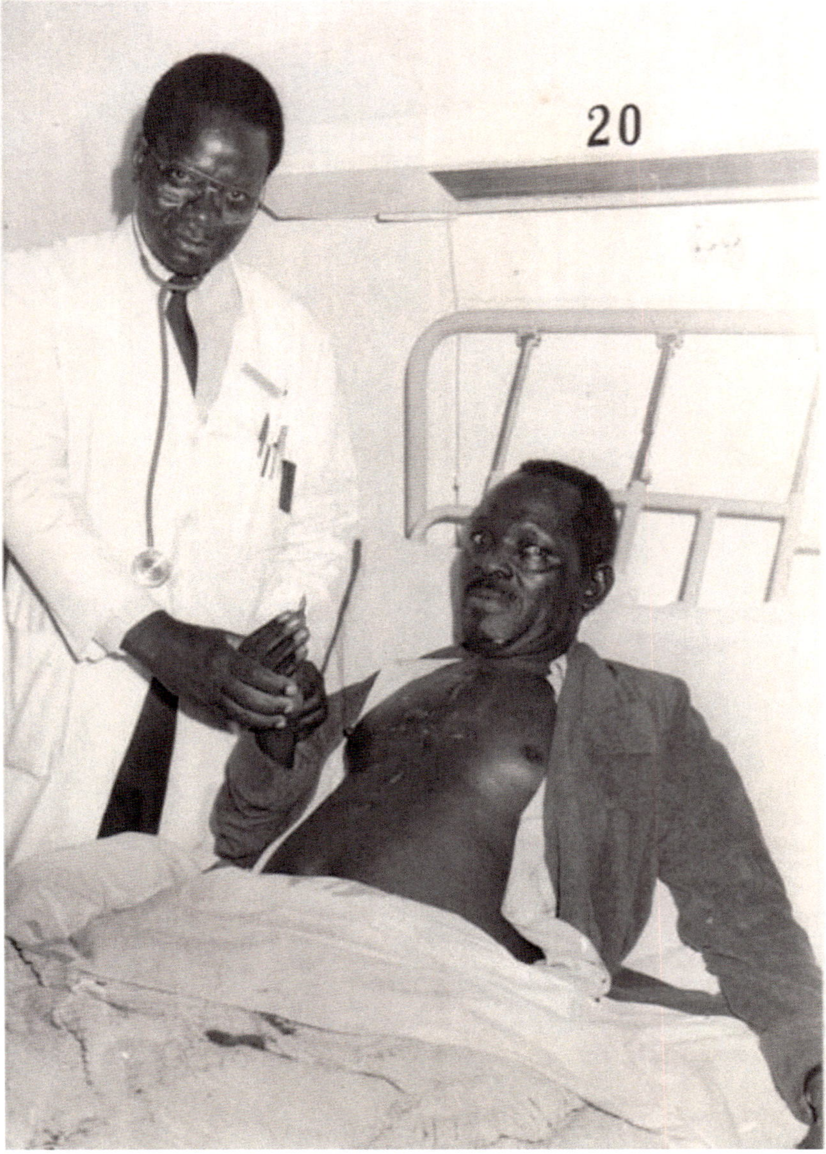

Freedom fighter Waruhiu Itote (*nom de guerre* General China) after surgery.

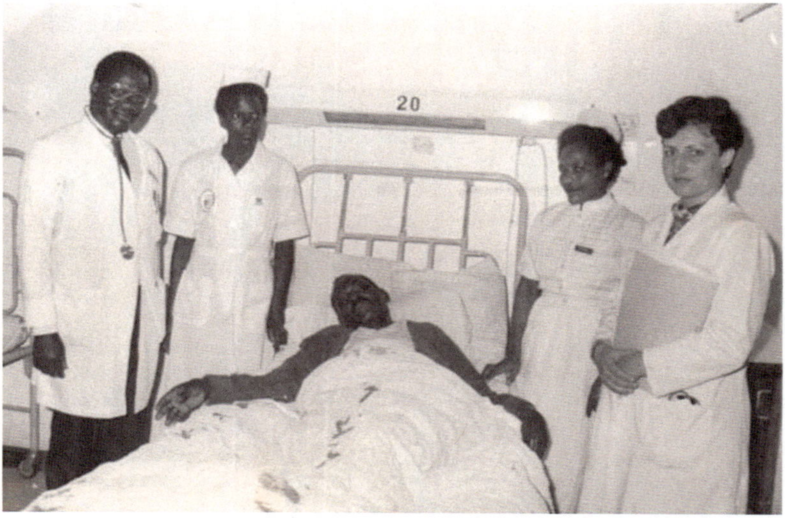

With General China and the team at KNH, 1988.

With Mrs. Waruhiu and Mary Waruhiu at the National Museums of Kenya.

With Mrs. Waruhiu and Mary Waruhiu at the National Museums of Kenya. Standing with us are the museum Deputy Director (left), the Director (second left) and the Coordinator, Mr. Nyaga (far right).

14

FROM KABATI IN KANDARA, MURANG'A, TO NAIROBI IN A 504 PICK-UP VAN WITH SHUJAA BILDAD KAGGIA

AS I HAVE previously mentioned, upon completing my six-month orientation internship at the Kenyatta National Hospital (KNH) at the end of August 1971, I was posted to Murang'a District Hospital. Its old name "Fort Hall" was still seen at times in official communication. The work was tough but enjoyable, with great teams at every level. There were several stretches when I was the only doctor in the whole hospital. The highway still passed through town and the hospital received many trauma casualties.

Socially, it was like I had been plucked from the city jungle and placed into a unique diasporic family, way beyond Murang'a town and Murang'a District. One did not see the indigenous Murang'a magnates and giants like the Rubias, Matibas and Michukis in the neighbourhood. If you looked for them, you might be told to go and check for them in Nairobi where they owned chunks of that jungle.

But there were two people who I got to know and cannot forget – one naturalized, the other native Murang'an. Ishmail Aluoch had lived in Murang'a from 1958. He had a spot on the pavement at a corner of the main town street where he ran his cobbling business. One of his legs was a bygone childhood mishap from poliomyelitis; he was disabled but not rendered unable. He fitted in so seamlessly with the place and the people that you also felt at home in his presence. Originally, he came from my own constituency (now sub-county) of Karachuonyo, but nearer Kendu Bay than me. He visited there in Karabondi (or was it

Seka?) from time to time, but for all practical purposes, he was a Murang'an. His wife, Njoki, was from the local neighbourhood. Here was a blend of self-confidence, humility, realism without apology, recognizable capacity and the connections that also encapsulated Kenya's history. Councillor Aluoch, as he was destined to be, was a larger-than-life embodiment of the saying "disability is not inability(!)"He was a friend, a brother, and a guide, my guide.

He showed me around Murang'a and its environs; the place was teeming with people from Luo-Nyanza, civil servants and sisal farm workers from nearby Makuyu. There was one person, however, that he wanted me to meet more than anything. I ended up meeting him over a month later.

On the appointed day, we left Murang'a town and went well beyond Maragua, turning at 'Kenol' (I think before it got that name) to *Shujaa* Bildad Kaggia's home.

I was immediately struck by the simplicity and humility of everything and everybody around him, not to talk of himself, a '*mzee-kijana*' ('young old man,' old but still strong, 'young' respected leader, 'young at heart,' if subdued, etc) par excellence, but sadly wasted by his own larger environment! His sister, Wairimu, was on hand to join his wife, *Mama* Mbugua, to receive us. Wairimu was herself a quietly seasoned politician. When she passed on much later - but before her brother - it was long after one last outward trip I made with her and her *shujaa* brother from Kandara straight to KNH in Nairobi in my personal pick-up van.

In the interval between that first home visit to Murang'a town to *Shujaa* Bildad Kaggia's last days after his discharge from hospital to his Nairobi house (Number 10-6 Lumumba Estate), we kept in touch off and on. Even when I moved back to Nairobi, my family and I paid them a couple of visits on their farm. On occasion, I would pick him from his humble shop at Kenol, take him to his home for the day, then return to Nairobi. I remember finding him sorting out heaps of old newspapers, very much as if he was trying to set the record straight. He would leave them there and we would go to his home. Whenever I could, I would go if Wairimu called and said he was not well. That is what happened the last time she called. The obvious decision at that time was to take him to hospital.

I fuelled my old pick up van (nicknamed *Matatu* by the family) and went for him. He sat between Wairimu and me in the front cabin of the pick-up; just the three of us!

I undertook to admit him under my own care onto the Amenity floor of KNH Tower Block and then mobilized colleagues in the various specialties as well as the 'young turks' or 'comrades' whom I could reach. I took responsibility for payments of his admission and treatment later, but soon enough. Trusting my word as an insider who was always serious and conscientious about my patients (a familiar trait of mine around), the Casualty Department allowed us in without paying a deposit, after a brief consultation with the bosses!

I commandeered his registration for that admission. Wairimu and I wheeled him to Ward 10C, which was on the 10th floor of the Tower Block of KNH, the Amenity Floor. I made sure that he was recognized for who and what he was. On all his papers, he was not "Mr." Kaggia but **'*Shujaa* Bildad Kaggia.'**

It was much later when the title SHUJAA became more frequently used, on the day, years afterward, when Kenyatta Day and Moi Day were merged into SHUJAA DAY, again, like setting the record straight.

Once we settled in the ward, I started mobilizing the political 'Young Turks' whom I could reach, both to spread the word of his admission and to fundraise for him.

As I recall it, the only people I could reach immediately were the Hon. Raila Odinga, whose father Jaramogi Odinga had been a formidable freedom fighter, and the Hon. James Orengo. Word went round fast. Contributions started in earnest. I think Wairimu might have handled some of the earlier donated money; but we soon agreed to centralize everything in the hands of the eldest Shujaa's son, Caetano. He was the elder stepbrother to Mbugua and Njoki (not Ishmail's Njoki). All went very well throughout his admission.

But just as the time came for *Mzee* to be discharged, we could not trace Caetano. I heard that he had returned to the USA. He did not leave any of the donated money with anybody, not even his aunt, Wairimu! I was struck speechless. I simply 'resigned,' flabbergasted! Wairimu and the others must have undertaken subsidiary fundraising to get Mzee discharged from the hospital. He was not taken back to Murang'a, but to his Nairobi house, Number 10-6 Lumumba Estate, near Jericho Estate in Eastlands. He stayed there until his very last moment. I had visited him there twice earlier, but I was not in town when he passed away! His 'disability' at the time of his demise was a mixture of poor physical health, age, stress and poverty – a very sad narrative after the history he had himself taken part in shaping for all Kenyans! May his soul rest in eternal peace!

By that time, his youngest daughter was a grown lady. Wairimu had died some time before that. Mbugua had died much earlier. *His* death shocked me, happening almost as a sudden event. When it came to friendship with that family, Mbugua was my best friend after Mzee. He was so humble and quiet, but something seemed to have subdued him; perhaps it was his father's frustrations!

I recall one night being called in to see a patient in the Male Medical Ward of the Nairobi Aga Khan Hospital. As I walked into the shared ward and headed toward my patient, there on my left was Mbugua signalling and greeting me! He was in high spirits and was discharged a couple of days after that. After a few months, word reached me that Mbugua was gone! I was devastated! That was long before the death of his mother; a little later, his aunt Wairimu passed, and finally his father, the Shujaa himself.

Caetano was the eldest stepbrother of Mzee's other children. His mother, Mzee's first wife, was long gone. The last I heard of him was when he came back from the United States of America to contest in an election. He did not make much headway. He was far away from being my hero. I did not bother.

Njoki ventured into business, but we lost touch. Her second elder brother was the humblest of them all. He and I never quite bonded with each other. All said and done, I lost touch with my hero family. Kenya owes them, the Mzee and his entire family, a huge debt!

In the meantime, Hon. (former Councillor) Ishmail Aluoch had spent two terms as a Councillor representing Murang'a town centre, but he also passed on later. It was then that we went back to Murang'a with Mama Jim (another Murang'a Hospital 'alumnus') to condole with his wife Njoki. We met their grown son Tom Mboya, named after the political leader who was assassinated, Thomas (Tom) Joseph Mboya.

Another Shujaa I encountered who was part of the "Kapenguria Six" was the suave Fred Kubai who, health wise, suffered more from heavy smoking! I had the humble privilege of repairing an artery in one of his legs. After some time, he developed a similar blockage in the opposite leg and was operated on by a colleague. It is likely he did not quite stop smoking and ended up having that leg amputated.

One must take serious note of my frustrations with tobacco and must understand part of the background of my uncompromising and unending war with tobacco itself, the tobacco industry and blind-folded tobacco consumers! Unfortunately, legislation, which is in place in Kenya, is a very unpredictable lifeline for victims of a disorganized lifestyle in an environment compounded with commercial greed, corruption and impunity, even without mentioning addiction, masquerading as "human right!"

Mzee Bildad Kaggia (right) with his family: Mama Mbugua (seated centre), daughter Njoki (standing, left) and some grandchildren. The youngest son was not at home. Caetano was in the USA.

From left: Njoki, Mama Mbugua, the Mzee and myself.

My pick-up van nicknamed *Matatu*.

15

DEANSHIP

PROF. GIDEON OKELO was elected Dean of the Faculty of Medicine in October 1991. Two weeks later, he was appointed Director of Medical Services. Prof. David Ndetei was appointed to act in his place, until the elections for a new substantive Dean were called in February 1992. I was approached by a host of colleagues to vie for the post, and I said okay, quite simply. It did not matter so much to me, but they urged me to just let them campaign for me. Prominent among them was Dr. Khama Rogo, but there were many. The actual election date would find me out of the country attending an all-India Thoracic and Cardiovascular conference in Calcutta, India. They assured me not to worry; they would do the winning job! 'Vintage' Khama urged me to write (not draft) my "victory speech" and give it to him in readiness for the occasion so he could read it in my absence!

There were three candidates. The acting Dean, a member of Faculty from another campus, and myself. As the campaigns entered their final stretch, word came to us that the one from the other campus was very busy telling Faculty that I had withdrawn my candidature in his favour. My team insisted that I show my face to rebut the manufactured rumour. I did. It worked. Then I travelled.

As stated earlier, the elections were due to be held in my absence. It was a resounding victory in my favour – there were combined votes of less than 30 for the two contestants against mine of over 90. Fair and square.

However, by the time I returned from the conference one week later I had literally forgotten about the elections. From the airport l passed through the Department to check my pigeonhole for mail. Suddenly I heard a voice calling, almost shouting at me from behind:

"Congratulations!"

More or less lost, I did not make the connection immediately, but I looked back. Sure enough, the person was talking to me! Unfortunately, I cannot recall who it was. The details were that I had been elected the new Dean of the Faculty of Medicine.

This was lunch time of Friday. I proceeded home and reported at the new office on Monday. The other two candidates were my friends and we continued as if nothing had happened.

Nevertheless, one could not help noticing that the acting Dean had decamped back to his Department immediately and without notice after the elections. He just abandoned the office of the Dean. Only Miss Alice Waweru, the very hardworking secretary, was there to receive, and 'hand over,' to me.

Alice Waweru

Professionally, Alice was a copy typist but was more knowledgeable, more diligent, more professional, more committed and, above all, more disciplined than many secretaries in the entire Faculty. She had a very good memory and knew the corners of the office like the back of her hand. That was one big plus for me during the take-off, or 'lone' launch, and the ensuing two years (plus another two and a quarter) up to 31st May 1996.

I had to 'learn' fast and take charge of the entire Faculty. It was one Faculty within one College, but it was bigger than that. Although there were twenty Departments in it, three of them were themselves potential Faculties, namely Dental Sciences, Pharmacy and Nursing Sciences. One day soon, they would be weaned off to be independent Faculties. That day did not come until July 3, 1995.

For now, one might say first things first, and fast! The infrastructure was in total shambles. More than 70 percent of the desks, benches and chairs in the two main lecture theatres were broken. Security lights were absent as students in search of pocket money had been stealing their parts like circuit breakers to sell. Even the projection systems were in dire need of repair and maintenance. I specify this because I caught one student trying to climb up into the Dean's office one early evening (dusk) while I was still in the office; he ran away very fast and changed direction upon landing on the ground floor! Soon after, another was brought to me and pleaded guilty to plucking out a whole circuit breaker to go and sell! Poverty is a curse!

On different occasions, I met the entire Faculty in my 'constituency' – the grounds men and women, then the maintenance department and administrative support teams (including the secretaries) on the KNH Campus and the rest. The bonding was instant.

Sometime before my trip to India and the elections, somebody had observed at a Faculty Board meeting that the School would be 25 years old come 3rd July that year, 1992! When I took over, I remembered this and determined that it was a must that we mark that day properly as our **Silver Jubilee** Day. We had barely four months to go! But I hit the road running with target committees (finance, fundraising, social, publications, editorial, etc).

Mid-March 1992 came fast; near the end I had another conference to attend without fail – that of the Convocation of the American College of Cardiology in Dallas, Texas, USA, to represent PASCAR as its President. A few years before this, Prof. Hussein Badawi from Alexandria, Egypt, then the President of PASCAR, and I as Secretary-General, had been invited to attend a conference of the American Heart Association. It was held in collaboration with the International Society and Federation of Cardiology (ISFC), which was later re-named the World Heart Federation (WHF). At the time, PASCAR had not been given any official recognition among other international cardiac bodies. No reason was given. We had registered our protest on behalf of PASCAR and gone ahead to attend just like other ordinary delegates. This time also, I was determined to attend the prestigious convocation.

Retracing our steps back here at home in early April 1992, we had only about two months to the historical ceremony. We worked very hard. The School moved as one.

But there were serious pitfalls, potholes and bumps. We committed funds we received into a special separate faculty account at Trade Bank. As we geared towards spending the money, the head of the Finance Committee, Dr. (later Professor) Nicholas Othieno-Abinya, reported to me that they had found that the bank had closed down. I went with him to go and find out what had happened. To our horror, the two brothers who owned the bank had fled to Canada after its collapse. All their customers were affected. More or less like other fellow customers, we had no immediate formula of following up. We remained only with the money from the central administration of the University.

The Editorial and Publication Committee also hit a snag with the printers who had been awarded the tender. They were not getting the proofs and yet the printers were demanding payment. As I piled up pressure on the committee to hurry up, three expensively dressed 'thugs' walked into my office like the forerunners of impunity and talked as if there was no problem, but sure enough betrayed gestures like people who already knew they were being looked for. I tried to get information about their printing press and its whereabouts, but they were quite cagey and slippery. Their body language was loaded, and they walked with carefree dare-devilry. Their location was supposedly along Luthuli Avenue, River Road complex, in the Central Business District of Nairobi City. I tried to follow their woolly directions and went there incognito. They were nowhere and the printing setups around did not seem to know them.

We were not deterred. The celebrations had to happen, and they did! We ran a couple of free medical camps in residential estates like Kibera and set up an HIV/AIDS counselling desk on school grounds. For the main formal part on the day itself, we organized speeches, special lectures and a dinner dance. The guest of honour for our silver Jubilee celebration was none other than Prof. Thomas Risley (TR) Odhiambo, Founder and Director of International Centre for Insect Physiology and Ecology (ICIPE). His keynote address discussed water and aquifers as vital resources of the planet earth, including their place in health and human/animal survival. Unfortunately, the entire written speech was later misplaced from our offices. Despite being duly filed, we could not trace it. We had all along assumed it was among our filed documents. This was during the pre-digital era. By the time we realised this when we wanted to include it later in our proposed 40-year celebrations, the professor had passed on! Despite our efforts and some help from both ICIPE and the African Academy of Sciences, we never got lucky!

The other special guests included Professor Francis Gichaga, (Vice-Chancellor, University of Nairobi), Professor Joseph Maina Mungai, (former Dean, former VC), Professor Nimrod Odundo Bwibo (former Dean and first College of Health Sciences Principal), Professor

Hannington Ouma Pamba (former Dean), Professor Frederick Onyango Ngao (Principal, College of Biological and Physical Sciences), Professor Jesse Mugambi (Registrar, Academic Affairs, UoN), Professor Samuel Sinei, (Principal, College of Health Sciences), Professor Hillary Ojiambo (former Chairman, Department of Internal Medicine) and other Chairmen of Departments.

In spite of the financial constraints mentioned above, we were able to obtain prizes, snacks, a Silver Jubilee cake and sponsorship for the dinner dance. The short rains of the season seemed heavier that year, especially on the evening and night of the dinner dance. The actual venue was quickly moved to the veranda in front of the operating theatre entrance where the rain still caught up with us. People danced ankle deep in the floods! The ever-supportive Vice-Chancellor, Professor Francis Gichaga and his team (Prof. Jesse Mugambi, Registrar, Academic Affairs and college principals including Prof. Fred Onyango Ngao) were present. The evening was a huge success.

Silver Jubilee celebrations, 3rd July 1992: Professor Francis Gichaga, the VC, addressing the gathering.

Silver Jubilee celebrations, 3rd July 1992: Cutting the cake at the gala dinner. I am standing far right. With the knife is Joyce Musandu (now deceased), who was at the time the Chairperson of the Department of Advanced Nursing, and later the first Director of the School of Nursing Sciences.

Part of the crowd taking advantage of the free clinic offered during the Silver Jubilee.

Silver Jubilee celebrations, 3rd July 1992: With Prof. Hastings Okoth Ogendo (School of Law, guest lecturer), centre and Prof. Jeckoniah Ndinya Acholla (Department of Medical Microbiology), left.

Prof. Hastings Okoth Ogendo delivering his keynote address at the Silver Jubilee arena. Session chairman Prof. David Gatei (centre) and I look on.

Silver Jubilee celebrations: L-R: Prof. Francis Gichaga, VC, UoN; Prof. T. R. Odhiambo, Director ICIPE and guest of honour; Prof. Samuel Sinei, Principal, CHS; Prof. Joseph Maina Mungai, Chief Guest; Prof. P. A. Odhiambo, Dean, Faculty of Medicine, Host; Prof. Hillary P. W. Ojiambo, Senior Faculty, ex-Chair Medicine; Prof. Jesse Mugambi, Registrar, UoN.

Silver Jubilee celebrations 3rd July 1992: Prof. Hillary Ojiambo signing the Visitor's Book.

TOP: The guest of honour, Thomas Risley Odhiambo, signs the visitor book. Looking on are, from left to right, Prof. Francis Gichaga, Prof. Joseph Maina Mungai, myself, Prof. Samuel Sinei, Prof. Hillary Ojiambo and Prof. Jesse Mugambi.

LEFT: Prof. Francis Gichaga makes a speech at the Silver Jubilee gala dinner. I am seated to his right.

I address the gathering at the Silver Jubilee gala dinner. Dr. Florence Odhiambo is seated far right.

We then set onto revision of curricula and syllabi. Surprisingly, there was no entry for the Faculty and its departments in the old university calendars except for the Department of Psychiatry. Even the postgraduate programmes were barely anywhere. I had a problem with the curriculum committee, but we managed to prepare quite a number from different Departments. On a priority listing were Pharmacy and Dental Sciences because they were now set to mature into independent Faculties under the College of Health Sciences. Nursing Sciences was much slower. There would soon be three Faculties under the College, namely Medicine, Dental Sciences and Pharmacy. In the end, we managed to deliberate and agree to name the new nursing faculty-to-be as the "Faculty of Nursing Sciences." It took me some effort to convince the chairperson and representatives that it was better for their discipline if it was named the 'Faculty of Nursing Sciences' rather than simply 'Faculty of Nursing.' They finally appreciated that 'simple' difference! They became a School much later after my two-plus terms as Dean.

The Faculty of Medicine itself continued to grow from strength to strength! The 40-year celebration date in 2007, long after my Deanship, did not materialize as proposed! Ten years later, in 2017, the School actually celebrated its Golden Jubilee. I was privileged to preside over the preparations and the programme.

The overlap between my Chairmanship of the Division of Surgery and my Deanship ended after the 'successful departure' of the IHG team and the hand-over to the next Chair of the Division, Dr. (later Professor) John Ating'a of the Department of Orthopaedic Surgery.

A major student affair soon after becoming Dean was the reorganization of the kitchens with the introduction of a Pay as You Eat (PAYE) system in the entire University of Nairobi. Before this, student meals in the halls of residence were free for the students; now they would have to pay to be served a meal. But soup or gravy, served on its own, was free; if one did not have enough money they could simply just buy *ugali* and ask for soup/gravy to complete their meal. That menu was unofficially dubbed "*Ugali* and Free" between students and serving/kitchen staff.

I joined hands with fellow Deans and Directors to oversee the process of this change-over. The physical adjustments in eating areas were undertaken when the University was closed, with no students on any of the campuses. The closure of the University had originally come about because of student unrest in one Campus over unrelated matters. The central administration seemed to have taken advantage of this and started working. It took many months!

Deans and Directors visited different campuses, including the Central Catering Unit (CCU), to assess the works as well as determine unit costs of portions of different food items on a subsidized scale.

When the University re-opened, I went to the dining hall at the first mealtime and ate with the students to reassure them about the quality of the food. All went quite well!

Very soon thereafter, the student leadership on the KNH Campus sought audience with the Principal of the College of Health Sciences, Professor Samuel Sinei and myself as the Dean. There were four student groups, with corresponding student organizations, according to the mainstream professional programmes at the College, as follows:

1. Association of Medical Students of University of Nairobi, AMSUN,
2. Nairobi University Dental Students Association , NUDSA,
3. Nairobi University Pharmacy Students Association, NUPSA, and
4. Nairobi University Nursing Students Association, NUNSA.

They wanted the Principal and I to explain to them why they had been sent home and why they ended up spending so much time away from their studies when it was well known in the whole University that students from the Faculty of Medicine never caused trouble, even this time round! They accepted our frank explanations and apology.

At the next Deans' committee meeting, in the interest of my students, I proposed that going forward, should there be any disturbance leading to the closure of the University, only the Campus or Campuses affected should be closed, rather than the entire University whose campuses were scattered widely apart. The unaffected campuses would have to be accorded extra security against striking students from other campuses to ensure continuity of programmes.

Within the next two or so years, a new crop of AMSUN student leaders raised their concern about the on-going six-year MBChB programme, whose longer duration had been implemented within the decade. The following were some of their points of concern:

1. Six years were too long,
2. It was possible to cover and complete the syllabus within the 'traditional' five-year period,
3. The holidays were unnecessarily long and could be shortened to permit more time in the class so as to finish sooner,

4. Medical schools in neighbouring countries did not have the luxury of our lengthy breaks, and
5. There would be no compromise of standards because the syllabus would still be covered adequately anyway!

I received several delegations. I was able to convince the first two. When they reported to their colleagues, they were rebuked that they had been 'bought' or bribed by the Dean!

They did not relent! Another delegation came!

Finally, I agreed to let them address the Vice-Chancellor on the matter. The VC agreed to meet them. I had no transport to ferry them to the Main Campus, three kilometres away! They were ready to walk. And walk they did! That day, that area of the city was painted white: a peaceful crowd, all in lab coats, marched right into Taifa Hall, the main hall on University of Nairobi's Main Campus.

The only other time I remember when the town was painted white with doctors' professional attire was much later after this, when the whole of the College of Health Sciences marched for about five kilometres in a long procession escorting the body of the late Professor Nimrod Odundo Bwibo from Chiromo Mortuary Parlour (owned by the UoN) to the All Saints Cathedral, close to Nairobi's Central Business District (CBD).

Inside Taifa Hall their spokesmen, Mr. Kirsteen Awori and Tom Chokwe, made a very passionate and impressive presentation, complete with slides and statistics, liberally quoting and referring to neighbouring institutions like Muhimbili and Makerere medical schools.

The Vice-Chancellor agreed to look into the matter and formed a committee that finally cleared the way for a return to the five-year programme!

Nobody boasted of winning over the other, although I later sensed that the two spokesmen seemed too shy to face me, even after their post-graduate education, one in Surgery (Kirsteen) and the other in

Anaesthesiology (Tom). I advised at least one of them to relax, and told them that that had been **dialogue** at its best!

When leaders ignore or overlook the importance of **timely dialogue**, and then belatedly and condescendingly, at times even desperately, plead for it only when things explode, then something is very wrong with their own managerial perspectives! True and honest dialogues do not break systems or subdue them in any way.

All this happened towards the end of my Deanship. Later on, I sensed some misgivings that it was not proper to have let the students walk to the Main Campus in white coats! I invoked Community Medicine and dialogue. The misgivings did not escalate.

But I was not yet off the hook. Not too long after I had handed over to my successor Dean, Professor Hannington Ouma Pamba, who had been re-elected for another (broken) term, he informed me that the Medical Practitioners and Dentist Board needed an explanation as to why the Faculty of Medicine had reduced the MBChB course from six years to five years! How would the University of Nairobi explain the lowering of standards as a consequence? He had been summoned by the Board to go and 'show cause.' Since I was the one who had presided over the changes, could I please go and represent him at the Board? I readily agreed.

Sure enough, it was a question of standards of the MBChB degree which seemed to them threatened by the reduction of the course duration. It was not a question of overworking students throughout the years, because the reduced holidays without subtracting anything from the syllabi had been the 'norm' in medical curricula in most, if not all, medical schools all over the world!

When I was given the floor, my presentation was short:

1. We had previously covered the same syllabi in five years;
2. The spread to six was to reduce the strain on the students who had to go through the tight programme;

3. The students themselves felt that they could do without the luxury of 'reduced strain.'
4. If you consider the full syllabus to be 100 percent and you must cover it, then you must cover it – if you can cover it, then it did not matter how long you took to do that! "Too long" itself might turn out to be a waste of time, or a state of mind!
5. By reducing the MBChB course from six to five years this time round, it was not the content that was reduced; it was the duration!
6. The difference between six years and five years given our content and our many "long" breaks within the previous six-year spell was negligible. Five years had been the 'norm' for generation after generation of medical students!
7. There was obviously a misunderstanding and misconception between time and content, somewhere!

For a brief moment, I did not look up, but I felt, rather than saw, glances and cross glances around the room. When I finally looked up, the Chairman said: "Thank you very much, Professor! You may go!"

I had spent far less than ten minutes in that room, including time for opening pleasantries! The Board's committee remained behind to continue with other items on their agenda.

Resumption of five-year programme was upheld! Again, **dialogue!** The storm that threatened to engulf the Faculty of Medicine cleared! The lynch mob dispersed. Indeed, there had been stalwarts at the ready!

It makes a lot of sense if one engages with their students as a parent would in both 'peace time' and 'tension time,' instead of drawing daggers at them when they have a grievance, genuine or otherwise. One should accord them the freedom of up-coming fellow intellectuals and future colleagues and leaders, and let them have their say. The old 'cane' is very tempting to use and might work but fortunately or unfortunately, the world has shifted! There still are rude, crude, stubborn, arrogant and even belligerent students, workers, etc - one might need a redefinition of "Human Rights" to include responsibility at individual and dependent levels! But dialogue will bail out management in more than ninety-nine percent of situations!

These days I see timetables and calendars moving back and forth. That content has increased is not the issue for doubt. One needs to be sure that somebody is not wriggling to increase more free time for the teacher!

The two episodes below emphasize the importance of dialogue. Before I became Dean, Senior House Officers (SHOs) – postgraduate students – had downed their tools in a grievance against KNH. It was threatening to boil over. I found myself in the presence of the group, assembled in the seminar room of the Department of Surgery. Whoever had requested me to talk to them I cannot remember (I think I just saw them in the room and walked in and started a conversation!), and although it was known that I could be radical when provoked, I was not there to flatter the SHOs with shallow support!

For what was possibly the very first time in their medical training, I tried to get them to see things from a new perspective. I advised them to bear in mind that they were students who had come to learn, and that the KNH factor was just one facet of their student experience. There were classrooms on both sides of the KNH-University divide, most of them run by university departments; on that occasion their complaint was not with the university. On a scale of priorities, their overall education, with its limited period of interaction with KNH, was far more important for their future. They actually might have been better off if they simply let their teachers address some of their issues for them! For their medical programme, I reminded them that they actually had more than five class 'rooms:' the actual room with a blackboard, screen and projector; the ward round; the outpatient clinic; the operating room (theatre); the logbook; departmental seminars and presentations; supervision of dissertations and theses, direct mentoring, allocations and projects, etc!

As far as I could tell, no one had broken it down that far for them or for any other batch of our students. I whispered to the chairman the gist of that conversation and asked him to take it from there! My memory tells me that that was the end of that 'strike,' with no ripple effects of any sort!

Then came the University of Nairobi staff strike of 1994: My promise to the Faculty of Medicine board had been that on the days when meetings were scheduled, I would adjourn the meeting at 4.45 p.m. to give staff enough time to pick their children up from school. School transport of any sort was yet to be widespread in those days. However, when the university staff strike was tabled as part of the agenda for one meeting, that day was different! When it got to 4.45 p.m. and I said that we needed to adjourn the meeting because the time had come, there was a louder "No!" than the ones we hear in Parliament:

"No, we finish this one first"!

The quorum was still intact! The meeting went on well beyond 6 p.m. It reached a point when the Faculty Board needed input from the Acting Principal. I called him. Those were the days of pagers, or 'bleeps.' You could not talk back. You just stood up and went, wherever! He came!

Then there reached a point during the same meeting when it was agreed that he as Principal, and I as the Dean, were to call and brief the Vice-Chancellor about the meeting as well as the position and recommendation of the School of Medicine. We had generated a **'back-to-work formula.'** We were to call the VC after the meeting, which finally ended a little after 8 p.m. The Acting Principal was to lead the way as the spokesperson of the College. By that time, it was still a one-College-one-Faculty situation. By protocol, he was the boss!

To my utter surprise, when we entered his office to make the call, he refused to call the Vice-Chancellor! I tried to plead on behalf of the Faculty Board; he refused!

I took the phone and secured an early morning appointment with the Vice-Chancellor for the next day! Could he, the Principal, come with me? The answer was another definite "No!"

After listening to me, the Vice-Chancellor constituted a "Back-to-Work Formula Committee." I was made a member therein. The only other two people whom I remember in that committee were the tough-talking Professor Jimmy Angwenyi and the suave, fatherly, solid-gold Professor Godfrey Muriuki. Jimmy ended up listening to, and agreeing with, the proposals from my Faculty.

With one brief to the Vice-Chancellor by the committee and some deliberations, the strike was over. We became very good friends thereafter.

Somewhere in the not-so-distant past, I recalled that back in 1959-60, long before all this, the motion of one of the school debates I had taken part in was:

"War is the only way of settling disputes!"

which I had opposed and won. Diplomacy encourages dialogue! However, taken at inter-country and international political levels, it is often abused. Ever so often, weak nations become extra diplomatic so as to get crumbs, ending up with monumental political, economic and intellectual self-mortgage of their peoples.

Proper dialogue must be founded and grounded on generic goodwill for communication to bear fruit. It is not meaningful, and may even be disruptive, if it is turned into a byword, a slogan, a platitude or a managerial escape route, just for some executive to cover up a complex or a failure, or pronounce some 'bravado' dictate! I wish some of our labour handlers took time to ponder this perspective!

The Unborn Baby – Our Brainchild: "University of Nairobi Teaching Hospital" (UNTH):

The year 1994 was also quite eventful during my Deanship for at least two other reasons. The Secretary and Head of the Commonwealth Secretariat for East, Central and Southern Africa, Professor Nonholi, spearheaded a project involving medical schools in the region for the purpose of harmonising the M.Med programme region-wide through their curricula. Such a mechanism would permit student and manpower exchange, with mutual recognition and employability.

The Nairobi medical school under my watch hosted about three meetings that deliberated on this proposal. When his extended contract ended and he left, the proposal died what seemed like an unnatural death. **But one reason might have been institutional transition without continuity. Provision for, and diligent patronage of, continuity of progressive traditions and dynamics, together with sharp focus, are a necessary basis of institutional building, viability, stability, growth and strength. The absence of such a culture is a phenomenon easily discerned in developing countries**. There could have been other reasons as well!

Computerization of the Faculty of Medicine took longer because of the corresponding reason of lack of, indeed even inability to ensure, continuity.

In 1995, I negotiated with the WHO Country Representative, Dr. Paul Chuke (a Nigerian, now deceased) to equip our administrative offices in the College of Health Sciences, the Faculty and Departments with computers. He agreed, *provided* the Ministry of Health office of the Director of Medical Services had no objection! Dr. James Mwanzia, the incumbent Director of Medical Services then, quickly agreed! He confirmed that the Ministry had no objection if the Country Office of WHO could come to the assistance of our institution. It was all in black and white; the consultations, requests and responses had been both verbal and in writing.

I handed over the deal to my successor at the Faculty. Soon afterwards, I gathered that the Faculty was going through procurement formalities of floating tenders in order to **purchase** computers. I held my peace!

In October 1994, two of my laboratory-based Associate Professors (Hannington Pamba and Isaac Wamola) attended an interview for promotion to (full) Professorship. Both of them succeeded at the interviews! They rushed back to brief me; they came together and found me in my office.

During their respective interviews, they separately complained about KNH and the shortage of facilities. The relevant part was the response from the interviewing panel.

"You people are always complaining about KNH! Why don't you build your own hospital in the Faculty of Medicine?"

It had been like a chorus from the panel. I sat them down and said, "If the challenge you have delivered is the seed, I am the fertile ground. It will germinate. There is no Biblical rock here: check your Bible! Both of you are already members of the committee that will do the feasibility study. All chairmen of departments will also be members."

The Faculty of Medicine lit up bright and sprightly! "At last!" There was no going back. The rest is history, and yet we still do not have a hospital as I go to press with my story in the year 2023. The dream for a University of Nairobi Teaching Hospital has yet to be fulfilled.

Two negatives failed to translate or transform, arithmetically, into a positive:

One was the incorrect view that the Medical School was planning (nay, plotting) to secede from the University of Nairobi. The connotation was that someone's empire was about to be dismantled. For a moment we forgot that institutional growth necessarily involves, includes and incorporates multiplication of campuses. Each and every new campus has innate potential and liberty to grow and prosper within the mother university, or even independently. Institutions are not empires incarnate like some corporate bodies. They are not political battlegrounds, and must never be made to be! Institutional growth is institutional life! It underlines its strength.

The second was that KNH would die a natural death if the University built its own hospital and moved out. This was ill-conceived and wrongly perceived. The proposed University of Nairobi Teaching Hospital (UNTH) was to be a facility that served the University with the dedication of teaching. History had it that, at the very outset and onset, KNH was the teaching hospital for the University of Nairobi. But over time, many things changed. There was both a political and financial grip on the hospital. It became a parastatal and, one might add, somebody's "milk cow." No problem with that 'for now,' but these were not the best ingredients for a teaching hospital. The medical school would never dream of leaving KNH. At most, there could and would be just two campuses.

The 'latter-day' or 'super-added' reasons were far-fetched, to say the least:

1. The fear of managing a hospital can and should never be a reason to choose stagnation over progress and academic as well as professional prosperity. The details of managerial strategies had yet to be elaborated on by the UNTH committee (almost politically, people just postulated and guessed). As pertains income generation, the UNTH would be owned by the University of Nairobi and managed as a three-tier institution, an integrated triad under a duly created 'Board of Trustees' under the University:
    a. An income-generating wing.
    b. A general wing as a service and teaching facility; a world-class centre of excellence.
    c. A University Health Services (UHS) wing for the care of University staff, especially senior staff and their spouses whose privacy should not be exposed to students.

The Vice-Chancellor was never intended to be the "CEO" of our UNTH, like some self-appointed 'advisors' implied, citing 'too much work' and 'too expensive' as the ultimate deterrence! It is foolhardy to sniff and dash for foreign donor money, or scramble for government capitation, instead of initiating, establishing and running an income-generating enterprise, and living off of it! There was, and still is, fairly fertile ground for the incompletely exploited sweet-sounding **'Triple P'** – "Public Private Partnership"

2. That there are already many hospitals within and near Nairobi. This was not the case when we started. One must consider the background and example of the mushrooming of medical schools, which were rushed without considering their critical mass, and now find themselves trapped and understaffed, when able-bodied and able-minded professionals go for private practice. The risk of losing quality while chasing quantity must be mitigated, if not completely eliminated. It would be foolhardy and myopic to build a hospital just to, or merely in order to, build a hospital!

When professionals and professional institutions start to listen to political conversations, tempered by, and inundated with self-interest, there can be no institutional growth, or very little of it, let alone plausible institutional or professional image, or development!

I took this project to belong to the then Faculty of Medicine; in terms of incumbency, initiation and push, it is actually my brainchild! The gestation continues. In fact, we were elated when, at the change of guard in January 2015, the new Vice-Chancellor, Professor Peter Mbithi, redeemed and took it on as one of his flagship projects. His predecessor, present at the time in Taifa Hall and listening to him, had literally, expressly, and I dare say brazenly, blocked our joint committee (the College of Health Sciences and the College of Architecture and Engineering had joined forces to push the UNTH project forward) during his entire ten-year tenure!

Then I remembered the 'confidential friendly warning' to our joint committee by a 'good Samaritan' from another campus that if we "made the mistake of letting the project slip into the hands of the main campus," then we "might as well forget about it!"

History is unfolding, but this project remains the baby of the School (Faculty) of Medicine! Even if the baby remains unborn 'today,' historically it is ours and mine in my retirement! Unfortunately, it might be 'delivered' after more than five generations of students, given the deteriorating 'mass production' type of medical education at the University of Nairobi and the country as a whole! The challenge then will be to capture, and perhaps recapture the nostalgia in reasonable time!

I have included the original drawings for three reasons:

a. Because I was very directly involved as the CAE team elaborated their concepts, drawings and plans;
b. For posterity to pick up the pieces of the dream, with whatever amendments, and
c. If I do not post them here, then this crucial aspect of institutional development will most likely be lost completely and forever in the history of the University of Nairobi.

I salute the entire committee of the University of Nairobi Teaching Hospital project. That committee comprised the 'home team' of the School of Medicine, representing the actual owners of the project (at the CHS), and the technocratic wing from the CAE, whose team was handpicked and released to us by the then Principal, Professor Crispus Kiamba and led by Professor Jerry Magutu. We could not have had it better!

Here was a template for intra-university-cum-inter-collegiate collaboration to contain costs, which may be emulated by sister institutions, today or tomorrow.

A number of private architects had been introduced to us, either as individuals or companies; some applied and presented themselves directly to the committee. But we said, "home is best!" And so, at that point, the late Professor Leander Saul Otieno and I marched to CAE Principal, Professor Kiamba's office on the UoN Main Campus, of course with due appointment.

The highlight was not so much his excited support for the proposed project, but that, after we left, he systemically handpicked a diversified and composite team of brilliant technocrats, then brought them physically and personally to the School of Medicine on the KNH Campus, and introduced them one by one to the UNTH committee!

When leadership clings to, and 'survives' on "low-lying fruits" ***only***, then the institution is in a more miserable place than an ICU! Academic institutions and academic freedom are about inspiration, adventure, exploration, discovery, invention, regeneration and conquest of knowledge for humanity and human advancement.

When you have a job to do, or you are given a job to perform, talk to yourself very seriously at the outset!

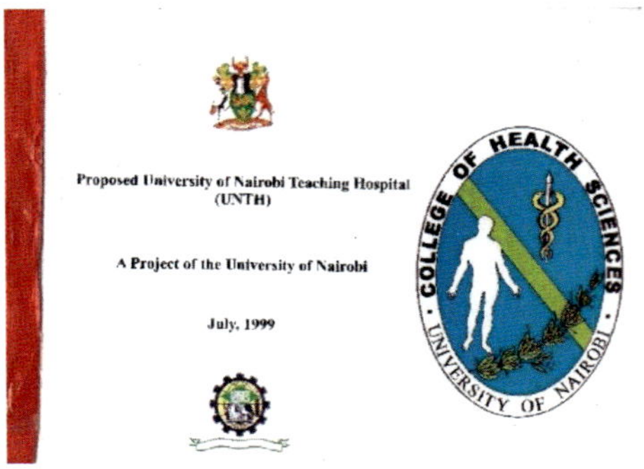

The project booklet (this shows just the cover) that was a collaboration of the College of Health Sciences (CHS), the College of Architecture and Engineering (CAE) and the College of Humanities and Social Sciences.

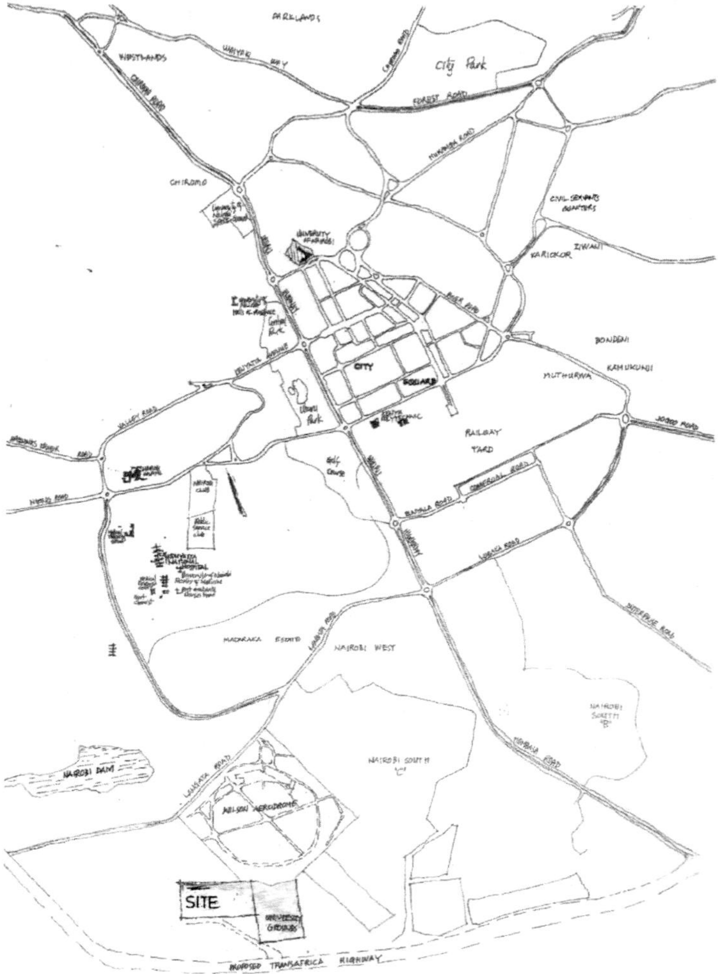

PROPOSED U.N.T.H. LOCATION IN CITY OF NAIROBI SCALE 1:20 000

The proposed UNTH site location.

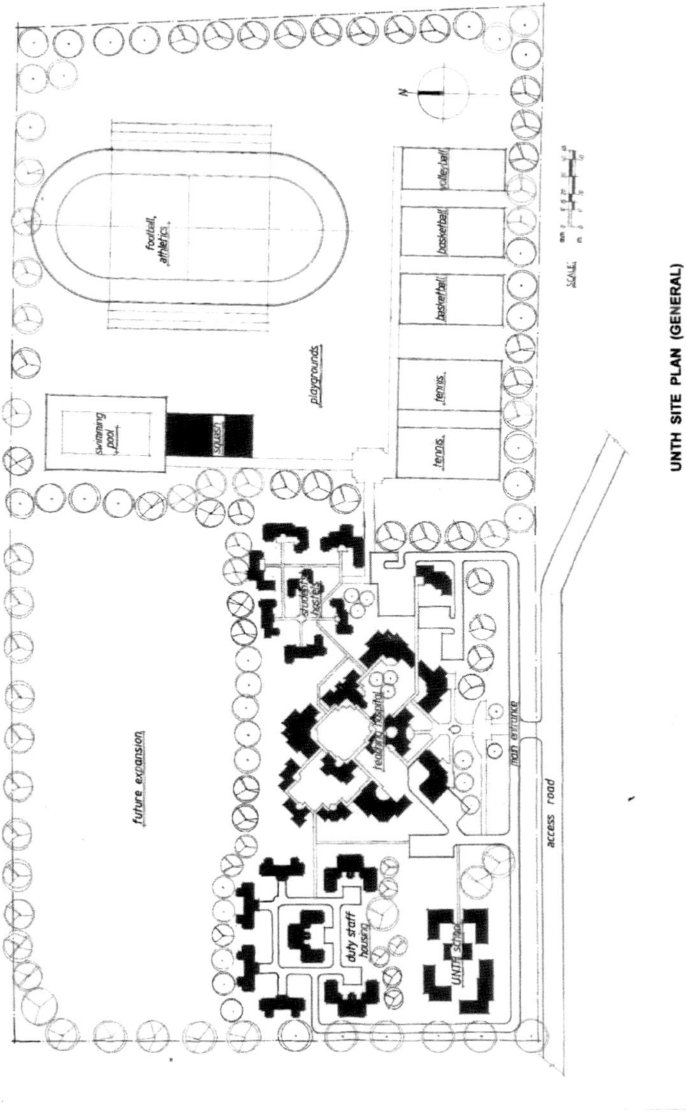

The proposed UNTH site plan

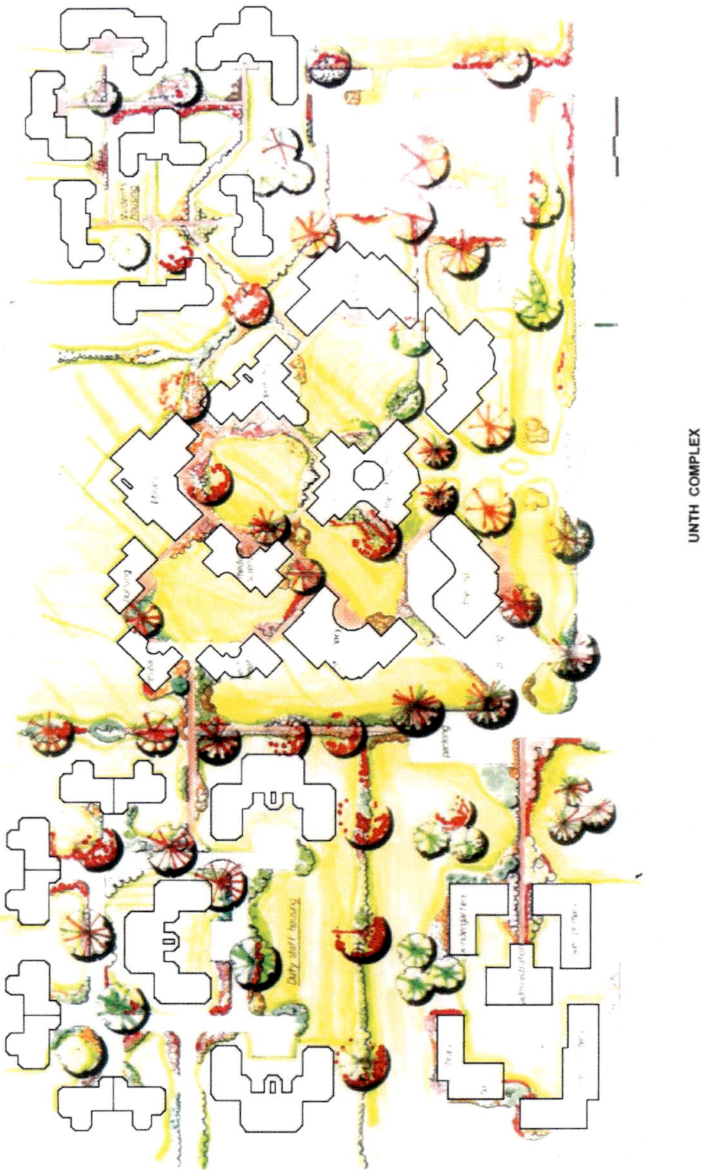

The UNTH complex comprising a central core with medical and administrative facilities (the teaching hospital), and peripheral buildings for staff housing, student hostels and a primary school.

THE HOSPITAL : ENTRY QUADRANGLE

A

The proposed hospital: the entry quadrangle.

HOSTELS : BIRD'S EYE-VIEW

Bird's eye view of the proposed student hostels.

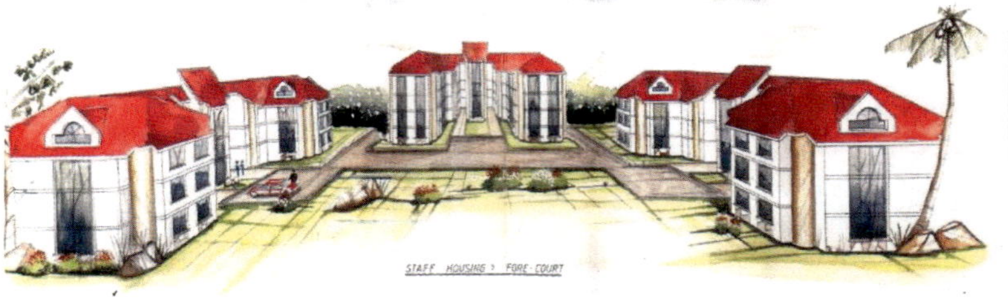

The proposed staff housing buildings.

The proposed primary school.

TOP AND BOTTOM: The UNTH committee at a retreat in Tigoni.

With the secretariat of the UNTH committee. Alice Waweru is on the left.

PHOTOS BELOW: The proposed University of Nairobi Teaching Hospital project site.

COLLEGE OF HEALTH
UNIVERSITY OF

FOR
FUTURE DEVELOPMENT
OF
THE PROPOSED UNIVERSITY OF NAIROBI
TEACHING HOSPITAL
COLLEGE OF HEALTH SCIENCES
UNIVERSITY OF NAIROBI

SITE
FOR
FUTURE DEVELOPMENT

What else for me as Dean?

We looked everywhere for a copy or template of a prospectus of the University of Nairobi or any one of its constituent Colleges, Schools or Departments. We found none; not even one said to have been published by the Institute of Development Studies on another campus. We geared up to produce one for the School of Medicine, which we did in 1995, with real scarce resources – the very first of such! I set up a committee headed by the late Professor Leander Saul Otieno (Internal Medicine), assisted by Professor Anastasia Guantai (Pharmacy). We did it. I reviewed it editorially. What we got was a modification of a standard prospectus, but it was a resounding wake-up call. Many followed thereafter, with even better designs, sizes, formats and production!

The Departments of Dental Surgery and Nursing were also represented. Technically, the three departments: Dental Surgery, Pharmacy and Nursing were categorized and treated as "Special Departments" because they were destined to be independent Faculties or Schools respectively on their own. Their fates were naturally mine to midwife. For each of them to be constituted as Faculties or Schools, the existing pioneer Departments had to be reconstituted and realigned. Each of them had to review and update, refashion or create their curricula along with newly established Departments.

Only Dental Surgery and Pharmacy managed to meet the deadline for weaning into Faculties, which was 3rd July 1995. These two Faculties were successfully launched on that date. The guest of honour was none other than Professor Francis Gichaga, the Vice-Chancellor. We fell just short of declaring and crowning him as **"The Friend of the School of Medicine!"** (He too just whispered to me, "Dean Emeritus,' as he tried to resist my return to the operating theatre)!

He had to move from one site to the next within the same morning, cutting tapes and launching new Faculties, or Schools, as they later became known. The newly introduced **Faculty Day** was a prominent part of the programme. But it was also the first and last of that aspect of the celebrations!

At the end of that three-in-one ceremony, the College of Health Sciences now had three Faculties: the original Faculty of Medicine, the Faculty of Dental Sciences, and the Faculty of Pharmacy. Nursing continued to be a "Special Department" in the Faculty of Medicine.

As it happened, during my term as dean of the School of Medicine, UoN, we undertook two big celebrations. The launch of the two new Faculties was one. The other was the earlier Silver Jubilee celebration held for the Faculty.

Over and above the determination to strengthen our institution, we recognized the practicality of staging such big functions within two years of each other. By the nature and magnitude of the two occasions, they stood apart from any other occasions.

My proposal was that we should formalize two-yearly observances and term them **"FACULTY DAYS" (or 'SCHOOL DAYS')**, quite distinct from the very welcome conferences now mounted jointly with Kenyatta National Hospital, but akin to "Open Days" of other institutions and in high schools.

The two occasions could be amalgamated, and the conferences organized so as to always overlap with alternate 3rd Julys, which would be sandwiched within the duration of the conference, to add pride of place!

The programme of the proposed 'Faculty Day' would necessarily include **'THE DEANS' HOUR,'** when past Deans and Chairpersons of Departments would reminisce on the past and dream about the future of the institutions. That way, the one above was the first one of them all!

To relieve busy academics, the function of organizing these occasions could be relegated and delegated to the office of the Dean, spear-headed by his Registrar or Senior Administrative Assistant.

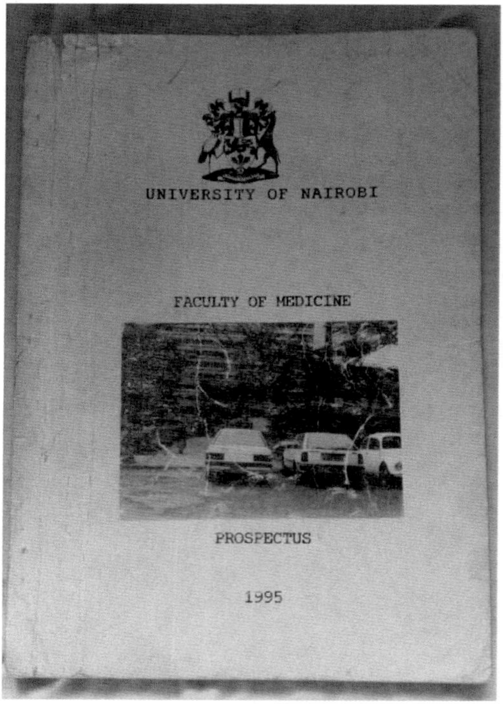

The very first University of Nairobi Faculty of Medicine Prospectus, produced in 1995.

Faculty Day, 3rd July 1995: The Vice-Chancellor, Prof. Francis Gichaga, leads the tour of the college. I am directly behind him. On the left is Prof. Julius Meme.

Faculty Day, 3rd July 1995: In conversation with colleagues. I am centre right standing next to Prof. Julius Meme.

Faculty Day, 3rd July 1995: Prof. Gichaga launches the Faculty of Dental Sciences.

Faculty Day, 3rd July 1995: The launch of the Faculty of Pharmacy.

Faculty Day, 3rd July 1995: Prof Gichaga signs the visitor book in the soon-to-be launched Faculty of Pharmacy as we look on.

Faculty Day, 3rd July 1995: Prof. Joseph Maina Mungai signs the visitor book in the soon-to-be launched Faculty of Pharmacy as we look on.

Faculty Day, 3rd July 1995: DEAN'S HOUR address by Prof. Joseph Maina Mungai.

Faculty Day, 3rd July 1995: DEAN'S HOUR address by Prof. Nimrod Bwibo.

Faculty Day, 3rd July 1995: DEAN'S HOUR address by Prof. Hannington O. Pamba.

Faculty Day, 3rd July 1995: DEAN'S HOUR address by my former college-mate, Prof. G.B.A Okelo.

Faculty Day, 3rd July 1995: DEAN'S HOUR address.

Faculty Day, 3rd July 1995: Prof. Gichaga presents an award.

Two New ('Conjoined') Birthdays:

The year 1995 thus witnessed three events in one, all held and marked on 3rd July, 1995, namely:

1. The twenty-seventh (27th) anniversary of the Faculty of Medicine.
2. The inauguration and launch of two new Faculties/Schools – **The School of Pharmacy and the School of Dental Sciences,** and
3. The observation and celebration of the first would-be **"Deans' Hour"** within the proposed "Faculty Day."

Hitherto, the College of Health Sciences had existed as a 'one-College, one-School' part of the University of Nairobi. From that date it acquired the two additional Schools listed above. In a way, the School of Medicine gave birth to, or weaned off, two of its three babies! The College of Health Sciences now had three Schools under it! The "Department of Nursing" was upgraded from 'special departmental' to full School status and weaned off from the School of Medicine a few years later! It became the **"School of Nursing Sciences"** (as originally proposed in 1995), the fourth School of the College of Health Sciences. Much later, the **School of Public Health** and several Institutes, centres and units, cropped up, but all quite distinct from the multi-disciplinary **Clinical Epidemiology Unit (CEU),** which had existed for some decades.

The Rockefeller Super-Star, Ms. Anita Prowl and the Undeclared 'Nyeri Declaration' (The Final Re-launch of "AFRI-CLEN") Or, INHERITANCE AND RESUSCITATION OF A MORIBUND UNIT:

Upon assuming the seat and duties of the Dean, Faculty of Medicine, I was soon introduced to a respectable and prestigious 'section' of the Dean's office by its Director, Dr. Harshad Sanghvi. Dr. Joash Aluoch was his Deputy. The official name of that section was 'CLINICAL EPIDEMIOLOGY UNIT," or simply the CEU. More than two years earlier, Professor Hannington Ouma Pamba, the Dean at the time, had presided over its launch at a venue in Mombasa. It was a mechanism for promoting and strengthening the subject of clinical epidemiology as well as encouraging research in medical schools in 'Third-World' countries world-wide in a collaborative manner.

Founded and championed by Dr. Scott Halstead, it was sponsored exclusively by the Rockefeller Foundation of the United States of America under the banner of the **INTERNATIONAL CLINICAL EPIDEMIOLOGY NETWORK, or simply INCLEN.**

The network was cascaded through regions then directly down to individual medical schools, rather than countries. As a new specially focused programme, cutting across the different specialties of medicine, it could not fit into any of the common or traditional Departments of the Schools and Faculties of Medicine. It fitted best in the Dean's office, almost as if it was an integral department therein, but yet not quite! Right across the collaborating institutions, the Units were patterned in a uniform manner, with a Director, Deputy Director and Members. The Dean played the role of an executive Patron, and was designated as THE SPONSOR.

All other constituted 'traditional' departments were headed by appointed chairmen without any designated 'deputies.' The Dean was the academic head of the whole Faculty or School.

That way, the CEU was like a special baby in the home who fitted into other departments but had the capacity to function independently as well as assist needy departments interactively on matters of epidemiology and biostatistics, for both lectures and proposal development. It ran a training programme for the School. Its original critical mass had by then been trained overseas at Harvard, North Carolina and other places.

So, by virtue of all that, I found myself already a sponsor of the CEU at the Faculty of Medicine, College of Health Sciences, University of Nairobi. Here was a Unit with a lot of prestige, visibility and clout. Surprisingly, even those who belonged to it seemed inclined to talk about it only in low tones!

Part of the reason for this incongruity was that our School had not quite come to own it, even though we had co-hosted its launch at a venue in Mombasa barely a couple of years before. Some members seemed detached, if not somewhat estranged. I suspected that as a novel section of the School's activities, it had not quite gelled in-house.

We were moving fast into mid-1992. The Silver Jubilee celebrations were fairly steadily on course. By early 1993, there was to be a conference of the "CLENs" (Clinical Epidemiology Networks) on the African continent in Cairo, Egypt. The multiplicity of activities in the School called for a multi-pronged response!

I felt that it was my turn and duty to encourage and facilitate Nairobi University's CEU as a very strategic commitment to strengthen the School, the College and, by extension, the University of Nairobi.

Come January 1993, a good contingent of members from Nairobi attended the Cairo conference of the African Clinical Epidemiology Network (AFRICLEN) with me. That included the Director, Dr. Harshad Sanghvi and his Deputy, Dr. (later Professor) Joash Aluoch. There were a number of international delegates. There had also been strong and ongoing support from the Rockefeller Foundation, without which there would not have been any conference, because the local hosts seemed to have an attitude problem!

The conference went very well, until the time for the business meeting, which came at the end. Our host Secretary of AFRICLEN, (from within 'Egypt-CLEN') went into a convoluted apology for the poor communication between him and all the six countries of AFRICLEN, claiming that the reason was because the African continent 'lacked this, that and the other,' including mails and transport! The hint was writ large; if Egypt could not do any better, no other African country could or would! The discussion that followed indicated that AFRICLEN was on its death bed, despite full sponsorship from a whole Rockefeller Foundation!

Enough was enough!

I shot up, gave a brief 'lecture' on apologetics that cover inefficiency as a curse in, on and around our continent. I further narrated how, barely three years before that meeting, but quite a long spell earlier (when it should have been worse), I had communicated effectively around the same continent, including actually flying from Nairobi to Dakar and, with the Senegalese Society of Cardiology, had organized a very well-attended conference of the Pan-African Society of Cardiology (PASCAR) in Dakar, Senegal in April 1989! Here in AFRICLEN, somebody had failed! It was all doable, despite the challenges! Those challenges were not absolute roadblocks! INCLEN would not die just like that!

Kenya would prove all that by organizing and hosting a special AFRICLEN 'recovery' meeting of all continental CEUs within the next few months. I invited everybody to come to Kenya for that historic 'get together!'

I deliberately adopted a decisive tone and spoke like the executive "Sponsor" of the Nairobi CEU that I was! Consciously and deliberately, I did not look at Director Sanghvi, because I did not want to witness or respond to any self-censoring body language from any member of my team! Later on, both Director and Deputy Director confessed their shock when I appropriated the challenge of reviving AFRICLEN on Kenyan soil, with our meagre and limited resources! Because of my 'outburst,' they were now 'destined' to be the micro-managers here; they were worried, necessarily! But we did it together, and everybody ended up being both happy and proud, just a little more than three months after Cairo!

We chose Nyeri's Outspan Hotel as the venue. We deliberately chose a location outside Nairobi as we did not want our delegates distracted by the hustle and bustle of the "City In The Sun." The Rockefeller Foundation was invited as both facilitator and official guide. They came in an institutionally very inspiring way.

Ms. Anita Prowl* was the 'ONE-WOMAN ROCKEFELLER SHOW' and more. She turned out to be AFRICLEN's 'Guardian Angel.' Beyond all else, she became everybody's star and a darling to match. On another level, she endeared us to African American ladies and made us feel very proud, just short of being baptized "ANITA PROWL!" Even her physical limitation seemed like an unmatchable strength (she walked with two elbow crutches). In short, she performed superbly and guided the retreat most smoothly, eloquently, exceptionally, efficiently and very effectively!

In one excited outburst at one point, we felt strongly that we were ready for a **"NYERI DECLARATION"** but we quickly sobered down and opted for a simple plan of action, because declarations had proven to be linguistic toys of political inaction, especially on the African continent. All said and done, Nyeri was a resounding success! The only missing piece was that the director had been unable to attend! He was very ably represented by his deputy, Dr. (later Professor) Joash Aluoch!

With whatever changes that followed, AFRICLEN never looked back. Kenya stayed aloft as a success story, if not actually a blessing to AFRICLEN, even a third mentor after Scott Halstead and Rockefeller! Under its subsequent directors (like Professor William Macharia, Mr. Erastus Njeru and others) and Dean-Sponsors, Kenya's CEU continued to march on, including hosting epidemiology training programmes for the Commonwealth region, WHO and others, apart from maturing as

*It would appear that there are several different ladies with the same name! For correct identification, this was the Anita Prowl affiliated with the Rockefeller Foundation, a highly knowledgeable and dynamic African American lady.

an inhouse training outfit, working closely with the School of Public Health of the University of Nairobi.

But there came a small hitch right there in Nyeri, about who would host the next of the regular meetings of the rejuvenated AFRICLEN, after the success story from Nyeri! For one reason or another, none of the other five members could host the meeting! We ended up heading back to Egypt at the University of the Suez in the Sinai desert, where I was invited to give a keynote address specifically to delve into the **"World Development Report"** of UNDP, **1993**.

Before I left the dual positions of Dean and CEU Sponsor, I had the privilege of leading our team from Nairobi to other INCLEN and AFRICLEN conferences. At two of those occasions, we had the privilege of hosting farewell dinners respectively for the INCLEN Founder, Dr. Scott Halstead in Chiang Mai, Thailand (1995) and international Director of INCLEN, Dr. Arturo Murillo at Victoria Falls, Zimbabwe in early 1996.

I never went for a specific training in epidemiology beyond what we got during the general medical and surgical syllabi and research, but because of my support of the Unit over time, I was 'unofficially' asked to hang on in there after my Deanship as an 'associate member' of the Unit and would be invited to give lectures to the Commonwealth and WHO training classes!**

Curriculum Development and Student Exchanges

I.

The plight and fate of a pioneer is to wade through, penetrate and clear the jungle and to eliminate any void that might stunt the vision! We had realized in around 1979-80 that in order for our open-heart programme to take any shape and to avoid premature burn- out, we

****See sketch in Epilogue II: "Planet Earth named Environment: My Take (Translating Policy into Practice).**

would need a very strong core of support staff in the surgical heart unit! By their training, the nursing staff was practically ready-made for those early take-off stages; they already had a good foundation for any further training, if need be. However, cardiac intensive care nursing was still a big challenge. Without a doubt, ward care for the pre- and post-operative cardiac patients was a daunting task given the broad and general nature of qualifications of the nurses, counting from nursing assistants, enrolled nurses, registered nurses and registered midwives.

All that was manageable! The University-trained Bachelor of Nursing (BScN) graduate was not in our horizon or within our catchment arena, it was somewhat in the distant decades ahead. The real challenge was in the area of cardiovascular technology – cardio-pulmonary perfusionists, cardiovascular diagnostic and monitoring technologists, and, because of a gross shortage of clinical staff, a competent cadre that would cover routine ward work, including clerking of patients.

In our setting, this was a yet-undefined category of health workers, much as one found them in established centres elsewhere in other countries. But even those other countries had no tailor-made reference that we could "cut and paste," as it were! But we knew what we wanted. It had to be done! Again, it was me!

But there was still another challenge! The trainees would need a certificate from a recognized institution in order to develop their careers and be promotable. Besides, we desperately needed a quick turn-over for the open-heart programme not to stall while waiting for degree holders! We found ourselves compelled to look for people with a good background of health work, one way or another. We settled for registered clinical officers as the most suitable pool from where to recruit trainees.

Kenyatta National Hospital was not ready or structured in any way for this kind of programme. For understandable reasons, even the School of Medicine was not suitable for us! But just next door were the champions of all certificate and diploma trainings of Kenya's health workers, the Kenya Medical Training Centre (KMTC), which later became the Kenya Medical Training College.

So, I walked into Dr. Migwi's office (he was the Kenya Medical Training Centre's Principal) to present a proposal for a new training programme, actually three programmes as post-graduate diplomas in Cardiovascular Perfusion (Heart-Lung Machine Technologists), Cardiac Diagnostic and Monitoring Technologists, and Specialized Cardiothoracic and Vascular Clinical Officers.

I left Dr. Migwi's office a very happy man! He understood everything, bought the idea and asked me to give him my draft curricula so as to align it with KMTC formats. The rest became history instantly. But for physiotherapy, a crucial and critical part of our specialty care, I crossed the street to teach within their established physiotherapy syllabus, having agreed and arranged with the Department that I cover areas relevant to the cardiothoracic surgical unit at KNH.

All these were some beginnings of what might nowadays look routine.

II.

A decade later, right from the outset, as I assumed the Dean's office, I embarked on the overdue task of revising and updating syllabi and curricula in all the twenty odd Departments of the Faculty or School of Medicine. A few years later, on a re-structuring spree at the Main Campus, those Departments were reduced to fourteen. In due course, nearly all Departments had elaborated new curricula by the end of my Deanship.

III.

Over that period and a little later, I also participated in drafting curricula for surgical training for upcoming institutions, specifically the Aga Khan University Teaching Hospital and Uzima College of Health Sciences.

There were institutions and hospitals that looked forward to collaboration with our School with a view to acquiring recognition as teaching hospitals. The Nairobi Aga Khan Hospital had approached the University of Nairobi for such an association in the early nineteen-eighties, but they did not meet certain basic criteria and requirements for more than a decade. When they finally hit the threshold, in terms of potential integral Departments, they turned to Karachi University, not Nairobi, for affiliation and mentorship. Just before that, they solicited a few academicians, including myself, to be members of a curriculum development team that finally midwifed the birth of the a plausible curriculum for several branches of medicine, ready for scrutiny by the Commission for Higher Education (CHE).

At that point what threatened to be a conflict of interest on my part turned out to be a blessing in disguise. The Commission for Higher Education (CHE), the forerunner of the Commission for University Education (CUE) requested me to review the submitted draft of the Aga Khan curriculum. I confessed that I had been part of the team that created that draft and that it would be wrong for me to be the adjudicator. They insisted. I declined again, but they still insisted. Then I issued my disclaimer. They sent me the document, which I knew very well.

To my surprise, I detected subtle alterations in the submitted draft that could have made Kenya just a transit for students and pseudo-students from other countries to go to USA and Canada. The draft had to be amended accordingly. On their part, CHE now included me in their panel that went to the Aga Khan Hospital auditorium where the curriculum was officially presented to them by the Aga Khan team.

IV.

Right in the middle of my Deanship, I led a team from the School that inspected three hospitals which, within the armpit of the Christian Health Association of Kenya (CHAK) who were keen and ready to start teaching in the area of "Family Medicine." That took us to three hospitals, namely Kijabe, Chogoria and Tenwek Mission Hospitals. Within a couple of years, the programme was launched.

V.

My international input into curriculum development was in Cape Town in May 1995 when I represented the Faculty of Medicine at the 4th Conference of World Association on Medical Education (WAME). I proposed that in curriculum and syllabus development, we must consciously, deliberately and structurally incorporate social, cultural and even anthropological dimensions in our teaching of all health and medical sciences, because there was a sneaking weakness in these areas in on-going evolution of our medical education, and yet therein might lie the ultimate core of primary and public health, and possible eradication of unguided, negative tribal cocooning, racialism and many other spin-offs for ultimate human health, whatever the specialty! Those sentiments were unanimously adopted and there is distinct mention of the same in the CAPE TOWN DECLARATION, the final outcome of that conference!

VI.

The School of Medicine maintained the spirit and tradition of regular curriculum reviews and revisions with well attended retreats. I still took part in some of them after my Deanship. Part of the time I chaired the curriculum committee of the Department of Surgery.

In the area of international collaboration for student exchange, I entered office when Germany had diverted their attention towards South Africa after the collapse of the apartheid system. We gathered that their students now went more to South Africa than elsewhere.

We entered into very productive collaboration with Universities in other countries. Of those, Tokai University in Japan, was most notable as we undertook full formalization for student exchange. Our own 4th year student, Zipporah Njeri Gathuya spent her elective term there most rewardingly. Professor Y. Sawada brought some of his students for an academic excursion as head of the tour.

We sent two of our students to Kansas State University. They brought me a precious emblem of that University in the form of a desk disc!

The late Professor of Anatomy, James Maina helped rejuvenate our long-lasting relationship with Pennsylvania State University. MEDUNSA University of South Africa visited us before it changed its name to University of Transkei. Unfortunately, the Dean who came over fell ill and our communication was interrupted. Oklahoma University visited us and took a video recording about our School; but my time was up as Dean, with no more leeway for follow up. The records remained for interested successors. To my recollection, it was only Professor George Omore Magoha who tried to follow up on the collaborations during his stint as Dean, but he was soon appointed Principal, then Deputy Vice-Chancellor, Vice-Chancellor, on and on, up to Cabinet Secretary (Minister) for Education in the Government of the Republic of Kenya! Cheers to him!

13th July 1995: Signing the exchange and collaboration agreement with Tokai University at the School of Medicine. I am far right.

13th July 1995: Signing the exchange and collaboration agreement with Tokai University at the School of Medicine.

With Prof. Sawada and his students at the Ngong Hills Hotel on 20th March 1998.

With Prof. Sawada at the Ngong Hills Hotel on 20th March 1998.

VII.

"Pearl Omega" – The Stigma That Almost Stuck!

Call it proactivity, motivation, research, innovation, discovery, or invention; any and all could have applied! At the time of the following narrative, I was the Dean, custodian of the **academic, professional and ethical image of the entire School of Medicine at the University of Nairobi.**

Let it also be known that Professor Arthur Otieno Obel, the researcher, was a good friend of mine. He was in my pioneer team of editorial consultants for *MEDICOM*. Many years before he came up with "Pearl Omega" for the treatment of HIV/AIDS, he had written a sharp, leading critique entitled, "Therapeutics, a Non-Starter," which I had published in our journal. His specialty was and is clinical therapeutics.

I had challenged our thriving media for always only going for what Reuters, the Associated Press (AP) and other (foreign) media houses had digested, and simply copying it for coverage in the local papers, instead of also getting health and medical material to report directly from local publications like the *East African Journal* and *MEDICOM*. We at Update Publishers (my publishing company that was behind *MEDICOM*) always gave them complimentary copies for whatever it was worth.

This time round, his article was splashed in one of the daily newspapers. The discourse was apt, and long overdue. Our academicians saw it and some of them came baying for his blood. He came to me, hoping that I could help tame the situation somewhat. I told him to hold his peace and tell whoever attacked him next to come to me. ***I*** was the one who had published his article, and with all due peer review, I would publish ***any rejoinder*** any of them would submit for the enrichment of science. I shared the same with others and I promised to publish their responses if submitted. Up to today, in *MEDICOM* or elsewhere, I never saw any rejoinder to that paper! Arthur continued with his academic pursuits. People learnt something: there was no need, and no good reason, to shout in the corridors. We could all participate in and enjoy **academic freedom.**

Later, Prof. Obel got involved in the research on Alpha Interferon for HIV/AIDS treatment with the Japanese at KEMRI (Kenya Medical Research Institute), which came a cropper. But he continued virtually alone, with some state backing, complete with a security detail. That period gave birth to "PEARL OMEGA," a supposed medicine to treat HIV/AIDS.

He got busy giving public lectures about his wonder discovery, which did not go down well with his former schoolmates and college colleagues. So, I invited him to my office and requested him to come and talk to us at the School of Medicine as fellow scientists. I was ready with a "red carpet" for him, "all protocols observed," including a visitor's book to sign and our secretariat to cover and capture the proceedings. Even if with some pomp, he came on the appointed day. Lecture Theatre-1 of the School of Medicine filled beyond capacity in no time with Medical School staff, 'big and small!'

After his presentation, there came time for questions and comments. Literally every hand in the hall was raised, itching to talk! We quickly brought in pieces of paper for those with questions to write them down and pass them to me in front. He would respond to as many as he would manage, then I would make the rest available for him to answer soon after, at his convenience.

The heap of papers with questions lay on the table before us. I picked and read the questions aloud. After a few questions, one of his 'aides' called off the session saying that the Professor was supposed to go elsewhere and would not answer any more questions.

They left in a hurry as I gathered the papers for safe custody for Professor Obel himself to come back soon and pick for his responses in writing if need be. That was never to be!

In the ensuing days and months, I extended more of the olive branch to vindicate his research. Could he give us a sample of the product for senior faculty to analyse and help talk to the profession and the world for the simplest possible credibility. The response was a straight "NO!"

Then we manufactured a 'patient' who was sent with a prescription to buy "Pearl Omega" as medication. But when tested there, he turned out to be HIV-Negative! He was told he did not need to buy the medication because he did not have the disease!

I gave up!

But by this time, there was a lot of keenness on the campus to know more about this 'wonder drug.' Suddenly, from wherever, somebody brought to me two big bottles, respectively of 1 litre and 2 litres, both with stickers duly labelled "Pearl Omega." The smaller bottle bore the dates of manufacture and expiry. The bigger one had a logo on the sticker but did not have any dates.

By that time, my term of Deanship was long over, and I was not going to spend time chasing up a 'ghostly' concoction, but I kept the bottles. However, when I finally gathered courage and opened them, they had a very strong and distinctive herbal smell; both were brownish in colour. One had developed lumps, like badly cooked *uji* (porridge). Obviously, these were now very different chemicals from whatever they might have been at "factory" level! I poured them down the drain and washed the bottles.

Earlier on, to my shock and surprise, I had gathered soon after the 'red carpet' reception (but kept mum about it) that the security detail that accompanied my honoured guest was very well armed and even had hand grenades in readiness for any eventuality, whatever that may have been. What we knew with some certainty was that the good Professor had been working with, if not also for, the State, which had expressly patronized his research. He used official vehicles. Most likely some of his research 'subjects' were derived from among the same pool; but this was more like a rumour than the truth!

Pearl Omega nearly became a sticky stigma on Kenyan research, but it sure did not stick!

When the Deputy Vice-Chancellor (Academic Affairs) at the time, the late Professor Nimrod Bwibo, had been sent to meet the College Academic Board of the College of Health Sciences on KNH Campus to get approval, support, recognition and some kind of certification of the earlier preparation from KEMRI (in which also Professor Obel was involved), Professor George Edward Kasili and I had quickly pointed out that we needed to distinguish between political-cum-politicized support and credible, scientific and professional support. The College gave the political support that was thereby officially solicited. Pearl Omega was not that lucky in the aftermath.

16

MY BRIEF LOOK AT SURGERY IN KENYA

THE FEW WORDS of this chapter are deemed relevant to all surgery in Kenya. The details of 'Thoracic and Cardiovascular Surgery' are contained in my other upcoming book covering the history of that specialty. Chapter 17 presents just the overview of the specialty.

The earlier phase of the surgical fraternity in Kenya saw a diffuse, if not amorphous, cohort of medical professionals who entertained some interest in surgery, even when actual capacities in some cases were grossly limited, as were facilities. The broad general base of training, complete with even a minimum of basic medical sciences usually given at the schools of medicine, helped a great deal. Ethics and ethical values compensated somewhat because it was hardly ever for money. Dedication to medical ethics in a noble profession with a robust public image was nearly always palpable.

That cohort included missionary doctors with the barest of surgical skills, but with enough spiritual overlay to inspire their juniors and instil confidence in their patients. As regards the history of surgery and general medicine in this country and region, no medical professional should display their own limitation of comprehension of and appreciation for who and what the missionary doctors were, as well as what their roles were in health care delivery hitherto, particularly given that basics are universal. Those doctors had enough basics and ethics not to butcher in the name of surgery!

Kenyan doctors started entering the scene. Some went on to train in surgery. Sometime in the middle of the nineteen-sixties, the World Health Organization (WHO) depicted the late Dr. John Otete (a

Bombay University MBBS graduate) performing an emergency operation at night in a small remote health facility somewhere in Kenya, using the headlights of a car parked nearby for the purpose!

Kenya's first trained surgeons, Mr. Michael Wilson Warambo (FRCS) and his contemporary, the late Mr. Kiragu, set the pace for the trail that followed, together with Mr. Michael Majale, Mr. Richard Wambwa, and Professor Ambrose Eric Onyango Wasunna, who soon became the first Kenyan-born Chairman of the Department of Surgery at the young University of Nairobi Faculty (School) of Medicine.

In those days, there was already quite a number of expatriate surgeons. There were two types: those who were hired or recruited as expatriates because of the gross shortage of surgeons and, therefore, contracted in a structural way, and those who fell into this category by virtue of some incumbency in institutions in the country. The latter predominated in the private hospitals. Some public hospitals also often benefitted from this general pool of surgical professionals. The overlap was notably seamless, especially in the eyes of the lay public!

With the establishment of the first medical school in Kenya in 1967, necessarily with dedicated academic staff and domiciled at Kenyatta National Hospital (its name had already been changed from the "King George VI Hospital") as the teaching hospital, there came incidental but distinct differentiation of employees, namely the Government-employed (through the Ministry of Health) and the University of Nairobi-based lecturers. The latter were also Government-employed in the Ministry of Education, but superficially seemed different from typical civil service! The hospital saw an emergence of two almost rivalling groups: 'Government doctors' and 'University doctors.' Ward beds were labelled 'University' and 'Government,' to distinguish teams from respective beds in the same wards!

That state of affairs lasted for the remaining part of the sixties and most, if not all, of the seventies. Something was not adding up! Without a doubt, University doctors were fully involved in patient care; they could only teach using their patients in the years of clinical training of their students. By that token, they simultaneously rendered routine clinical service, doing both teaching and treating. On their part, 'Government' doctors also could not avoid teaching, anyway. As part of their focus on patient care, they ended up also teaching clinical, paramedical, nursing and ancillary staff. There was a gaping shortage even of those who would support the latter consultants in the wards for the total care of their patients. Critics of the unwarranted dichotomy, including some of us, persevered and persisted.

Things might have looked different if the two teams were given completely different wards, but by the early to mid-eighties, many wards had dismantled the artificial boundaries, as clinicians worked together in peace, so to speak! There had always been regular synchronised "grand rounds." These continued and attracted all surgeons at Kenyatta National Hospital as well as the private ones in town. In due course, other growing and expanding hospitals outside KNH evolved their own grand rounds, notably at Aga Khan, Nairobi, MP Shah and The Mater Hospitals, all in Nairobi.

One other phenomenon was unavoidable. With the confirmed surgical training locally, the number of surgeons grew fairly steadily, if not fast. Emergence of specialty surgery was like a given part of the increase, even if not enough, and part and parcel of explosive growth and development of surgery as a major component of health care globally.

The surgical specialties became so attractive, fashionable and prestigious that general surgery in itself became threatened! We could, albeit inadvertently, soon wean ourselves of general surgeons. That would be our undoing as watchdogs of medical education and a sorry state of things in a teaching hospital! For all-round teaching, that was not desirable. But even before we embarked on remedial thinking, the upsurge of specialist surgeons appeared to also threaten the entrenched expatriate general surgeons, who staged a semi-diplomatic mission by engaging regional governments under the guise of technical advice to simplify and skew surgical training towards mass production in order to "offset," so to speak, the shortage of surgeons in the region as a whole. There came proposals like the "The District Surgeon" and books like "Cutting Along The Dotted Line," by even non-surgeons who thought they knew the needs of the place better.

I found myself championing the promotion of general surgery for teaching and training purposes and for extended services, especially in hospitals less equipped for any specialised work in more rurally situated facilities and smaller towns.

In exactly the same breath, I also reacted sharply against the over-simplification of general surgery through 'miniaturizing' and minimising the basics; in one such instance, a non-practising physician and a non-surgeon, with WHO funding, wrote a surgical textbook for guiding would-be surgeons, without so much as any tribute to basic medical sciences. This trend was further compounded by [trained] surgeons who literally succumbed to the sweetened name, "The District Surgeon," again ostensibly to deal with the shortage of surgeons, parallel to, and in the face of, a properly structured ongoing programme (M.Med, Surg.), as if the rural hospitals would be served better by those 'pre-devolved' multitude of half-baked middle-of-the-road surgeons! I saw no need to reinvent the wheel; for sure, a digital, technically developed robot is better than a walking, breathing 'pro-robot,' whose thinking ability and thought process has been calculatedly stunted by being drilled through and into shortcuts, without basic medical sciences in real terms! It would appear that sponsorship, vested interest and remuneration were silent variables in this quagmire of 'underdevelopment!' I think there are remnants of such challenges that the surgical fraternity must still address!

As fate would have it, my singularly unmarked crusade came to a head when, at Afya House, I bumped into two of our newly qualified M.Med (Surgery) graduates sitting on a waiting bench to see the

Director of Medical Services (DMS) for posting to their respective home areas – Dr. Peter Kimanzi Kimende to anywhere in Ukambani and Dr. Joseph Oraya to anywhere in Nyanza, especially on the Homa Bay side! I knew both of them as very good students and competent surgeons.

I mock-rebuked them for being so tribal; then on a serious note, 'ordered' them to stand up and "come with me:" I had a job for each of them. They came out with me and never saw the DMS.

First and foremost, they needed to recognize and appreciate "General Surgery" as a very good and important specialty! Secondly, we needed them in the medical school to help us teach and produce more general surgeons, before catching up with the specialties.

Dr. Kimende ended up joining the Department of Surgery on the University side, as Dr. Oraya joined the KNH side. I had been Dr. Kimende's supervisor for his dissertation on "Penetrating Chest Injuries."

The emergence and exponential growth of surgical specialties in Kenya, as elsewhere in the world, also witnessed the mushrooming of surgical societies in Kenya, all admirably active. Over-arching bodies like the Surgical Society of Kenya (SSK) continue to be very active and, indeed, vital to the entire landscape of surgeons, and must always be duly patronised.

I am happy and proud to have been associated with its beginnings. I had the honour and privilege to serve it as first Vice-Chairman under its Founder and Chairman, the very sober, professionally dignified Mr. Michael Wilson Warambo (FRCS) for five years and later, during its resuscitation time. I doubled as Acting Treasurer after the late Mr. Hasmukh Harilal Kamdar (MS, FRCS, FACS) passed on in 1996. With SSK withering under the weight of an absentee Secretary-General, I tripled as acting S-G to help my Chairman. I persuaded him to convene a 'salvage and resuscitation' committee that put together a revival conference that saw it take off again, to date! Kudos to the new generation!

I had the very rare privilege and special honour of delivering its inaugural keynote address on 6th September 1991, on a topic that addressed the raging debate of the time. My chosen topic of the talk was – **"COULD THERE BE OR SHOULD THERE BE 'KENYAN' SURGERY?"**

After that, many felt that they had just attended the funeral of the "district surgeon," but the lull that followed among some of its key officials bordered on sabotage, suspiciously in favour of the Association of Surgeons of East Africa (ASEA), which was not called for at all! Practically all surgeons in Kenya were members of ASEA, with no conflict of interest! In my address, I had seen the two as potentially good collaborators! Some thought SSK (a national outfit) had been formed to kill ASEA, a regional giant! Far from it! Mr. Warambo and some of us had been grossly misunderstood, ostensibly at the behest of the outgoing (self-made) "expatriate" surgeons and their local protégés!

At the regional level, the Association of Surgeons of East Africa (ASEA) was playing a big role in keeping surgeons in the region together and the specialties as near the cutting edge as possible. Its conferences were always popular and very well attended. Nevertheless, its leadership was labouring under diehard paranoia; hence, not surprisingly, it was jolted by the inauguration of the SSK. The post-colonial survivalist strategy by 'foreigners' to make 'locals' fight one another still works, especially among politicians! It did not work as effectively here!

My inaugural address referred to above sure seemed to have calmed the waters somewhat, but the simmering unilateral tension between ASEA and the SSK lingered on, especially among some of its Kenyan members, hence the (sponsored?) paralytic cold shoulder of the Founder Secretary-General, who later became its second Chairman anyway. In all fairness, and on a serious note, everybody just wanted professional progress in surgery, in Kenya and the region.

One might be inclined to see that as a triumph for the SSK. So it must have been! The forward head-current was too strong! Those who felt guilty jumped on to the unstoppable bandwagon. It was an interrupted dream whose time had long come. Cheers to pioneer visionary and Founder Chairman, Mr. Michael Wilson Warambo who, almost single-handedly at the forefront, mobilized the entire surgical fraternity in Kenya to form and start that Society!

By the way, Mr. Warambo was the first supervisor of my M.Med (Surg.) dissertation before the late Professor Nelson Awori and the late Mr. Ben Obonyo (Ugandan) took over upon his retirement from Government service.

That dissertation was on "ENLARGEMENTS OF THE PROSTATE." Being composed of two parts, an inner glandular and outer fibrous, parts, I proposed that the prostate should anatomically be re-named **"URETHRO-PROSTATIC GLAND" (UPG),** and enlargement of the prostate to be termed **"URETHRO-PROSTATIC ADENOMA OR ADENOSIS (UPA)**, which to-date does not seem to have caught the eye of any of our urologists, since I retreated back to heart surgery, which I had started with in Calcutta, India. Curiously at some point, that dissertation disappeared from the shelf of the School library after I drew attention to it at a "Grand Round" of the 'Division of Surgery' at KNH, to expound on some discussion at the meeting and to tickle or stimulate thoughts on the anatomy relevant terminology!

At the local academic level, the first Chairman of the Department of Surgery, Professor Douglas Roy, played a key role in founding the Department. He was followed by Professor P. Dhall, then Professor Edwin O.W. Knight in an acting capacity. The late Professor Ambrose Eric Onyango Wasunna came in next (also as the first indigenous Kenyan in that Chair), followed by the late Professor Nelson Wanyama Awori, Professor Julius Kyambi, the late Professor Michael Mbalu, Professor George Omore Magoha (deceased 2023), Professor Zipporah Ngumi, Professor Herbert Ouma Oburra, Professor Stephen Oduor Ogendo, Professor Peter Larry Waweru Ndaguatha and Dr.

Julius Kiboi. I had acted on this Chair for nine months many years before, in 1990-91 when Professor Kyambi took his sabbatical leave, just about one year before I was elected Dean of the Faculty of Medicine in early 1992. Within the nine months, I re-established our Departmental library by donating a textbook entitled *Vascular Surgery* by Rutherford.

My substantive Chairmanship of the Division of Surgery, which combined KNH-based and University-based surgeons (1989-1993) overlapped with Professor Kyambi's Chairmanship of the academic Department of Surgery. I was a member of his Department; he was a member of my Division. We jovially chaired each other respectively and jointly, with a very pleasant and great working relationship! For as long as it lasted, we changed the face of the Division of Surgery!

It was through that docket of the Division of Surgery, in collaboration with all Divisions at KNH, (Obstetrics & Gynaecology, Medicine and Paediatrics-and-Health), that we were able to help save KNH from collapsing in the hands of the aforementioned expatriate management team called the **International Hospital Group (IHG),** whose case went up to State House. Their contract was terminated through a Presidential Commission of Enquiry as I have elaborated in another part of this book.

It chanced that all this happened during my tenure as Chairman of the Division. I had spent most of my surgical life there, within the Division and the Department at the KNH Campus, almost like working at 'home.' I knew the place well. It was a rewarding phase of my input into management. In the preceding chapter, I have narrated fully my other experience as Dean of the Faculty (School) of Medicine. All else is really the content of this whole narrative about myself. But perhaps I should say something about the Departmental **"JOURNAL CLUB!"**

After my initial (uncompleted) surgical training at the Postgraduate (PG) SSKM Hospital in Calcutta, India, I worked in Murang'a for nine months, literally like a District Surgeon, between September 1971 and

June 1972. The 'former incumbent' surgeon, Mr. (later Professor) Jeshrani had gone to complete his own surgical training at the new Master of Medicine (in Surgery) programme at Makerere University, Uganda, where it had been started ahead of Nairobi. In due course, I was soon to catch up with, and complete, my own post-graduate training in Surgery, but in Nairobi, Kenya.

From Kenya, surgical trainees usually went on to complete their courses and practical clinical hospital experience before taking Parts I and II examinations of the Fellowship of the Royal Colleges of Surgery in United Kingdom. But at this time, plans for starting the local programme of Master of Medicine in Surgery (M.Med-Surgery) were at an advanced stage. The days of FRCS would soon be over. When I joined in June-July 1972, the batch ahead of my class were retained as the first class of M.Med (Surgery) in Nairobi. The three were Mr. (later Professor) Gerishom Mudanya Sande (deceased 2019), Mr. Peter Ochola Abila (deceased 2012) and Mr. (later Professor) Benjamin Mbindyo (deceased 2020). They were now preparing for their Part II (Final) examination of the FRCS in UK, except for the new development in training. All necessary arrangements for the M.Med (Surgery) programme were more or less ready, hence their retention as the pioneer class. Of the fifteen (15) of us in the second M.Med.(Surg.) class, only three of us made it through Part I in March-April 1973. The other two were Dr. (later Professor) Joseph Samuel Oliech and Dr. Kapasi.

Immediately after announcement of the results, these two classmates of mine independently left the country to pursue their continued training abroad, the former to the United Kingdom, the latter to North America. I remained alone in a class of one student!

Touting my own surgical training in Calcutta, surgical work experience in Murang'a and a problem of one person alone in a class, I appealed to the Department of Surgery to permit me to join the senior class and do the final (Part II) examinations together with them. I was allowed! We became a class of four as the first batch of the locally qualified surgeons in Kenya. Peter Abila had actually been behind me at Kisii High School. Now we were classmates. No sweat – we had travelled very different pathways in the intervening years! Soon after qualifying, we joined the academic Department of Surgery at about the same time.

In our final year of the M.Med (Surgery) class, we formed a study group and started a journal club, of which I was the convenor-coordinator. We apportioned or assigned about three reputable peer-reviewed medical journals to every one of us to read and select important papers for presentation to the group, one after another. We always met in the (old) Seminar Room of the Department of Surgery at 8 pm, until we graduated together in August 1975.

In the meantime, the usual Departmental meetings and discussions of Saturday morning got interrupted when Kenya changed to a five-day working week, instead of the six-day weeks before! Now there was no non-clinical work on Saturdays! The Thursday "Grand Rounds" continued.

After joining the Department as a Lecturer, I introduced the journal club system to postgraduate students for Thursday mornings. This went on very well for some time but slowed down and fizzled out! I did not find any club when I returned after two years sojourn abroad for my thoracic and cardiovascular surgical specialization training! This time round, in mid-1980s during Professor Awori's Chairmanship, I proposed the re-awakening or reviving the journal club. Repeatedly, it was not being included in the agenda of Departmental meetings. So, at a 'next' meeting, I raised it as an AOB at the end of the meeting. Professor threw it back at me that if I wanted it "so much" then I should become the convenor and organize accordingly. The response to my push and organization from both staff and students was very gratifying! **The Club** took off and soon doubled up as a forum for other presentations like dissertations, study and research proposals, and protocols for robust discussions, like was already happening in some other Departments of the Faculty of Medicine, University of Nairobi. The tradition continues!

Specialties

Circa late 1980s: The Department of Surgery after the death of the late Prof. Nelson Awori (I am seated second from right). Before Prof. Awori was Prof. Ambrose E.O. Wasunna who presided over the upsurge of surgical specialties, including thoracic and cardiovascular surgery. Prof. Julius Kyambi succeeded Prof. Awori.

A visit to the Department of Surgery today finds a specialist in almost every area of surgery. That was bound to happen as highlighted above! It was a necessary part of the development of surgery in this country. Traditional general surgery merged with gastro-enterology. Curiously, however, all these have not fully stemmed the tide of medical tourism by patients and their relatives seeking health care in overseas destinations!

17

THORACIC AND CARDIOVASCULAR SURGERY: WHERE DO WE GO FROM HERE?

PROFESSOR EDWIN KNIGHT from Jamaica was the pioneer head of my specialty of "Thoracic and Cardiovascular Surgery" at KNH. He performed the first open-heart surgery in Kenya on 14th June 1973 on an enrolled nurse who had an atrial septal defect (a hole in the heart).

Actual commencement of dedicated open-heart surgery as a continuing programme kicked off with the assistance of the Japanese in June 1975, after Professor Knight had left Kenya at the end of his contract. Dr. Onishi lead the Japanese team, together with Dr. (later Professor) Fujita. Mr. Terence Paul (FRCS) from Sri Lanka took over from the Japanese. I was privileged to train with Professor Knight as a postgraduate student and with Mr. Paul (deceased) as his senior registrar and junior colleague. No open heart operation was performed during the short stint of Dr. James McCoy from Houston, Texas, mainly because the facilities were not yet adequate. Mr. (later Professor) Francis Omaswa (Ugandan) joined our Unit in May 1979 up to around August 1981. I did my first independent open heart operation in Kenya, by a Kenyan, as it were, on 1st February 1979, upon returning from Guy's, Charing Cross, and Cardiff (all in the UK) and Montreal, Canada. The rest of this story is in ***The History of Heart Surgery in Kenya***, a book meant to be published soon after this one.

In my invited talks to the Lions and Rotary Clubs in the 1980s, I said it, and it is already happening, but only to a small extent:

a) That there was a need to take such specialized treatment like heart surgery to the provincial (and now county) hospitals. The upsurge in the level of open heart surgery centres is so noticeable that one wonders why some parts of the country are still so shy to start at all! Along with the number of centres in Nairobi, one can now count Mombasa (Coast General and Teaching Hospital), Eldoret (Moi Teaching and Referral Hospital) and Tenwek Hospital in Bomet. When Professor Christine Jowi and her cardiology colleagues lined up patients for heart surgery at Jaramogi Oginga Odinga Teaching and Referral Hospital in 2009, and Professor Steven Ogendo and I performed two closed heart operations in Kisumu (strategically to prompt the largest regional hospital), Kisumu did not and still does not seem tickled to any provocative extent for action. Later on, I raised the matter of training heart surgeons for the same county with the first Governor of Kisumu County, together with his Health Minister, but nothing happened!

b) There would be a natural progression towards super-specialization and inevitable separation, even if partially, of the three main subsections of the combined or compounded specialty. We were bound to see peripheral vascular surgery leave cardiac and also let general thoracic surgery remain as a super-specialized area. That is already a reality. Paediatric cardiac surgery, even peripheral vascular surgery are showing strong signals of 'going it alone.' Only remember, as I advised our younger colleagues, that the environment, and even economic level, will remain big challenges. In a little while, the public will be sufficiently aware to make their own choices. But until then, if a specialist in this area wants to split away and off to pursue only one of the super specialties,

> let him and her ensure their own proficiency in the other (remaining) two during training before spreading out and beyond.

Jokes aside, in this environment of ours in Kenya and the region, a general thoracic surgeon must know how to operate on the heart, and vice versa. Whoever wants to take on cardiac surgery must know how to remove a lung. A peripheral vascular surgeon must know how to put a patient on to cardio-pulmonary bypass and do the operation accordingly.

This voice is for the sake of education, training and practice, say ***safe practice, in fairly closely related areas of surgery*** best incorporated in the curriculum. **General surgery is key to all surgery because the general surgeon should and must be able to enter any body cavity safely and to come out equally safely!**

In this part of the world, 'public-private mix' has been more of a slogan than a fertile stimulant/stimulus to development. I still think that the (non-toxic) private sector would play ball much more if and when their corporate social responsibilities, including funding research, are recognized and rewarded by the tax collector in the form of incentives such as **tax rebates, or tax holidays** (whatever these terms mean in effect), as reverse, indirect or reciprocal compensation for their contributions.

In my sense of "PRIVATE" here, I do not include tobacco, *miraa*, alcohol, cocaine, even so-called medical marijuana "private" and underground businesses, hence the word "non-toxic!" These dangerous merchants and their lethal merchandise hover around researchers-in-the-making, choking them with skewed vested interests, including "blood money." Their sponsorships for research, sports, school activities, etc. are always meant to corrupt the ruling and management systems for their own selfish interests, irrespective of the health and economic damage that their products cause at individual, national and environmental levels! They deserve to be taxed many times higher than other friendly businesses that promote health and economy, and spare, if not also promote, the mind and the environment!

You cannot retain or sustain – let alone enjoy – your national so-called independence, or cultivate development and prosperity within a country for which the above is the case, where there is an appetite for what you are given and not what you create or craft! Medicine, technology, economy or any other human development cannot thrive in a thwarted atmosphere! Over and above these, super-specialties in medicine require strategic active patronage! Kenya has had, and still has, the chance to be the hub of this and other specialties in the entire region and beyond!

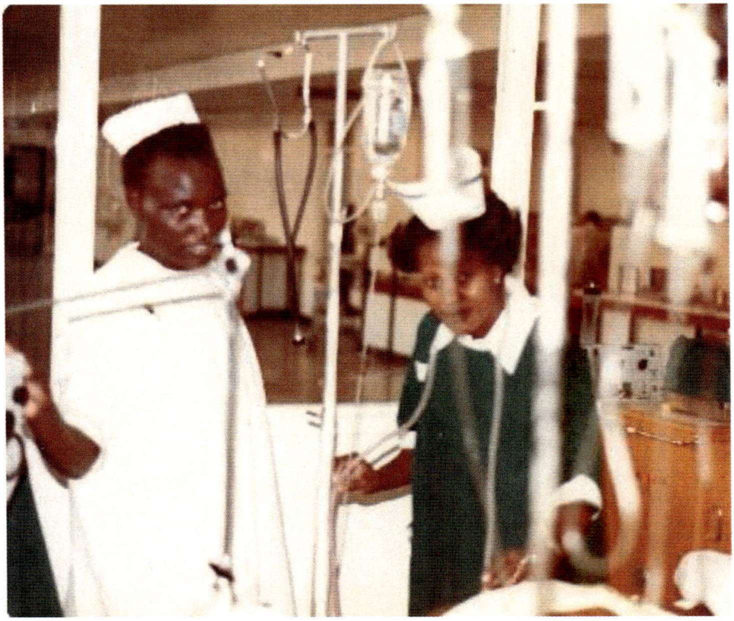

1st February 1979. Sisters Onsongo (left) and Florence Mutiambei (right, partially obscured) on the day of the operation (Day 0) after settling my first dedicated open-heart patient, Agnes Muthoni Kariuki in ICU. She had undergone an operation to close an atrial septal defect (hole in the heart).

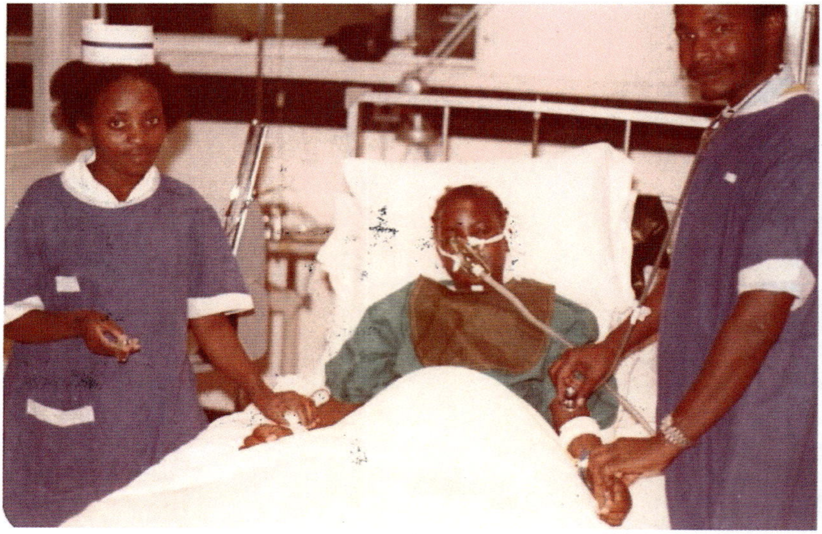

February 1979: Two nurses, Sister Kariuki and Mr. Maina with Agnes on Day 1 (first post-operative day) in ICU.

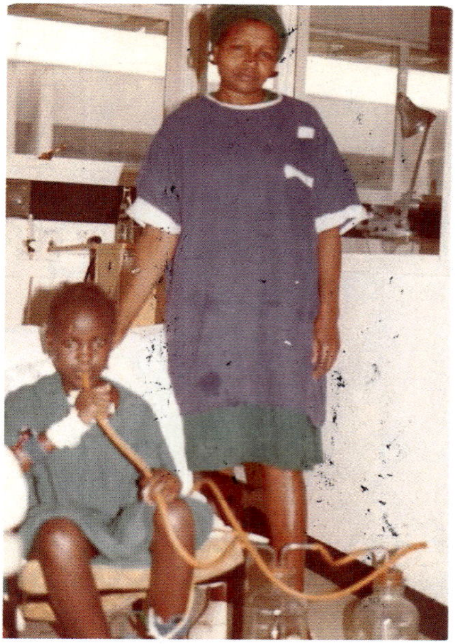

February 1979: Wambui, our very efficient patient attendant (she happened to be deaf and dumb), with Agnes on Day 3 (third post-operative day).

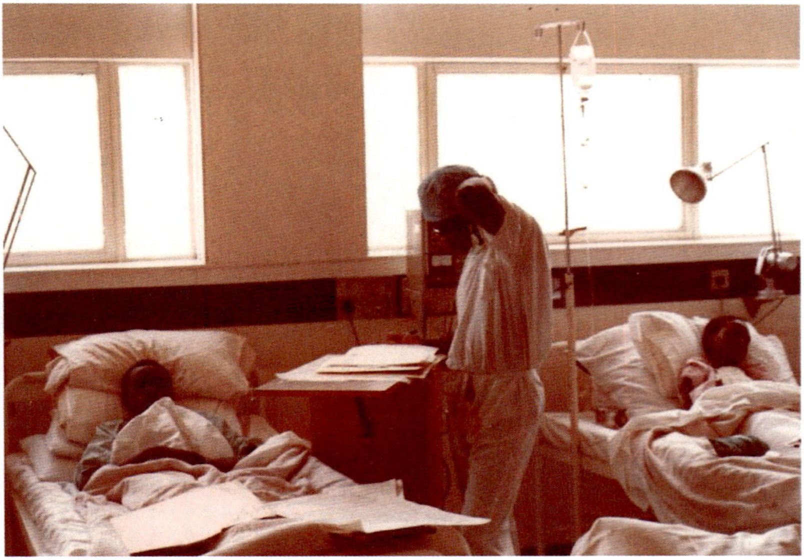

In the ICU after theatre. Assessing a patient and writing orders.

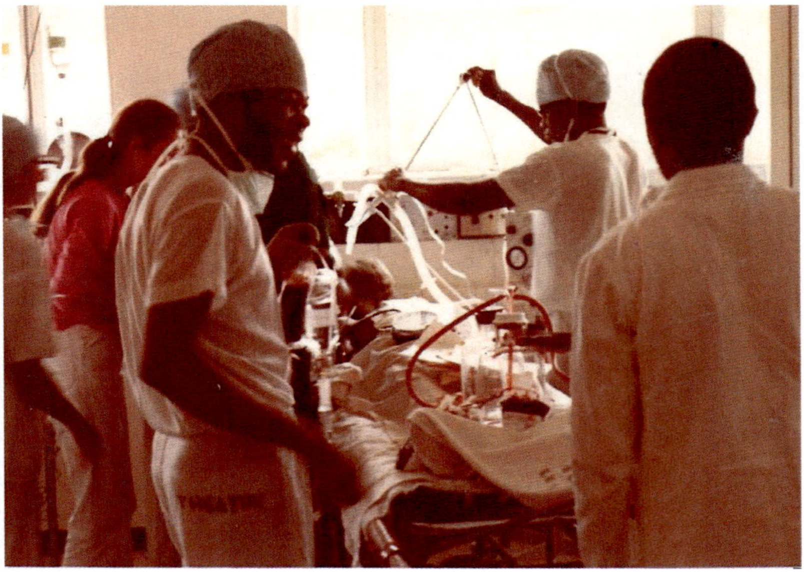

Mr. John Ang'iro (left) moments after we wheeled a patient from the operating room. I am second from right holding the tube.

With two key theatre nurses at the time, Sister Eva Gituma (left; the in-charge) and Sister Julia Kibe.

Left to right: Sister Margaret Gikonyo (the in-charge at KNH Ward 4B) and Esther and Mary who were both in the haematology and blood transfusion unit of KNH. They made open-heart surgery tick!

LEFT: April 1977. In London with Dr. Fujita, who I met at a conference. He formed part of the Japanese cardiac team who performed the first open heart operation at KNH in 1975.

BELOW: 1991. Flying Doctor Service. Standing with Prof. Emmanuel Ayim (left), a nursing sister and the pilot (right).

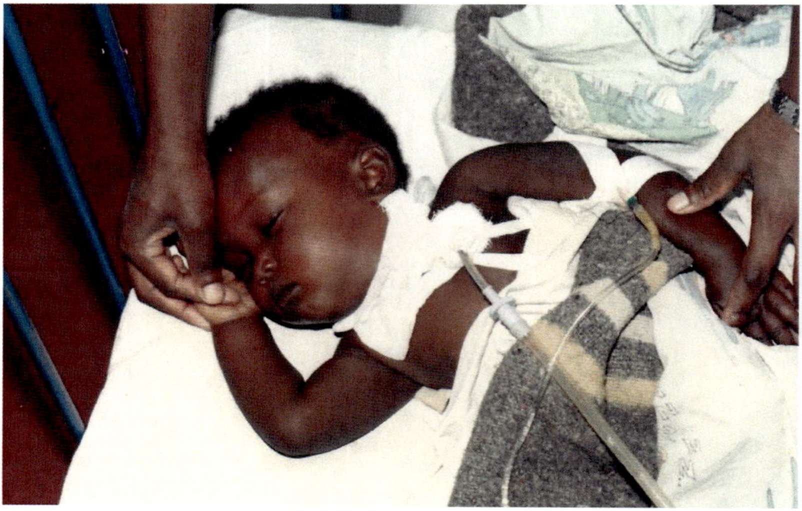

1991. Flying Doctor Service. Chest operation patient at Wamba Hospital. That experience motivated me to reinstate the rotation of flying out with AMREF teams around the country as part of our surgical training when I became Dean of the Faculty of Medicine a year or so later.

The KNH heart unit, including cardiologists, anaesthetists, surgeons, nurses and technologists. I am in the centre flanked by Prof. Elijah Ogola and Hasmukh Harilal Kamdar.

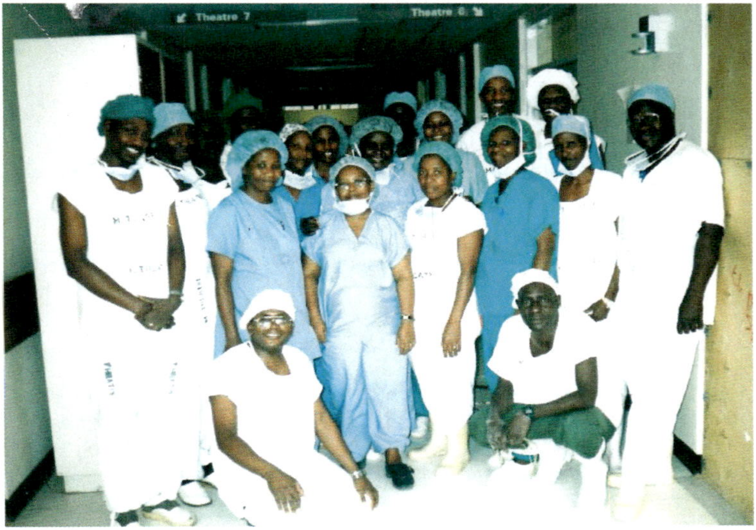

The KNH theatre team. I am standing far right. The only perfusionists in the country at the time were Fred Mwololo and Philip Ochieng (both squatting). They were trained through our initiative in the team. The rest of the team included some very senior nursing staff who were just right for the young unit. The sister in charge at the time, Sr. Matu, is standing behind Fred.

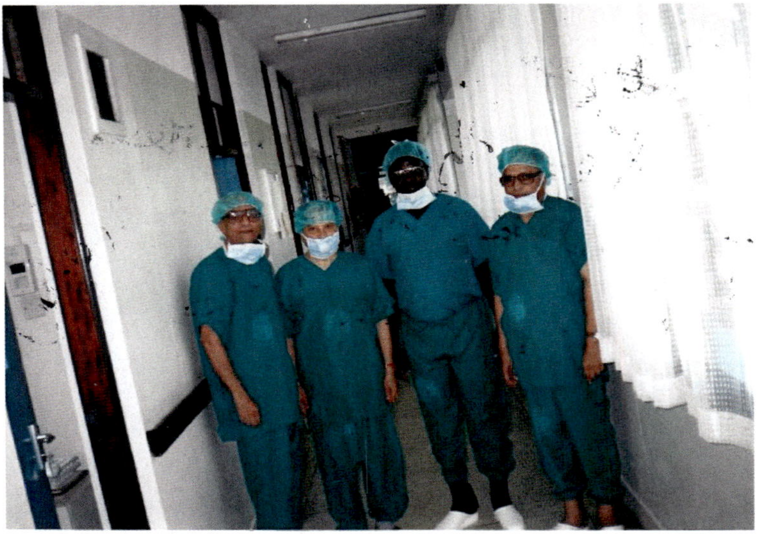

With the Doshi brothers at the Mater Hospital. They sponsored a series of open-heart patients who were operated on by the heart team at the Mater Hospital.

With the Mater team and the Medtronic Medical Company-sponsored team from South Africa who were led by co-director Steve Sutherland (fourth from left). The cardiac perfusionist is in front of Steve. I am squatting in the front.

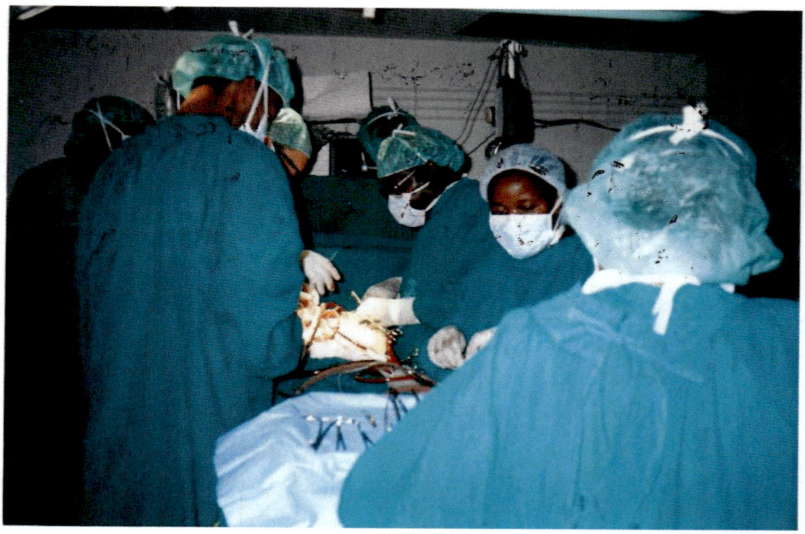

The collaborative team from Mater and South Africa during surgery.

The Kenyan team together with the Medtronic Medical Company-sponsored team from South Africa. I am standing far right next to Steve Sutherland.

With my first closed-heart operation patient in Kisumu

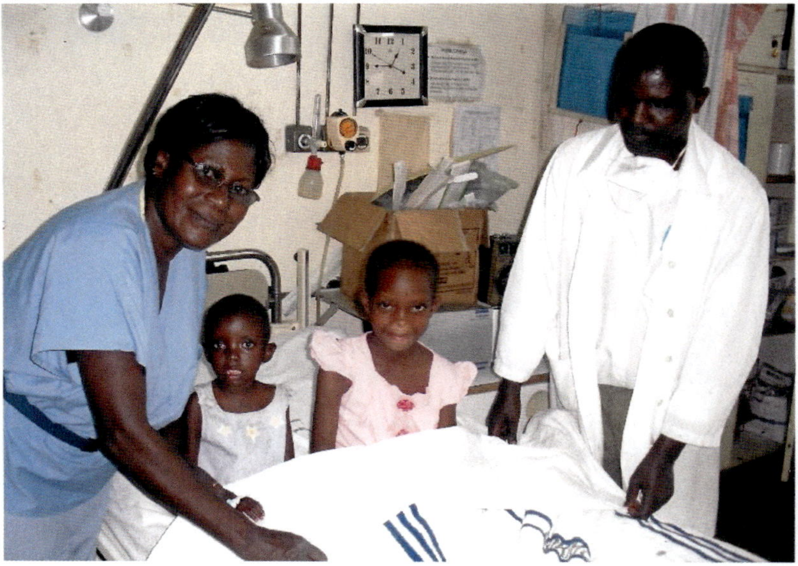

My first closed-heart operation patient in Kisumu

18

THE 'ORPHAN' STATE OF (SOME) KENYA HEART PATIENTS AND THE SALVAGE: THE KENYA HEART PATIENTS' ASSOCIATION (KHPA)

AT THE CLOSE of the 1970s and into the early 1980s, it became quite apparent that something was missing for our patients. On the one hand, there was a mystique surrounding open heart surgery, even among health workers. Patients and relatives were also hard put to go through with doctors' plans. We set out to demystify open heart surgery. It meant being close to the patients, so that they would not stress themselves out with what the doctor 'found' but was not talking about, be it good or bad news.

On the other hand, there were a number of patients who had been operated on overseas and had returned - and were presently in the country. Even if referred out there by local doctors, they would require surgical review. Many people are fearfully sensitive about the heart and scars on the chest. But the direct challenge for this earlier batch of patients was that they had left their surgeons behind, abroad, in the countries where they were operated on. Even local cardiologists could only do that much better with surgical consultation. The net situation was that these patients were surgical orphans!

Some did not have detailed reports, but as long as the cardiologist referred them for surgical review in our clinics, we accommodated them, even if they had been referred and sent abroad privately.

Both groups, the actual catchment for local care, as well as those who had left their surgeons abroad, needed human ears, human eyes, human hands, human understanding and humane service, if not also human feelings; another human heart and, above all, actual cardiac care skills! Those not yet operated on wanted to see survivors, so to speak, so as to reassure themselves before they gave consent for their own forthcoming respective operations. There was dire need for a counselling forum where their symptoms, ailments, fears, 'overrated' trust and other problems would be addressed.

The surgical team at Kenyatta National Hospital resolved that a Kenya Heart Patients' Association be formed. It was imperative that the correct procedure was followed for the Association's formation, including a proper constitution and official registration. There would be, within the constitution, a provision for a Patron. The Association's forums would necessarily include sharing of experiences among themselves, reassuring one another and inviting cardiac workers to give them talks and answer their questions. I became their first Patron and stayed on for the number of years that followed. Surprisingly, after more than a decade, my successor had more to blame them for than I dared to try and understand!

The benefits to patients were more than we had anticipated, or bargained for. I have said more about this in a separate volume, ***The History of Heart Surgery in Kenya.***

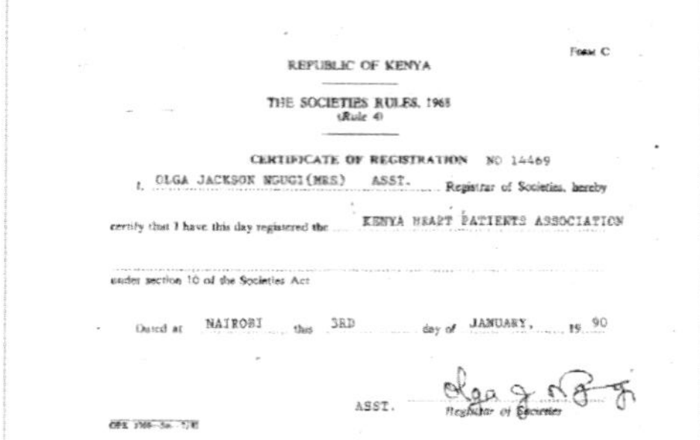

Form C

REPUBLIC OF KENYA

THE SOCIETIES RULES, 1968
(Rule 4)

CERTIFICATE OF REGISTRATION NO 14469

I, OLGA JACKSON NGUGI (MRS) ASST. Registrar of Societies, hereby certify that I have this day registered the KENYA HEART PATIENTS ASSOCIATION under section 10 of the Societies Act

Dated at NAIROBI this 3RD day of JANUARY, 1990

ASST. Registrar of Societies

The KHPA registration certificate.

With the first Chairman of the Kenya Heart Patients' Association, Mr. Geoffrey Chepkwony (right), and a member, Ms. Njoki Gichia (previously operated on overseas at Hammersmith Hospital in London).

19

DRUMS OF WAR, OR JUST ANOTHER FATALISTIC AFRICAN REHEARSAL?

THIS WAS A TRUE SOS call from a good neighbour! A vehicle convoy belonging to a head of state had been shot at and the President had sustained injuries. The call came to Kenya as an emergency appeal through the protocol of Foreign Affairs, Defence, Ministry of Health and the main National Referral Hospital in Nairobi, the Kenyatta National Hospital. It was presumed that the President of that country had been shot. Could Kenyan doctors go and help?

The then Director of Medical Services (DMS), Prof. Tom Ariba Ogada, coordinated the whole operation overnight. He quickly put together a team of four to be flown to Mogadishu immediately. They were:

1. Head of the team – Mr. Joab Bodo (FRCS), Orthopaedic Surgeon and Deputy Director of KNH. Nationally, Chief Orthopaedic Surgeon.
2. Consultant Anaesthetist Prof. Emmanuel Ayim.
3. Chief Physician and Neurologist Dr. Samuel Mwinzi.
4. Thoracic and Cardiovascular Surgeon Prof. Peter A. Odhiambo.

I was woken up by Mr. Bodo. We had to leave that night. By 3am we were all assembled at the Eastleigh Air Base. Our plane was an army helicopter, a buffalo. The seats and improvised patient coach were suspended with chains from a level above.

When we arrived at daybreak, we were very well received and taken straight to the hospital. We clerked the patient together. The unanimous opinion was that there was no serious injury to warrant special care. We made clinical recommendations.

After that, two other things compelled us to tread very carefully:

1. The very simple fact that it was the head of state who was involved.
2. The potential psychological and politicized impact on the local doctors, should anything go wrong in their hands after we left.

We were the ones to protect and salvage confidence in them locally. They needed an antidote against the phenomenon of overrating anything and anybody 'foreign' by 'locals.' Together, we consciously felt we needed to leave them with some confidence in themselves. That was not our main mission, but we saw it as contribution to a possible shift in the paradigm.

We unanimously agreed that we would fly back to Nairobi with the President. But we had to talk to them and reassure them that they had so far done just fine, and we understood their hidden political predicament as 'locals.' It was an African phenomenon!

Time to leave! By that time, we had been told that two other countries had been invited and their doctors were already airborne. Italy had just turned back on hearing that Kenya had landed. Saudi Arabia was approaching. While on our way back to our helicopter to effect final touches in readiness for the President, a fairly large civilian-looking aeroplane circled overhead and landed.

That was Saudi Arabia's **air ambulance**, complete with gadgets and resuscitation facilities! We needed not to know more! That was it! An fully-kitted air ambulance versus a buffalo helicopter with a "swinging bed" and no medical equipment to talk of. There were other considerations:

1. There was already a presence of alternative rescue.
2. The flight on board the Saudi air ambulance was bound to be more comfortable, patient-friendly and enabling for any

doctor's intervention by virtue of ambulance facilities on board.

3. Predictably, there was likely to be easy religious and cultural bonding with the environment and health teams in Saudi Arabia.

We graciously stood down and recommended that he be taken to Saudi Arabia. That was it! We flew back in our buffalo helicopter without the super-patient.

That Kenya responded so fast and was the first to land in Mogadishu, was a welcome **plus** between good neighbours and among medical colleagues at the hospital. That was a distinct diplomatic score!

By the way, we never checked the circumstances surrounding the shooting at the Somali head of state's convoy. Within two or so years, he had been toppled. There was no 'medical' post-mortem to do for that. We were very simple medics. We just stayed home! For decades now, both KDF (Kenya Defence Forces) and Amisom have had a very big job there.

20

WALKING AND LOBBYING

One step at a time: There is no need to re-invent the wheel. If met with hostility as you pursue the path of justice, apply the ***'Submarine Formula!'***

I WOUND UP my Deanship with the election of a new Dean on 31st May 1996. Within the very next month, June 1996, I was re-elected Chairman of the Kenya Cardiac Society (KCS). That made me fourth Chairman of that Society, counting from myself in 1980 to 1987! It was like being recycled after those founder days.

KCS elections were held every two years. The Constitution provided for two consecutive terms for office-bearers; it chanced that I was re-elected in 1998.

By that time, KCS had long been affiliated with the International Society and Federation of Cardiology, the ISFC (its name later changed to the World Heart Federation), in collaboration with the World Health Organization (WHO). That affiliation continued seamlessly. We were bound by the spirit of global collaboration on and for cardiac health!

That year, 1998, the World Heart Federation (WHF) selected the last Sunday of September and named it World Heart Day, to be marked and observed every year with a 'Heart Walk' by all health workers concerned with heart health, together with other stakeholders all over the world. That was in line with the WHO's Tobacco-Free Initiative, through which member states were expected to domesticate their commitment by forming their own National Tobacco-Free Initiative committees. KCS staged its own heart walk to join the rest of the world affiliated with the WHF to mark the first World Heart Day.

Our guest of honour was the Director of Medical Services (DMS), Dr. (later Professor) Richard Muga. He did the entire 10 kilometre walk together with me and my Vice Chairman, Professor Elijah Ogola, leading a long line of heart health champions, including some of our already operated-on heart patients.

While walking, we chit-chatted. One outstanding part of our conversation (after prompting my Vice-Chair to stay close) was to drive the point home to the Director that he was presiding over a bombshell at the headquarters of the Health Ministry. Very soon, non-communicable diseases would engulf the country – under his very watch! It was important and urgent that he woke up and strengthened the sleeping Division of Non-Communicable Diseases so as to save the country and its people, particularly its people.

By coincidence, along with the KCS happenings, the tobacco control desk of the Kenya Medical Association, in consultation with the Ministry of Health, had solicited the Law Society of Kenya (LSK) to help draft a bill to be enacted into law for the control of tobacco in the country. KCS was soon invited to join the team. It fell upon me to represent the KCS on that 'drafting' committee. A relevant coincidence was my 1976 paper on lung cancer in Kenya.*

KCS made its contribution towards the elaboration of the bill. The Law Society of Kenya continued as the main technical advisor.

By 1999, a fair copy of the draft bill was ready for presentation to Parliament. In Parliament, there followed an annual cycle of tabling, lapsing, and re-tabling, repeated almost like a ritual, for close to a decade. Those days, when the National Assembly broke for December recess, any and all bills not discussed would lapse and wait to be re-tabled afresh, without any prioritisation, together with other old and new bills in the following year!

*Odhiambo PA, Gatei D, Knight EO. Is Bronchial Carcinoma Increasing in Kenya? *East African Medical Journal,* 01 Jul 1976, 53(7):383-388

First Kenya Cardiac Society Walk, 1998. With then Director of Medical Services, Dr. (later Prof.) Richard Muga as the guest of honour (right). Heart patient Fiona (centre) took part in the walk.

First Kenya Cardiac Society Walk, 1998. Dr. Stephen Oduor Ogendo (now Prof.; in blue jumper) and Dr. Elijah Ogola (now Prof.) form part of the leading pack.

First Kenya Cardiac Society heart walk; the 1998 participants gather for a photo.

1998: The youngest World Heart Day walker, now Dr. Jowi.

LEFT: First Kenya Cardiac Society heart walk, 1998: Warmup exercises.

BELOW: Heart walk participants on the KNH grounds. Ms. Penina Apiyo Ochola leans on the car. Next to her is the soon to be KNH Quality Assurance nurse in charge and to her right is Dr. (later Professor) Christine Yuko-Jowi.

In the new year of Parliament, the Minister for Health would make his or her move, virtually like a bid, and still find his or her bill listed near the bottom to await another December recess and another ritualistic lapse! It was a '*fait incarnate,*' as long as you did not look around, or forgot to remember your friends (and enemies)! The influence of the tobacco industry was palpable, ostensibly sacrosanct in the corridors that dictated your fate as a Kenyan citizen with supposed enshrined rights! There are corresponding replicas in many other parts of the world – alive but studiously, commercially, financially, psychologically, intellectually, morally and biologically defaulted in readiness for the scourges of lifestyle abuse!

The seemingly simple coincidence that a bill would be time-barred appeared innocent until you were told in plain language that it was done deliberately, and with a purpose, to derail legislation on tobacco control for as long as possible, without making it look like a premeditated act, which would provoke uproar and protest, at the very least. For now, it appeared ordinarily circumstantial or 'natural' that it was just time-barred! That it was the calendar, not the Assembly Clerk! Or was it?

That is the exact situation for which I would re-borrow the term **'manufactured ignorance,'** engineered by lubricated collusion with key operatives in the cogwheels and joints of national development. The situation tastes rotten when one reminisces about how, quite recently, slaves were sold in exchange for beads, perishable goods and other useless ornaments! What about a contemporary sermon about wheelbarrows on a stomach full of grabbed wealth! There is also the vocabulary of "hustling" sold as unmitigated misery while retaining the in-built dangerous connotation of grabbing by whatever method for the end to justify the means as wealth starts flooding around!

Later, in those days, the system in Parliament changed! Bills not discussed when Parliament went into recess would stay in their positions on the order list without lapsing, and new bills would now be listed further down the page. This ensured some predictable continuity and progression towards issues ultimately being debated!

While the draft bills were criss-crossing between the Ministry of Health and Parliament, the teams represented in the exercise did not relent.

At the level of documentation and policy, everything was in place. What Professor Muga needed to do was to implement and purposefully reactivate the Division of Non-Communicable Diseases which, at the time, was housed under the Division of Mental Health! The head of that Division was responsible for both Divisions.

They did a very good job nonetheless, particularly when the Framework Convention on Tobacco Control (FCTC) was under preparation at the WHO, in Geneva. The Inter-governmental Negotiating Body (INB) went through some tense moments, pitching the developed against the developing countries.

Kenya was represented by Dr. David Kiima, a psychiatrist of no mean dimension, then the Head of the twin Divisions of Mental Health and Non-Communicable Diseases.

Together with delegates from other developing countries, they formed a strong African and 'Third World' front that ensured delivery of the FCTC as it is came to be in its first edition. I can say, confirm and repeat that Dr. Kiima did Kenya proud!

That lobby with the DMS during the first Heart Day Walk appeared to have achieved something! We in KCS also followed up with the DMS. His positive and strategic responses and actions determined what followed in the immediate aftermath, for up to a decade.

In due course, the Division of Non-Communicable Diseases was separated from the Division of Mental Health. Almost simultaneously, but preceding that development, a tobacco-free initiative committee was constituted and set up. I was appointed its Chairman; Dr. Charles Maringo headed the newly 'independent' NCD Division, soon followed by Dr. Ahmed Ogwell. There was no looking back! We knew that in dealing with a ruthless, heartless, sadistic industry determined to sell death, we were in for a rough and bruising war. The grip of the tobacco industry on governments of the world, and worse, in developing countries, was and still is well known! We knew that they never slept on their goal. For the sake of our country, we could not afford to so much as to blink on ours.

A curriculum workshop. The National Tobacco-Free Initiative Committee. I am seated far left.

We quickly consolidated ourselves and formed close working links and alliances with, among others, the National Agency for the Control of Alcohol and Drug Abuse (NACADA) under its first Director, Mr. Joseph Kaguthi. As an institution, NACADA was an appointed member of the National Tobacco-Free Initiative Committee (NTFIC). Ministerial memberships and representations included Health, Information, Education, Agriculture and Labour. Along with them was the other founder member, the Kenya Medical Association (KMA).

Other stakeholders represented included religious groups as one category, and civil society, also represented by one person from among themselves.

True to themselves, the tobacco industry agitated to be included in the membership of NTFIC, and later even in the Board itself! The response was simple, clear and categorical – when one plans to invent an insecticide to control, even kill, mosquitoes, one does not invite the lethal insects to join and help in preparing the insecticide! The Committee, the Board, the Ministry of Health, KMA and the Government were unshakeable! The tobacco industry was **not** a stakeholder in tobacco control, except to the extent of the default of 'democracy' and 'trade license;' even then, not when their activities impacted negatively on basic human rights! From our campaigns, it became generally understood that the whole of the tobacco industry and its activities were stakeholders in death, not health!

Seen in context, the approach, tactics and trickeries of the tobacco industry towards legislation amounted to four major chapters of intrigue and human sacrifice, namely: DELAY, DILUTE, DERANGE AND DESTROY. We remained awake to this ruthless strategy.

With or without job description, this was a very special and unique committee; not just because it was a WHO agenda, but also because it instantaneously acquired its own relevance and dynamic for this country, the entire African continent and the whole world. The FCTC itself was the first-ever international treaty on health endorsed and adopted by United Nations member mtates! That alone was a strong message that there was something very wrong and dangerous with tobacco! It was vital and urgent that the world paid attention and acted! Individual nations and states had no other options but to join in and save their peoples.

But, for this country and this continent, it encapsulated additional overwhelming responsibility, provided one was disposed to see depth, meaning and correlation in history!

For and from the most indigent among us, to the most 'self-fortified' end of the scale, this committee had historical templates and challenges of the renaissance, abolition of slave trade and independence struggle, all wrapped in one; of note is that slavery is still rife in its overt and covert forms! The successor bodies like the Tobacco Control Board would, necessarily and inevitably, inherit these challenges in their corresponding forms. It is for the people to decide what they want for themselves, their children and the children of their children. But the responsibility was self-evident, prescribed and apportioned! For the limited time of my appointment into the committee, we set out to cover a few key aspects and areas of tobacco control, as follows:

1. Create awareness and educate the Kenyan public about the dangers of tobacco and tobacco-related products. For this we quickly produced a leaflet of information about the dangers of tobacco; additionally, we traversed the country, talking and lecturing.
2. Highlight environmental, economic and social dangers of tobacco.
3. Institute and ensure control of tobacco, tobacco products and tobacco use by children.
4. With the Ministry of Agriculture, explore and implement crop substitution to save those entrapped and involved in tobacco farming and other tobacco related activities.
5. Outlaw smoking in public places to stem the tide of second-hand smoking and exposure to second-hand smoke.
6. Legislate:
    a. against the lethal trade to **control supply,**
    b. to increase tax on tobacco and tobacco products, so as to **reduce demand** by the factor of difficult affordability,
    c. to provide for compensation for the damage caused and done, by levying a 'tobacco control tax' and establishing a **"Tobacco Control Fund"** and

d. to promote healthy living and a healthy environment.

7. Join the rest of the world, through **collaboration**, and otherwise, in the fight against tobacco.

In summary, our modalities in the war included leaflets, posters, books, talks and lectures. We visited schools and lobbied Parliamentarians. We supported litigation against the tobacco industry by victims of tobacco products.

We observed all "World No-Tobacco Day" occasions on 31st May, every year, at first just in Nairobi, but later we went round the country through Provincial and County Headquarters, and elsewhere!

Initially, in Kenya, it was commemorated late to avoid a clash with preparations for Madaraka Day, which falls on 1st June. As we settled down in the committee, we realized that that was not friendly to tobacco control. We reasoned that Madaraka Day rallies were very fertile grounds for **advocacy** and continued lobbies with the public and the Government itself! Since then, Kenya observes World No-Tobacco Day, with the rest of the world, on 31st May every year.

And so, we fought on! The decade-old tobacco control bill was finally passed by Parliament and given assent by the President in October 2007. The law was now in place!

In 2008, I had the honour of being among those from different countries to receive that year's World No-Tobacco Day Award at the 48th Regional WHO-AFRO Conference. Later the same year, the Minister for Health appointed me first Chairman of the newly constituted Tobacco Control Board. It took that long because the tobacco industry, led by British American Tobacco (BAT) had pleaded for time to change the labels of their cigarette packets to be in line with the new law!

The battles raged on. We had long prepared our tobacco policy document; the strategic plan was also done. We needed to implement the Tobacco Control Act. In order to do so, we needed Tobacco Control Regulations. We undertook the exercise of public participation by sharing it widely with the public in 24 counties, with members of the Board physically going around the country. The tobacco industry itself was invited to stakeholders' fora at the School of Government. Among those present were representatives of the different tobacco companies and the tobacco farmers, respectively. The Regulations were gazetted on 4th December 2014.

Once again, true to themselves, the tobacco industry sued the Ministry of Health and the Board, claiming that they were not consulted. This was for no other reason, except to block the Tobacco Control Regulations. They lost at the High Court. They then moved up to the Court of Appeal where, again, they lost! As if that was not enough for them, they jumped up to the Supreme Court, where they were given a hearing in April 2018. Their defence focused on public participation, which BAT and Master Mind-Kenya claimed were not done, further insisting that they were not invited! With the likes of the tobacco industry that we know, I dare say that it might still seek some other interventional mechanisms to cow Kenya. Should that happen, then even as 'retirees,' we shall go back to the trenches and deliver Kenya! In any case, the entire tobacco control fraternity in Kenya, with its institutionalized fronts, is a force to reckon with: talk of the Kenya Tobacco Control Alliance (KETCA), of which I was the founder Chairman, now with Joel Gitali and Thomas Lindi on the front-line! The public is much better informed than it was decades ago, especially when we started.

Meanwhile, WHO recognized tobacco control achievements in Kenya by awarding Kenya's Tobacco Control Board itself with the 2016 World No-Tobacco Day award. My term as first Chair of Kenya's Tobacco Control Board expired in August 2017. I am happy and proud to have been part of this line-up of "Shujaas!"

Removing a lung, or repairing a sick heart and waiting for another to come, and then another, is not holistic health care. What I have done, still do and will continue to do to eliminate tobacco is an effort, not in futility, but in dealing with a major cause of many diseases in many specialties, including mine!

That is my new pet subject! I call it ***Preventive Surgery***. Surgeons in both the clinic and the operating room see much more of what should be prevented than public health workers do. It is high time that surgeons appreciated this as their unique opportunity to contribute more to health care delivery, right from the primary health care level up to organ replacement and extirpation of cancer.

That is my challenge to fellow surgeons of today and tomorrow!

Thank you!

The National Tobacco-Free Initiative Committee meeting in Nanyuki. I am seated in the centre.

TOP AND BOTTOM: Championing alternative crops for Migori tobacco farmers at a demonstration farm.

We are shown the inside of a tobacco curing kiln in Migori.

A congenitally deformed child born into a tobacco-growing family in Migori, Kenya.

Receiving the World No Tobacco Day Award, 2008 – Yaoundé, Cameroon.

WORLD NO TOBACCO DAY

31 MAY

2008

The World Health Organization awards this Certificate of Appreciation to

Professor Peter Amollo Odhiambo

Professor of Thoracic and Cardiovascular Surgery, University of Nairobi, Kenya

in recognition of outstanding contribution to tobacco control

World Health Organization

The certificate of appreciation I received.

A consultation with the then Provincial Director of Agriculture and his team. He briefed the NTFIC team about the unfortunate effects of tobacco and tobacco farming in Mbeere, Embu county. I am seated far right.

The making of a preventive surgeon: Press conference in Embu.

2014: Tobacco Control Board public participation mobilisation in Kisumu

Follow-up group photo of public participation for tobacco control regulations and gazettement in Garissa town. The group included police officers, municipality officials, and the Tobacco Control Board team.

2010: Receiving Hon. Beth Mugo, Minister for Public Health, at Laico Regency Hotel on World No-Tobacco Day. Looking on is Dr. James Maina, Head of Non-Communicable Diseases.

The 'Omboga Declaration' of 2011: **"We, the students of all Secondary Schools in Kanyaluo, Karachuonyo, Homa Bay County, hereby resolve to say "NO!" to preventable diseases and deaths, including tobacco, among us in this great nation, Kenya!"**

The Tobacco Control Board and the students of Kanyaluo schools, Homa Bay County. See Omboga Declaration.

The Kanyaluo community that attended the Tobacco Control meeting at Omboga, along with seven secondary schools of Kanyaluo ward, Homa Bay county.

2012: Attending the 5th Conference of Parties (COP-5)of the WHO in Seoul, South Korea on the Framework Convention on Tobacco Control (FCTC). With Dr. Ahmed Ogwell, formerly of the Division of Non-Communicable Diseases, now at the regional WHO office in Congo-Brazzaville.

2012: At the 5th Conference of Parties (COP-5) in South Korea seated with a delegate from Samoa (left).

14th March 2014 at the Nairobi Safari Club. Forum for 'Preventing a Tobacco Epidemic in Africa.' With Prof. Ratemo Michieka, Secretary-General of KNAS (left), and Mrs. Noel Abudho, the administrator.

14th March 2014 at the Nairobi Safari Club. Forum for 'Preventing a Tobacco Epidemic in Africa.' Introducing MEDICOM to Mr. John Mututho (third from left). Others, from L-R: Prof. Ratemo Michieka, Sec. Gen. of KNAS and Prof. Raphael Munavu, President of KNAS. Looking on is a high school student who was an awardee at the event.

Washington D.C, 2006. World Conference on Tobacco. I am standing far left.

The Tobacco Control Board. I am standing front and left.

Eastern Africa Awareness-Raising Workshop on the WHO Framework Convention on Tobacco (WHO FCTC).

November 2003: National Tobacco-Free Initiative Committee (NTFIC) with MPs and NACADA in Mombasa. In the group, among others, were MPs Hon. Joe Hamisi, Hon. Ocholla Ogur and NACADA director Joseph Kaguthi. I am seated far right.

One of a number of KETCA retreats. I am standing in the centre.

21

SERVING ON SCHOOL AND OTHER BOARDS

I
THE RAMOGI INSTITUTE OF ADVANCED TECHNOLOGY (RIAT) AND THE FUTURE

I WAS APPOINTED Chairman of the Board of Governors of the Ramogi Institute of Advanced Technology (RIAT) in February 2014, and inaugurated on 4th May 2014. My term expired in 2017 and was renewed. The long and short of the story is that I found myself presiding over the **rebirth** of RIAT. The giant had slept long enough. It was now out to awake, rise and take a leap to become the true giant that it has always had the potential to be!

As I write this, RIAT has 400 acres of land. Out of those, 150 have been the target of forced dispute. It will for sure regain that property. Currently, for the first time, we are in the middle of a "RIAT Master Plan" for the entire space as a living institution that would take care of its survival and future goals.

The Master Plan may see the emergence of a SUPER-RIAT which should grow and live long after my Chairmanship, especially if successor Boards embrace the plan. I can only urge the reader to watch this space!

The "Tilapia Tri-Lateral Cooperation" with Germany and Israel which I found in place, was a notable success when it ended over three years ago!

In-house development of infrastructure, like constructing a new gate, fencing and new Departmental buildings were already in progress when I left. I hope that my push for RIAT to expand its aquaculture to include income-generating fishing and fisheries will finally prosper!

I welcome the German ambassador to Kenya to RIAT.

At RIAT in Kisumu with the Trilateral Tilapia Collaboration of Israel, Germany and RIAT.

The German ambassador to Kenya inaugurating a water project at RIAT, Kisumu.

At RIAT in Kisumu with the Trilateral Tilapia Collaboration of Israel, Germany and RIAT. Planting a tree to mark the occasion.

II
THE NAIROBI HEALTH MANAGEMENT BOARD

Under the chairmanship of Dr. Betty Gikonyo from 2004 and for both of the terms in which she served, I served as the Chairman of the Clinical and Curative Committee. At this time, Dr. James Nyikal was also at Afya House as Director of Medical Services, the headquarters of Kenya's Ministry of Health. Plans to decongest Kenyatta National Hospital were effectively consolidated at the time.

Without continuity, when management conscientiously tries but fails to reinvent the wheel, any past problems are bound to recur.

That seems to be at least part of the story at this Board!

Until the retrogressive issues of attitude and empire creation are dealt with, our institutions are set to perfect lacklustre performance and can achieve their own high scores in the spate of growing mediocrity!

The Nairobi Health Management Board at its Lady Northey offices.

The Nairobi Health Management Board at its Lady Northey offices. I assist with watering a tree we planted.

III
OMBOGA SECONDARY SCHOOL
OH, OMBOGA, MY HOME (MY BIRTHPLACE).

I spent most of my Primary School education at Omboga Primary School in the early nineteen-fifties, before it was re-located to a new site near the local shopping centre in the nineteen-sixties, to give room for the new Secondary School through a lot of community participation!

I was born right in the middle of that original (and still the present) compound, with only a make-shift church building as the only structure. In 1952 my parents moved out of that compound, along with another two families, to respective new homes in the neighbourhood. My parents moved us just about 2 kilometres away to a place known as

Ong'eche (land of monkeys), because of the many monkeys that used to harass farmers in the larger area! We renamed it "Ong'eche-1" when I moved out of my father's homestead and 'established' my own place, which I named "Ong'eche-2;" I have spread out to other 'Ong'eches' ("Ong'eche-3" in Kisumu, which my son Jim made everybody call "Summit" on RIAT Hill, where we buried him on 8th August 1998). Then there is "Ong'eche-4" in Rongo. All those places have had stories of monkeys creating havoc on farms!

Omboga Secondary School was closed from 1989 to early 1991, because of so much mismanagement that parents removed their children to other schools one after another, until the numbers were unsustainable, compelling closure of the school!

This school is located nearly 28 km from Homa Bay town, within Homa Bay County. Omboga Mixed Secondary School (now Omboga High School) is not to be confused with ***Ombogo Girls'*** Secondary School, which is in Kochia, about 10 km from Homa Bay town.

In April 1991, the then Minister for Education, Hon. Oloo Aringo, and his Assistant Minister who was also the Member of Parliament for the area (then Karachuonyo Constituency), Hon. Lazarus Amayo, went to the school, inspected it and reopened it. I attended that meeting. The Minister appointed me the Chairman of the school's Board of Governors with immediate effect.

Despite a consciously and participatorily hatched out strategy for the school, there was a lot of negativity from the pupil catchment area around it. With the new headmaster, we planned and brainstormed. I told him he was not posted to close the school yet again! With polite, creative planning and constant communication, I kept the clan, including the area Chief, away from the school. I told the Chief he could attend board meetings, but he was not to otherwise enter the school compound without good reason. The only way he could help us was by keeping peace outside the gate and perimeter of the school, and providing us with all necessary security. For those who infiltrated (at least two tried), I got them impromptu one-on-one meetings, discussed a little and then told them not the try the same again as long as I was the Head of that 'homestead and family.'

In good time, the negativity against the school changed into a scramble for admission. In the 15 years of my chairmanship, with the same dedicated and hard-working Principal, the school's performance improved tremendously. Omboga Secondary School climbed to the top 100 District Schools and remained there for five years. We were ranked number 15 nationally in our best year.

When I left the chairmanship of the Board, all hell broke loose. Some elements in the clan came forward to harass the Principal again! They agitated for his removal due to clan animosities. He was demoted and transferred far away to another school in a different County, Siaya. I did not belong to the same clan, but I re-joined the dynamics to try and see, along with the new Board, how to offset the risks of his transfer and attendant disruption of the school. We won back some of his credibility, and subsequently, soon enough, the Teachers Service Commission (TSC) re-promoted him back to school headship – but in a different school elsewhere in another County, Kisumu!

Despite all that, back at the school, things seemed destined to deteriorate further! They did! Results and grades at national examinations plummeted year after year! The Board of Management (BOM), the community, the political big mouths and overall stakeholders were transfixed in their depressed, frustrated and (almost) self-blackmailed edifices!

When I encouraged organized groups in the area to act, lethargy (for lack of a better word) seemed the order of the day! The incumbent BOM Chairman was being defied quite blatantly, very freely, and literally routinely, by the new Principal! Some of his own home relatives urged him not to bother, even after he consulted me and I told him to take action, because insubordination was a serious lapse of institutional management and discipline!

Soon enough, quietly and independently, I resumed my status as a triple stakeholder:

1. Omboga was my birthplace.
2. My eventful Chairmanship of the same Board, and
3. My status as an alumnus, not to talk of my rightful role like an ordinary stakeholder, like 'all of us' in the neighbourhood!

I contacted the Teachers Service Commission (TSC) and physically visited their offices on Nairobi's Upper Hill to discuss the matter with relevant officers.

It amounted to sitting in a waiting chair nearby for four hours, because the officer in charge, a Mr. Farrah, was at a meeting. His secretary told me as much, twice, when I moved to her desk for an update!

Finally, a curious member of staff approached me and asked who and what I was waiting for! When I mentioned the name of the person I had been referred to, and said I did not know him physically, she told me that the man had just passed by me on his way for lunch! Could she assist, she asked me? The secretary did not witness that conversation but maintained her official poise as I could see her on her desk from where I sat!

My volunteer hostess told me that she had just returned from leave and was yet to re-occupy her desk. She walked me to a makeshift table within the big hall-like office space and absorbed my story!

I introduced myself a little more. I had been Chairman of the School's Board, for fifteen years from the date I was appointed by the then Minister for Education, Hon. Peter Oloo Aringo, accompanied by the M.P. at the time for Karachuonyo, Hon. Lazarus Ombai Amayo, also his Assistant Minister, when both toured the Constituency and visited the school. The School had been closed for two years between 1989 and May 1991 because of reasons narrated above, and that the Ministers re-opened it and appointed me as Chairman; I told her a little more!

On that earlier occasion in April 1991, after the Minister's left, with a core of other local stakeholders, few of us remained behind and immediately embarked on a structured, serious serial talent hunt by ourselves. Nobody would again come and play with the opportunities and chances of the children of our community!

The next morning, armed with the name of our chosen talent, Mzee Johnson Ng'oma Aneya and I drove to consult with the District Education Officer, Mr. Kavuludi. Mr. John Omollo Onyango, our choice, was then the Deputy Principal of a Secondary School in Mbita. Our request was that he be posted on promotion to come and head Omboga Mixed Secondary School as we joined hands to resuscitate the school back to life. His story is within these pages.

This time round (2012), yet again, we were being forced to go down the same road! ... "NO, thank you!"

I took responsibility for the petition, ignoring the variables which included cowardice! The incumbent Principal was busy enjoying himself like a systematic strategic saboteur! The main part of my petition was just his removal! After that TSC would best decide what to do with him.

I declared that I was ready to put my case in writing for ease of reference, memory, personal responsibility, and as a basis of official action.The beautiful "good Samaritan," Ms. Reginah Opondo, gave me paper. I wrote my case by hand and signed it.

She turned out to be the sister of a much younger but now fairly senior medical colleague. At the TSC, she was at the rank of a staffing officer able to run key offices at the Commission at both Regional and Headquarters levels! Omboga School and its entire community owe her a lot for the survival of their school, even if the school continues to limp! The Omboga that Mwalimu Omollo and I left is yet to be fully resuscitated!

Soon enough after my visit, TSC followed up on my letter with action! When they physically visited the school, some of their own findings were shocking! One of them was that the incumbent at the time was reportedly not qualified to head any school, not even Omboga – whoever had dumped him on us?! When our local community-based organization (CBO) talked of building a university in the area, he went out of his way and mobilized the school's "Parents and Teachers Association (PTA)" to block it, even before we had determined any proposed site, and even though the school topped the list of choices!

Purely on the grounds of his curriculum vitae, he was summarily transferred on demotion to a school some 30 kilometres away in another County altogether! I have no idea, and I am definitely not interested in, whatever subject he taught, if he taught at all!

It has now been much more than a decade. The school has not recovered from the shock of that commotion. Its history is and will remain a glaring lesson on perennial negative attitudes, loose talk, disunity, opportunism, cowardice and procrastination around the school.

As I express this lamentation, the school already needs an Intensive Care Unit (ICU) kind of therapy as it appears that its dynamics are too much for the recent heads! Somebody needs to help Omboga fast! I kind of feel relieved that the recently appointed Board Chair, Mr. Boaz Waruku, might help turn things around!

The main feeder Primary School for Omboga High School is Omboga Primary School. It had its own "slow-motion" story of survival!

As stated above, that was my Primary School in the early fifties. It was relocated to its present site to give way for the Secondary School, less than two kilometres away, nearer to Omboga shopping centre.

In the mid-eighties pupils were still learning under trees, seated on the bare ground, although that was also to let construction of some permanent classrooms go on!

I chaired the School Committee between 1984/5 and 1991/2. When I started, the Headmaster was none other than Mr. Jonathan (Jona) Onyango, the eldest brother of Mr. John Omollo Onyango, who later was to become Principal of the re-opened Omboga Mixed Secondary School (see above). Even at that time almost the same intra-clan feud reared its ugly head! But before it burst open, I convened a meeting of the entire School Committee to discuss the trumped up blame-game circus from their own first cousins! In a strict and serious business manner, the perennial complainants disarmed themselves by presenting no substantial issues! The matter ended there!

In the year 2002, Omboga education complex was 75 years old. The Secondary School marked that **"Platinum Jubilee"** occasion with a researched book on the history of **Omboga as a School,** which had been started in 1927. Wazee Yustino Onyango Omollo (aka 'Osuri;' father of Jona and John Omollo) and my own father, third teacher at the school, were our leading management resource people! There were a number of others in the clan, but these two led the scene.

Omboga Primary School students learning under trees in 1987.

Omboga Primary School students learning under trees in 1987.

Front view of Omboga Mixed Secondary School.

The 4th Board of Management at Omboga Mixed Secondary School. The principal, John Omollo, is seated far left. I am seated second from right.

Omboga Mixed Secondary School staff. John Omollo Onyango stands front and centre.

Omboga Mixed Secondary School student officials.

Omboga Mixed Secondary School Education Day: Joining the students' song and dance presentation. I was board chair at the time.

LEFT: Omboga Mixed Secondary School Education Day: I present the guest of honour David Siele (right) with a ram in acknowledgement and appreciation of his gracing the occasion as our chief guest.

BELOW: Omboga Mixed Secondary School Education Day. From left to right: District Officer, myself, Mr. (later Dr.) David Siele, Provincial Director of Education, Nyanza, and Mr. John Omollo Onyango, Principal.

Donating books to Omboga Primary School. From left to right are the Principal, Mr. Agure, committee member Jane Achieng' Goga and Deputy Principal Jane Obel.

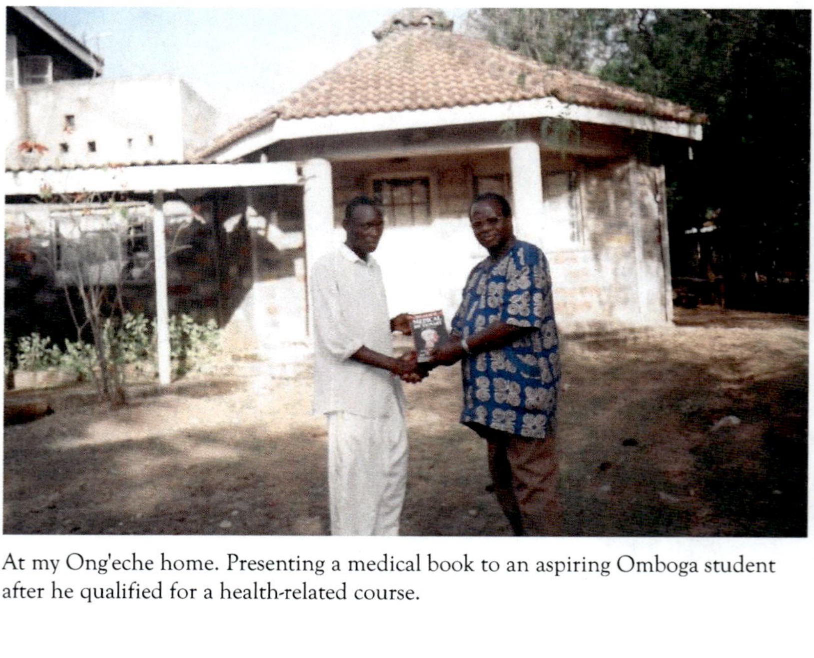

At my Ong'eche home. Presenting a medical book to an aspiring Omboga student after he qualified for a health-related course.

TOP: My book donation to Omboga Primary School pupils. Principal Agure, committee member Jane Achieng' Goga and Deputy Principal Jane Obel stand behind three students.

BOTTOM: Tank donation to Omboga Primary School.

22

MEMORIAL LECTURES ON SOME OF KENYA'S RENOWNED DEPARTED MEDICAL HEALTH PIONEERS AND PROFESSIONALS

AS I WRITE THIS, I can count up to seven 'Memorial Lectures' in memory of some outstanding Kenyan Doctors and Professors, all of them health professionals with notable landmarks and legacies in Kenya. They included some of Kenya's outstanding firsts and pioneers! These were all invited lectures through the following medical and surgical associations, on diverse dates and at different venues as listed below. Some lectures were delivered more than once on the same person to more than one body:

1. Kenya Medical Association (KMA)
2. Kenya Cardiac Society (KCS)
3. Surgical Society of Kenya (SSK)
4. Kenya Society of Haematology and Oncology (KESHO)
5. Kenya Orthopaedic Association (KOA)

It was my very humble pleasure and singular pride to lead medical professionals in remembering our professional heroes. Some of them are remembered every year, through **"Annual Memorial Lectures,"** each time by different lecturers. On my seven occasions, I was called upon to remember the following:

1. Prof. Hillary Peter Witts Ojiambo, MD, FRCP: Kenya's first Cardiologist.
2. Mr. Hasmukh Harilal Kamdar, MS, FRCS, FACS: General and Cardiothoracic Surgeon.
3. Prof. Edward George Kasili, FRCPath: Clinical Haematologist, Oncologist and founder of Nairobi Hospice; ex-Chairman, Department of Haematology and Blood Transfusion, School of Medicine, University of Nairobi.
4. Prof. Nelson Wanyama Awori, FRCS: Urologist and Kenya's first Kidney Transplant Surgeon; Ex-Chairman, Department of Surgery.
5. Prof. Thomas Ariba Ogada, MD, FRCP: Clinical Haematologist; former Dean, School of Medicine; former Director of Medical Services and former Ambassador of Kenya to the World Health Organization (WHO), Geneva; former Director, Aga Khan Hospital, Kisumu.
6. Prof. Ambrose Eric Onyango Wasunna, MD, FRCS: former and first indigenous Kenyan Chairman, Department of Surgery; former Dean, School of Medicine, former WHO Consultant.
7. Mr. Michael Majale, MD: Kenya's first Orthopaedic Surgeon.

Over and above their respective curricula vitae, I dealt with certain pertinent issues that impacted upon the medical profession in Kenya, as follows. (Some I gave more than once, to different associations).

a) Professionalism.
b) Evidence-based and scientific basis of medicine.
c) Need for continuity in healthcare (under the heading "The Future is here!").
d) The malignancies of the heart.
e) Lung cancer.

f) The place of the environment in determining lifestyle patterns among professionals.
g) The compelling need for accredited and registered Professional Associations and Societies to craft their own "Honours" recognitions and awards to their outstanding and distinguished members, instead of always dreaming of political and politicized awards and recognitions by the Government (This is already happening!) .

Although I did not give Professor Nimrod Odundo Bwibo's lecture, I researched and compiled the information that formed his eulogy.

May all their souls bless Kenya and rest in eternal peace!

June 2016, Eldoret: Kenya Orthopaedic Association Annual Scientific Conference. Attendees at the memorial lecture on the late Michael Majale, Kenya's first orthopaedic surgeon.

June 2016, Eldoret: Kenya Orthopaedic Association Annual Scientific Conference. Receiving the keynote address trophy.

23

"WRITER AND DEBATER"

THE YEAR WAS 1968, final year for the 1963 Calcutta Medical College intake batch. The only other black student in the same class with me was a fellow Kenyan, the late Dr. Willie Mwaura. I am sure that he also found the following to be a great source of wonderful memories.

As a farewell and memorial gesture to one another, in our final year at the Calcutta Medical College, we published an album with our pictures. The interesting part was that we anonymously wrote poetic, and funny (but factual) captions about one another in three or four short lines that would help us remember one another with fun and pleasure! To this day, I do not know who wrote mine, but I liked it and continue to treasure it. More than that, I was and still am very grateful for the overwhelming goodwill, even camaraderie, that I enjoyed in that class and the whole College.

Next to my passport-sized photograph, it read:

"Writer and debater, Peter's a pride,
Any topic he can take in his stride,
A Kenyan, he is liked by all,
Bosses or students, big or small."

Also see the "DEDICATION" section at the beginning of this book! I have kept that book very carefully. My surprise is that repeatedly, the students in their final years in Nairobi with whom I have shared it (for the simple reason that it is a worthwhile idea and a 'landmark' for people who will travel very different paths in life, even if all are medical doctors), have not shown any notable reaction. I have even tempted several batches of my final year medical students, especially my designated mentees, to do the same, in and for their classes, but the idea never gelled. It could be a generational thing - our 'modern' students are loners, to an extent, even in 'cells.' Frankly, I do not know how best to phrase that!

PETER BEN AMOLLO ODHIAMBO
Omboga School,
P. O. Kendu Bay,
S. Nyanza, Kenya.

Writer and debators Peter's a pride
Any topic he can take in his stride
A Kenyan, he is liked by all
Bosses or students–Big or Small.

My photo and the accompanying poem in the album of the 1963 batch of students at Calcutta Medical College.

That said, literally out of the blue ten years later, I was given a direct challenge by a leading scientist right here in Kenya, Professor Thomas Risley Odhiambo (TR). My fellow 'victim' was a former high school classmate, who had bonded together with me and three other friends, to form an unofficial club which we deliberately and inspirationally called the **"Thinking Club."** He had been my seconder in the 1959 Form III debate at Kisii High School when I opposed the motion that **"War is the Only Way of Settling Disputes."** I had gone to India; he had gone to Puerto Rico and then the United States of America. He got married out there to a fine lady, Caroline Okite.

Now we were both in Nairobi, he lived here with his family, and was a very dynamic journalist. He had started a private monthly magazine called ***People.*** He later left for exile in the USA, after undergoing an ordeal at the Nyayo House torture chambers. He went blind from the 'burns' of acetylene lights beamed directly into his eyes there (over and above effects of his high blood pressure). He was able to learn braille and continued with his writing out there, but the monthly magazine died a natural death back here in Nairobi.

Back to the prior story. While this former classmate was still in Nairobi, the late Professor Thomas Risley (TR) Odhiambo, one of the founders of the African Association of Science Editors (AASE), challenged the two of us to start a health science journal; my partner saw it as very doable, but merely as a lay-reader forum of health information. I saw it as an opportunity to start a serious, solidly ethical and technical-cum-professional medical journal, similar to the *East African Medical Journal*. Finally, he agreed with me and charged me with the task of coming with a name for the new publication! In no time, **"Medical Communication"** (***MEDICOM***) was born. The journal evolved fast, and in due course changed its name to *MEDICOM - The African Journal of Hospital Medicine,* and, finally, to what it is today – **MEDICOM** - ***The African Journal of Hospital and Scientific Medicine.***

I salute the two resourceful scientists who contributed to the subsequent and final amendment of that name: namely, my good old friend and senior college-mate from Calcutta, Professor G. B. A. Okelo, who proposed we add "Journal of Hospital Medicine," and Professor Violet Kimani, a social scientist in the Department of Community Health, now the Institute of Public Health, whose recommendation added on the word "Scientific." The rest is history, because despite all the challenges, this journal still pulsates with a hospital and scientific 'heartbeat.' It has made careers for many and has been featured on the University of Nairobi website. I have put together and published a compilation of all my editorials over the four decades of *MEDICOM – The African Journal of Hospital and Scientific Medicine,* or simply "MEDICOM."

At the African Association of Science Editors with Prof. T.R. Odhiambo (convenor) and *MEDICOM* marketing staff, Ms. Peris Awuor Okombo-Oweggi, the influential lady behind the successful take-off of *MEDICOM*.

I find it interesting that a good number of people now look at me more as an anti-tobacco fighter than as Kenya's first heart surgeon, who has trained a core of other now long-matured heart surgeons, some already retired from public service.

This chapter was inspired by my class album of 1968, which was created for the 1963 entry batch of medical students at the premier University of the East, Calcutta Medical College – a unique breed indeed!

As I celebrated my own fifty (50) years as a doctor in 2018, counted from the date of graduation in 1968, my classmates out there had counted from our year of admission in 1963 and celebrated fifty years with another album in 2013. They sent a classmate, Dr. Mohammed Yasin, to bring me that album in August 2018, as he, his wife and fellow ophthalmic surgeons toured Kenya.

After all those years, we no longer looked the same physically; even the Mohammed of those days, a slim, agile cadet after his brief spell in the army, was now a greying successfully retired ophthalmologist!

My friend Alpana Ghosh (née Gupta) also aged gracefully. Her father, a general medical practitioner, had been very good to me! She had belonged to a youthful group called **"Friends Forum,"** and had played a very big part with her friend, Ms. Ratna Sen, in mobilizing me to participate in my last debate in India, this time outside the academic institutions. Word had gone round, and it seemed as if some people wanted to hear me debate. Like in my first (high school) debate, I opposed the motion (whatever it was)! The difference was that I was not permitted to sum up my case before or after the mover of the motion! That seemed deliberate, to limit my chance of finally disposing of the motion!

Alpana tracked me down after decades through the internet in the recent past and we have been in communication across the geographical divide. But I lost touch completely with other friends like Swapna Banerjee (medical school), Biplab, Biswas, Gupta and a few more! Saradindu Ghosh, a patient of ours at the Post-Graduate (PG)(SSKM) Hospital, himself an artist, lives on in my memory with his drawing and picture that symbolized true Kenya-India friendship (see chapter 26,"Ties that Bind"). Mohammed Yasin brought my classmates that much nearer! Of the rest, I cannot fail to mention Professor (Ms.) Shushila Shripad (a cardiothoracic surgeon), who was my Senior Registrar at the PG Hospital, where I started my cardiothoracic training under India's great Professor Ajit Kumar Basu, my mentor, with a great team under him. That team included Professor Somen Sengupta, whom I met later in the late nineteen seventies at a thoracic-cardiovascular conference in London. Together with Shushila, Dr. Sankar was another senior of mine. I met both of them in February 1992 at an all-India Cardiothoracic Conference at the Birla Heart Institute in Calcutta. Dr. Sankar actually gave me a tour of Calcutta, including his own home and our Alma Mater, the latter in late evening, well after sunset!

Circa 1977: Serendipitous reunion with Prof. Somen Sengupta (centre) at a cardiothoracic conference in London. The man on the left was one of his students.

I presented a short paper at that conference on our experience with cardiothoracic surgery in Nairobi, Kenya. During my few days in Calcutta, I made sure I contacted and visited Mrs. Basu (Prof. Basu had passed on some years before). One of her two sons was in India; the other one was in the United States of America. I did not have any more time to trace or contact all my old friends in Calcutta!

While all that was going on, the Faculty (School) of Medicine in Nairobi was holding elections for the Dean, something that slipped my mind as I felt so much at ease in Calcutta, only to return home and find I was elected with overwhelming majority in absentia, on or around 14th February 1992 as detailed previously!

24

"LAKE TAKU," NOT "VICTORIA" (AND THE FORGOTTEN HOBBIES)

TOWARDS THE finalization of this book, I was near-lynched by my wife and (former) singing partner, Mama Jim/Mama "Jordan," because I had left this chapter out; actually, mainly because I had said nothing about the twenty-odd unrecorded songs that I had composed while in India.

My children knew about those songs; they saw my guitar in the house. They even kept track of who borrowed one and did not return it. Before that I had actually disposed of an older one in exchange for a typewriter. Somehow, I nearly always found myself buying another, even when I was no longer fiddle-playing! To date, I still have one, which I no longer "own!" I left it with my second daughter, Olivia, after she and her siblings failed to stir me back into playing again! Music was my favourite 'background guardian,' whenever I was studying or operating in the surgical operating theatre (until my car was broken into, and the portable player stolen); it was a huge loss when over five hundred (500) cassettes went missing while moving houses from Nairobi's Kileleshwa Estate to the Upper Hill area.

So far, my domestic fans have not succeeded in making me dispose of the old clay discs of singles and long-playing albums! The souvenirs include the players as well. I am yet to transfer them into compact discs. In the end, I shall probably let the attachments go and dispose of them, or model some kind of archive and keep them!

Back in the operating theatre at the hospital, the team later acquired a radio-cassette. It had become routine to play music in theatre. At the very beginning, junior staff would run to a side room and make rhythmic dance-like moves, but that had died out a long time back once everybody noticed and understood that it was for work, not simple entertainment or romance!

All the same, it somehow seemed like it was easier for me to let music lie than to escape from the ever so regular peer pressure into some form of group leadership or the other, so long as it did not veer towards career politics!

By the time I was returning from India, I had written over twenty songs. I hardly ever did any practice on them until I got to host one of the leading Benga musicians, George Ojijo, and his band at the two RIAT fundraisers in Murang'a in late 1971 and early 1972, events where music and dance were the main accompaniments.

During those 'dancing sessions' my Murang'a team, who were not a band as such, sang some of my songs, among them ***Pongezi kwa Wazee, Taabu Za Dunia*** and, more notably, ***Lake TAKU***.

My Murang'a residence.

LEFT AND BELOW: Penina (Mama Jim) and I entertaining the crowd at the RIAT fundraiser held at the District Hall in Murang'a. I used George Ojijo's/Continental Band's guitar.

Infront of my Murang'a residence with members of Continental Band. I am standing far left. Penina, in the nurse's cap, is seated second from left.

Continental Band in Murang'a for the RIAT fundraiser. Standing from left to right: Kiche, Odera and Ouko. Squatting from left to right: Tobias Not, John Yogo, Onyor and George Ojijo (band founder, owner and leader).

Now George and his band knew that I could compose and sing! When I returned to Nairobi, specifically to pursue my postgraduate studies in general surgery, George paid me several visits at my residence at the Registrars' Flats of Kenyatta National Hospital (KNH). On one of those occasions, he came with a couple of his band members and requested that I compose spoken lyrics for his English-language song, entitled ***Birthday.***

I did, literally in a 'couple' of minutes! We practised and rehearsed it that same evening, and that was it! He did not even think of editing what I wrote! He was so keen to record it that he quickly booked a recording session with a music recording broker, a Mr. Daudia (owner of MELODICA on Tom Mboya Street, Nairobi), at a studio in Agriculture House, a short walk away. He insisted that I join the recording and do the poetic talk for them. Again, I did! That is what you hear on the airwaves, once in a while today, these many years down the music lane in Kenya!

It was only a short time afterward that he recorded a song in loving praise of his fiancé Millicent, now better known as Joan Ojijo, who was still training as a teacher at a Teacher Training College. They married soon after she completed her training.

That particular song, ***Millie,*** started with the words **"Oyawore Millie owada!"** ("Good morning, Millie My Dearest"). It was composed between 6 am and 7 am in my sitting room, immediately after we had reached my house from Kiharu Hall in Murang'a after a packed marathon 'RIAT Night.' That was his second and last visit and performance in Murang'a at our invitation to fundraise for RIAT. On both occasions, every town in Central Province was represented by highly motivated and supportive Nyanza people who worked in the entire area. The most inspiring part was that a large number of local friends and others from other parts of Kenya came! On the second occasion, there was no dancing space! Led by the late Ezra Opar ('Opar Taya,' then Provincial Police Commissioner for Central Province who later joined politics and got his nickname "Taya" - lamp - from his election candidate symbol), we had to urge people and show them how to **dance vertically** in order to move at all!

RIAT or no RIAT, that was the face of Kenya proper! Yet, we were but a fairly small, even junior group supporting and championing the RIAT wave in Central Province! Part of the bigger picture was that that wave swept across Kenya as a contagion – every region soon started their own institutes of technology, some are now Universities. Even the Technical and Vocational Education and Training Authority (TVETA) may be traced back to the very promising beginnings of RIAT! The ultimate driving force, indeed, the clarion call, was the dictum of the founding fathers that "***RIAT MUST BE BUILT!***"

I left Murang'a in June 1972. By that time the fundraising for the proposed institute was at a very advanced stage. The Murang'a team never regrouped after my departure. I presented a full report to the RIAT Treasurer, the late Hon. Dr. Odongo Omamo (then also a Government Minister for Agriculture, based at Harambee House) and the Central Committee which included prominent Luo leaders and scholars. The late Hon. Dr. Grace Ogot was the most prominent lady in that team.

And there ended my romance with RIAT, until 43 years later when fate, in the person of Professor Jacob Kaimenyi, Minister for Education, ushered me back there by appointing me as Chairman of the Board of Governors of RIAT, now a long-established institution! For sure he had no inkling about my earlier dalliance with RIAT!

I found a giant sleeping on 400 acres of bush land with mostly the very original structures perched somewhere in the middle at what was supposed to be the 'main campus,' ever so often jostling with trespassers and squatters, as entrepreneurs salivated for camel-style collaboration!

My instant dream of a huge complex through a **"RIAT MASTER PLAN"** has not quite woken up this potential truly international giant! Either my predecessors had cast the threshold in iron or the contemporary executives and staff feared being dislodged and dislocated by anything too big for them to fit into, or both! The threshold, or any leverage, did not seem so futuristic at all! Suffice it to explain to the reader here that my proposed "Master Plan" would see four components earmarked and developed:

1. Current RIAT being developed to become a centre of excellence, even better than the "National Polytechnics" in downtown Kisumu.
2. A 'Technical' University par excellence, to match the likes of the Technical University of Nairobi and Massachusetts Institute of Technology (MIT).
3. A 'traditional' University in its own right, on 50-plus acres of its own, in memory of one of the region's prominent early scholars like Professor Wasawo, Professor Simeon Ominde, Professor Thomas Risley Odhiambo (all deceased). In my shortlisting, the late Professor Simeon Ominde came on top because he hailed from the next-door Nyahera Clan.
4. An unrivalled income generating complex with no dream limit, but without bypassing the lake, Kenya's shop window of all inhabitants of the lake shore! All along, neighbouring communities further inland thought that it was the lake fish that made the Luos, for example, so clever, if at all! How could RIAT sit barely 12 kilometres from the lake and not study, eat and trade in fish? That bothered me quite a bit, many, many times, even before the late Professor Ben Mbindyo's challenge to me!

Whereas all four components of RIAT would be largely autonomous for purposes of respective institutional output and growth, to uphold the original spirit of RIAT, they would best be managed by an over-arching body, which I tentatively called "**Super-RIAT,**" subject to further crystallization, perhaps into a semblance of a **Board of Trustees**.

While the two sets of Board members, during my two terms of three years each, got very excited about these ideas and plans, the series of executive management during my whole tenure at the "Institute of **Advanced** Technology" continued to be supportive, but there seemed to be intangible, if not invisible, diplomatic slipperiness, ending in zero net progress! With me (and 'my two regimes') gone within days to weeks, I did not see the need to push my agenda any harder because it seemed destined to be forgotten and the giant retired into another slumber! Continuity across phases of leadership on our continent seems to be an exceptionally rare phenomenon. So, I desisted from the assumption that my ideas and proposals would 'one day' necessarily be entertained by my successor(s)!

What I have referred to above as one of my forgotten hobbies, music, peaked with the RIAT fundraising campaigns in Murang'a. That is why I have aligned relevant bits with RIAT here.

Stepping back to my dalliance with music, plus my collaboration with my distant clan uncle, George Ojijo, who was actually younger than me: I now knew the manager, producer and owner of MELODICA, and the location of the recording studio at Agriculture House.

Mama Jim, one of my singing team members in Murang'a, had returned to Nairobi to pursue her own further studies in Midwifery and a Diploma in Advanced Nursing; much later she proceeded to Harvard University's School of Public Health for her Master's in Public Health, but that is her own story!

At this time, she joined the push that I also record my songs. She already knew some of them from Murang'a. In the end, I succumbed, in spite of my very tight study programme at the University of Nairobi and the KNH Campus.

With her as my only singing partner this time, we recorded two of the three listed above: ***Taabu Za Dunia*** (Problems of the World, or Humankind) and ***Pongezi kwa Wazee*** (a tribute to some of the early

African freedom fighters). The other songs were to have followed later, which they have not to date!

Top of that subsequent set was one admonishing East Africans to change the name of our lake from "Victoria" to "TAKU." Fortunately, or unfortunately, it (the song) was never to see the light of day! But I got the proposal published in the mid-seventies as a very short letter to the editor in a daily newspaper. That did not provoke any reaction among readers! Here were people who had shed blood to be "independent' but were not bothered by the name of a queen from very far! To date, that is how it went!

Below is a portion of the song:

LAKE TAKU

"Fellow East Africans!
We've got one Lake – Lake Victoria
We should now name it 'Lake Taku':

"Ta" for Tanzania, "K" for Kenya,
"U" for Uganda –
Queen Victoria now may rest in peace!

Water, water, and "Ngege" the great...
Queen Victoria may now rest in peace!"

Beyond that, there may be just three parts of my dabbling with the hobby of general writing to mention here:

1. Contributions to some aspects of contemporary literary fora.
2. Pioneering and initiating or founding publications in the forms of magazines and journals, and
3. Writing this book and those lined for publication after it.

My attempt at authoring a story book while I was still in India was aborted when the Kenya Literature Bureau turned down my draft entitled ***A Thing Called Life***. They saw it as a camouflaged story of my own life with "personal aggrandisement" in parts, which it was not, as far as my drive to write a story book went!

When I returned from India and contacted one of the reviewers who had communicated above editorial sentiments to me, he thought that I could work on it a little again and he would review it once again himself! To my amazement, the man remembered the draft almost to the letter! But by that time, I had lost interest in that line of writing and the style and trend of editing! I left the draft alone! It remains in that draft form on my shelves.

That was in my youth, in the mid-nineteen sixties. I thought it to be an inconsiderate verdict on aspiring writers who were yearning for positive patronage in a newly independent country with bubbling potential and enthusiasm.

It could be that that whole saga played subconsciously in my future challenges to provide a medium of training for young medical authors when I found myself starting ***MEDICOM: The African Journal of Hospital and Scientific Medicine*** to, among other services, assist young professional writers take off with some confidence in their effort at academic, professional, scientific and intellectual writing. This effort acquired legs to walk after the challenge from Prof. T.R. Odhiambo as narrated previously!

At about the same time of my brief storybook dream, while still in India, I wrote some pieces that were published in the Medical College Magazine – like **"Science, Leisure and Common Sense."**

The ***East Africa Journal*** also published my "letter to the editor," which I had submitted as an article, entitled "Is Witchcraft 'Psychiatry'?" during my second year in medical school.

My small article in the College magazine entitled **"Namushkar and a Lump of Ice"** ('Breaking the ice of friendship,' or establishment of friendship between foreign students, read me and local mates) was warmly and fairly well-received on Campus.

Then there was the writing competition staged by the same *East Africa Journal* just before that. "Independence" had arrived for the three East African States which formed the "East African Community." With great challenges of development for these three countries, the essay competition as a question and was captioned: **"What is the Greatest Problem Facing East Africa?"**

The late Professor Elisha Atieno Odhiambo, then an A-Level high school candidate, championed the much rehearsed three-in-one slogan of **"Poverty, Ignorance and Disease"** and won the competition. I was listed fourth among the top ten competitors.

My diagnosis, which I would repeat today, was the deep-seated problem of "attitude and pattern of thinking" in the entire region, which to me was different from, and worse than, "colonial mentality," but somehow included it.

It was quite obvious to me that, very much in spite of loud political bravado, we were still very deeply steeped in colonial thinking. That was bound to impact on how we ruled ourselves, and would be our undoing! It required starting with 'dry cleaning' and decolonizing the minds of both the leaders and the populace.

As I look back today, it is clear to me that the late Tanzanian President, Julius Kabarage Nyerere, got it right. The late Tom Mboya Ndiege, to me the fastest political sprinter of them all, still came second to the "Mwalimu!" We missed the 'train of thought,' and we are still grappling with all the three political bywords, even though we have made visible strides! But remember, we are just about to celebrate our **platinum jubilee** of **"INDEPENDENCE!" Our 'age-mates' like Singapore and South Korea are plucking medal after medal of development as we gaze and marvel as tribal cocoons with no accredited "chieftainships," innately distinguished by our deafening political melodrama!**

During my tenure as president of the African Students Association, India, or simply ASA-India, we undertook to support the South African freedom struggle with what was supposed to be an annual magazine named the ***South African Tribune***, which I edited and published there from '*The office of the President!*' In it we highlighted the gross and totally undemocratic anomalies between eleven (11) million Blacks and Coloureds, on the one hand, and the minority four (4) million Whites! Only that one edition saw the light of day, as my successors did not maintain the effort! I ceased to qualify for an office in the Association after I graduated, even though I stayed on in India for more than one year after leaving medical college.

Within that 'extra' year of my stay in India (1969-70-71), the publishers of ***Africa Diary***, which was a product of the **Indian Council of Cultural Relations (ICCR),** the main sponsor of foreign (mainly African) student scholarships, also organized an essay competition for African Students on the fertile subject of **"Indo-African Relations."** I participated.

A senior postgraduate journalism student from Nigerian won the first prize. I came second. The two of us were invited to New Delhi to receive our prizes on live Indian television.

The Nigerian was already stationed in New Delhi. I had to travel 900 kilometres by train from Calcutta. Luckily, Kenya now had her first High Commissioner to India, who had already met us Kenyans in Calcutta when he conducted his familiarization tour of India upon his posting there. My runners-up score in the essay competition made him very happy and proud for both Kenya and himself!

Upon getting news of those results, he gladly invited me to go and stay with him and his family for the few days of my encounter with my 'Africa Diary' hosts. Forget about the debating trophies: that reception and the hospitality I received at the High Commissioner's residence in New Delhi was the climax of my stay in India. It was a real home away from home! We became very good friends.

This was the family of the charismatic, suave, diplomat incarnate, His Excellency Leo Odero (retired), nicknamed on the side by a very old Indian lady as "Oh-Dear" at a cocktail party he hosted during one of his visits to Calcutta where some of the prominent among our local Calcutta hosts were invited! I remember his not-so-young family like yesterday!

Celine Anyango, the eldest daughter, was in high school right there in New Delhi, closely followed by Siprosa Achieng' (called "Achienge" at home), then Albert and two other much younger female siblings.

Later on, in the early to mid-seventies, after a stint in Lusaka, Zambia, Celine remained there (in Lusaka) to complete her University degree. I met H.E Odero and his two elder daughters a few times in later years in Nairobi. I could not bear the shock when I learnt that that their mother was fatally knocked down by a moving motor vehicle in their very small hometown, Awendo, in Migori County, where she ran a shop.

That family encounter with the Oderos in New Delhi almost overshadowed my main mission of receiving a prize! Notably, it was my first time ever to appear on television, much as I had already donned the title "Doctor!" My prize was also very memorable – my very first briefcase!

This is all in my travelogue **"Goodbye India,"** along with two other pieces from my Zimbabwean friends –Peter Mavengere, a roommate at the International Students Hostel in Calcutta , and Mushariki, one of my mentors out there during my first year in India at the Hindu College, Old Delhi. He left at the end of that same academic year (1963) after completing his master's degree in History. Both wrote back to me, describing their respective return journeys to Salisbury (present-day Harare), via Mombasa, and the twists and turns on the high seas of the Indian Ocean, ever so familiar to me, because that was how I had also travelled out there.

Among my hobbies, I enjoyed dancing as well, but consciously desisted from making it a 'habit' or a regular diversion! To this day, some of my friends think that it was among my favourite pastimes!

Whereas I easily managed to wean myself from literally all these hobbies, I did not manage to escape from associating with different welfare organizations, always deliberately stopping short of joining career politics. Perhaps this is due to my contempt for the way politics has acculturated itself in Africa, and for the 'neo-freedom non-fighters' who have perpetuated human deprivation on the continent.

25

BEREAVEMENTS

I.
BYE-BYE, MUM!

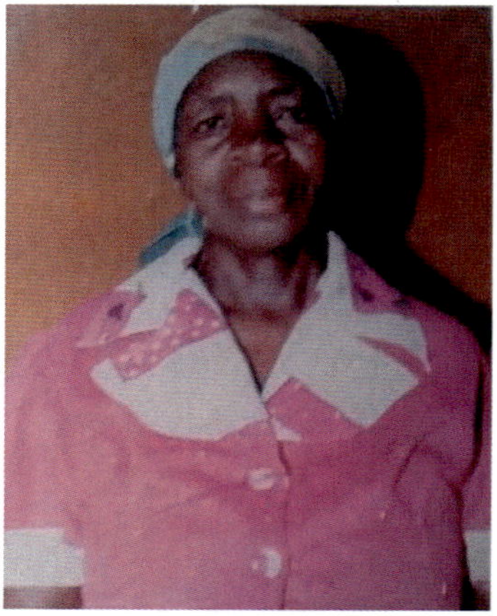

IT WAS JUST before midday on April 21, 1989, inside Theatre 11 of KNH. The team was fully bonded and ready. All arrangements were in place. Pre-operative presentation and care of the patient may depend on the stage at which the patient presents; but the diagnosis and planned operation is among the most challenging, even for those in well-established thoracic and cardiovascular specialty centres. The diagnosis here was "Thoraco-abdominal aortic aneurysm," the longest aneurysm that a surgical team can ever encounter. It spans and crosses two body cavities, namely the chest and the abdomen. That was the first and last time anyone ever tried the operation at KNH up to this narrative.

It meant extensive bypassing of the aneurysm, which involved the entire length of the aorta from the upper chest down to the lower abdomen. The operation involved replacing that whole length of the aorta with a large, long artificial tubular vascular graft, and replacing its vital branches with smaller grafts anastomosed to punched-out holes along the wall of the large (main) graft for continued blood supply to abdominal organs. The procedure was a **replacement** as opposed to simpler term and procedure of **'bypass,' because every one of the vital branches had to be anastomosed directly or through an artificial graft to the different vital organs supplied!** The small grafts were the time consumers. We had to ensure that the stomach, the liver, the small intestines, the large intestines and the kidneys were connected safely for their own blood and oxygen supplies and for their individual and respective structural and functional survival. That bridging of the distances between those organs and the main graft, by anastomosing the smaller grafts, directly or through stumps of their branch supplies, was a big challenge, but we managed!

Right in the middle of the operation, at around 8pm, a telephone call came into the operating theatre for me. In those days in rural Kenya there were only a few sporadically scattered and isolated centres with 'landline' public telephones, kept in booths. The functional status of any one of them was always unpredictable! The nearest to my rural home was six kilometres away at a place called Adiedo, a shopping centre along the road from Kendu Bay to Homa Bay. It was out of order! The one at Kendu Bay was never reliable. After these two, the next one was in Homa Bay town, thirty kilometres away from our home, or twenty-four kilometres from Adiedo.

Two or three of my cousins led by one John Ombura Singa (a schoolteacher and church elder) were sent by my father in the late afternoon to send me a message by telephone. Having bounced at Adiedo Shopping Centre, 6 kilometres away from our home, they resolved to proceed to Homa Bay, 24 kilometres from Adiedo, rather than return home and report that they had failed. There was no public transport, leave alone roads! They just walked! Fortunately, the phone in Homa Bay was working. And so, the phone call came through to the main hospital switchboard, and on to the extension of Theatre 11. Coming in from that far, I had to get the message before proceeding with the operation!

The message was delivered! Of course, everybody in the operating room heard it all!

My mother was dead!

In a split second I made up my mind that I was not going to lose two people on the same day. My mum had died in the afternoon or sometime during the day.

I cannot remember what I might have said but I for sure talked to myself from within and was quickly composed enough to proceed with the operation. Without a twitch or further reference to the telephone message, I continued with the operation. My body language must have been sufficient to carry everybody along with me. The mood was set! We did not finish the operation until 2.00 a.m. or after. I did not leave until we closed the very long and wide wound from the left chest behind the heart down the whole length of the abdomen to the pubis, with a sideward extension that we had to make for fuller exposure and access.

Because of our unique circumstances, two of the things that I taught in surgery are relevant here were:

1. The surgeon does not leave theatre when there are no other operations to follow, until the operated patient is ready to be moved out of the actual operating room to the ICU/HDU recovery area, or is actually awake. Almost as a rule, the surgeon must go with the patient to the ICU or HDU.
2. The surgeon who actually does the operation is the one who writes the operation notes, even if he/she is a junior being assisted by a senior.

I did neither that night, but we had taken photographs of different stages of that operation. I left theatre immediately just as the gloves dropped from my hands. I still needed composure because I had to drive some 400km to where mum's body was and take her to a mortuary in Homa Bay. In the end, I did not have to take her that far. There were some "experts" near home who could preserve her body right there at the home, in spite of the very warm ambient temperatures. We buried her in about one week.

As I look back, only two things come alive in me:

1. The words of Pastor Walter Ogwai (deceased soon after) who came to lead the burial ceremony. He had said, 1 admonishing us who mourned our parents. "You do not dramatize your tears for your parents when they die if you did not and do not help them or care for them when they are alive! The time to "weep" for them is when they are alive! You are there to fend for them and to let them die in gratitude!" I had been very close to both my parents; my conscience was and remains clear and at ease!

2. A soothing dream about her several years after her death. There she was in a bright yellow dress, surrounded by, and flying with, beautiful yellow butterflies in front of our home over her spring water well sites which she had been so keen to dig, just to get clean water nearer home, like homemade 'surface' boreholes; she always got water! In that dream, she looked very happy, and that was my additional healing! That was the true ***NY'ANDING'O,*** at peace with her homestead and her people!

Anding'o was her birthplace: a hilly place in Kasaye, Upper Nyakach, Kisumu County. It is full of rocks, some of whose sizes and heights would challenge **Kit Mikayi** in Seme, also in Kisumu County, and the "Crying Stone" of Ilesi, Kakamega County, any day!

Heaven is yours. Stay well in your Heaven Mummy! I am peaceful!

II.
14 YEARS LATER, ANOTHER DRAMATIC SHOCK. MZEE WAVES WITH HIS LAST BREATH: EXIT 'ADUNDO' (SMALL MAN), THE CLAN GIANT AND FOOT-BALLER!

The date was August 13, 2003. Mr. John Omollo Onyango (the Headmaster of Omboga Secondary School) rang me in the morning and told me that he had had to rush my father to the Homa Bay District (now County) Hospital the previous day. The old man had suddenly fallen very ill, literally collapsed, after learning that a notorious young thief, a boy within the clan and living barely one kilometre away, had stolen his favourite ram!

He had been admitted that same day and spent the night there. Mr. Omollo, a cousin and a friend, told me that the Mzee had been very upset, had become very agitated and suddenly looked unwell, hence the rush to the hospital.

My effort to get my friend and former student, Dr. Ojwang Lusi, the senior District surgeon at that hospital, to check on him and help with treatment found him attending to another patient in or around Migori, more than 50 kilometres away.

Meanwhile, my youngest sister, Elsa Molly Atieno Oloo, had been visiting with my family at our Spring Valley residence in Nairobi. We had planned to travel home together before that telephone call. I was to drop her near enough to take public transport to her own marital home a few kilometres beyond Ahero town in Kano (now Nyando Sub-County). I would then proceed to my own home, Ong'eche-2 in Kanyaluo, Homa Bay County, another 70 kilometres or more.

With news of Mzee's hospitalization in Homa Bay, the plan changed; we would now go together to the hospital first and then home. We bought for him a Fanta soda on the way.

We arrived at the hospital a little after 4:30 p.m. and found him just a little weak but awake, alert and talking. Clinically, one might have thought that he was only mildly dehydrated, but he was on an intravenous infusion drip of a crystalloid. We found our stepmother with him in a ward packed with other patients and their relatives. It was still "visiting time."

Upon seeing the two of us from Nairobi, he brightened up immediately. He thanked us for the soda, especially Elsa who actually handed it over to him. He wanted it opened and he enjoyed drinking all of it.

After chatting a little, we encouraged him to take it easy and rest, without a lot of conversation. At about that point, both Elsa and our stepmother stepped out of the ward to talk outside. I sat on a chair at the side of his bed.

Barely fifteen minutes after them, Mzee made like moving and raised his left arm in front of him, as if he was waving. As I moved closer, he put it down, and that was it! The Mzee had just waved his final "Bye-bye!" and went without another word!

I checked his pulse and heartbeat, and gave him a massage pressure shake onto his chest a few times, but he was gone, barely two hours after our arrival! All this was in full glare of everybody as the ward was full, with no screens! I had not dozed; I am sure I did not blink, as Mzee just exited right in front of me! I had sat near him just like I would sit next to my ICU patients after an open heart operation in those almost 'lonely' pace-setting days, with a trained eye for the tiniest warning sign of collapse or change in condition of the patient.

I think I called a nurse before going to call my stepmother and youngest sister. The rest were the usual formalities, up to the hospital mortuary. All three of us finally left hospital for home much later that night.

The drama of Mzee's "Bye-bye!" wave sure caught the attention of those in that ward that evening. One of them, a middle-aged man, happened to have been a fellow Nairobian; he had also gone to visit his father and was a few beds away. It further turned out that he was actually my churchmate at New Life Church in Nairobi. Sometime later, he spotted me in church and came straight to me. He introduced himself. He went ahead and narrated what he had seen at the ward with my father that fateful evening! He never missed to come and say "Hallo!" and always recalled the occasion every time we met in church thereafter! His own father had also passed away a few days later.

III.
JIM, BIG JIM. "JORDAN."
JAMES HILLARY ANG'AWA OCHOLLA ODHIAMBO.

To us, his parents and his friends, he was simply 'Jim.' To his paternal relatives, 'Big Jim,' differentiating him from my brother David's much shorter third son, 'Small' Jim (deceased 2013). To his friends and later to the entire nation, he was 'Jordan,' or 'Jordo,' out of recognition, admiration, appreciation, encouragement and respect for his stellar basketball prowess deemed akin to the great basketballer Michael Jordan formerly of Chicago Bulls in the USA!

Born on 14th January 1974.

Shot dead by police on his way home from university on 27th July 1998.

What a life! What an end!

It rattled the nation. Or so it seemed at the time, at least. It was only 3 years later that Allan, a third-year medical student at the UoN Medical School, son of Justice Gideon Mbito, was also gunned down in the early evening hours by the same Kenya police while in the company of fellow medical students from the Public Service Club nearby, very early in the evening of the serial fateful day!

As the 9 p.m. news started on 27th July 1998, my sister-in-law, Mrs. Dorine Adhiambo Alwar, called me on the phone. She had just seen **"BREAKING NEWS"** flash on KTN (Kenya Television Network) news showing a car that "looked like" ours, a Land Rover Discovery, KAK 608F, at the Uhuru Highway/Kenyatta Avenue roundabout, commonly called "GPO" due to its proximity to the General Post Office, a nearby landmark. There had been shots heard and the car was shown in that breaking news segment, but Jim was not shown in that initial news flash! He often drove home from his classes at the United States International University (USIU) at night. He had driven the Land Rover Discovery, his mother's car, that night. The other car, a saloon Peugeot 504 (registration KPS 192) which he used more routinely had a mechanical problem that day! KTN interrupted their ongoing programme just to broadcast this episode which happened just below their windows at Nyayo House!

There must have been a big problem.

I was still in my office at Continental House, a fairly short walk away. (Continental House was later acquired by the National Assembly). I quickly made one strategic phone call and left. I went via Wabera Street near the Standard Newspaper's old offices and picked up a journalist friend, Caroline Ger Onyango, the one whom I had telephoned from the office before leaving. For this exercise and for the rest of the night, I introduced her as my niece as an 'undercover' way for her to cover everything that happened thereafter, uninterrupted and literally incognito.

We went to the roundabout mentioned above. There was nothing. The whole place was clear. There was no sign even of broken glass. We headed straight to the Central Police Station (CPS), parked my car and walked past an open pick-up parked at the entrance of the reception of the police station block.

At the reception, I said I was looking for my car. The policeman at the counter confirmed that the car was behind the building. He took me there and I confirmed that that was our car. But where was my son?

"I am medical; I can help if he is injured!"

He said they were waiting for the Officer Commanding Police Station (OCS) to take the matter from there.

In no time, a crowd began to swell. Many family friends who saw the news flash had rushed to the same Central Police Station (CPS) and found me with my 'niece.' Police still insisted we wait for the OCS and the Officer Commanding Police Division (OCPD). The hallway was nearly full. We were then taken to a room upstairs with a long table and chairs, like a smallish boardroom. Time was really passing! The Police did not seem to have any concept of time, or life, or death, not to think or talk of public relations and public service! 'Public relations' was conspicuously wanting and absent! "UTUMISHI KWA WOTE" ("SERVICE TO ALL"), the loud National Police Service motto was suddenly a foreign dialect, or safely secured in the archives of the 'Force!'

As we sat there, I urged everyone to try as hard as possible to stay calm, even if for appearances only. It was imperative that we listen to every word the police would utter. Open emotions might only assist in and encourage a cover-up, I told them.

When the police finally re-appeared at around 2 am, it was the duty officers, and then their bosses.

As the duty officer began to stammer, I pulled out my notebook so that my 'niece' would take her own notes without interruption. Those who had any semblance of notebooks and paper also took theirs out. It was a perfect camouflage for a thorough scribe to put it all in black and white!

It was all becoming very long-winded, so I asked, point-blank: "Is my son alive or dead?"

He confirmed that Jim was dead!

Before he could tell me where his body was, friends of Jim, led by Benjamin Gakuiya (Benji), stormed the room and demanded the truth from the police because they had just found his body at the City Mortuary. We all headed there. I found the body of my son, as white as paper. He had died from profuse and massive bleeding with no sign or evidence of any therapeutic or first-aid intervention.

My thoughts went back to the open pick-up truck that we had passed at the entrance of the CPS building. I wondered if his body might have been lying in that pick-up while the police detained us to wait for their bosses!

The next morning, the newspapers carried a huge banner headline saying that a carjacking "thug" had been shot dead at the GPO (General Post Office) round-about, having been followed by the Flying Squad of Police from Pangani Police Station after a distress call from a victim of carjacking. Sure enough, Jim had passed through Pangani on his way home from USIU, in Kasarani, heading for Ngumo Estate on the other side of the City. Directly behind him, there had been a university van carrying his fellow students, including foreign students, who were being taken to their different accommodation locations after class. They had witnessed it all and had pleaded with the police at the time, saying they were all coming from USIU! They were immediately bundled and taken into the cell of the Central Police Station (CPS), barely three metres from the reception desk where I had reported upon arrival there! As we had talked and waited, they had remained locked up in there, absolutely without our knowledge. Later, so we gathered, they must have been intimidated or threatened, as there was not a word from them regarding the incident in the legal battle that ensued. Among them were foreign students from Uganda and other countries.

The second morning after the killing, 29th July 1998, the same papers carried the correct story, with his picture, which I had pulled out from a family album, and which is now a permanent reminder of the pain that extra-judicial killings can cause, especially when carried out by cowardly police. Jim's car had stopped at the roundabout, as any car normally would, in response to traffic lights. The shots rang out totally unprovoked from the rear of his car! Even after he crawled out with his hands up and collapsed onto the ground, they were still shooting like psychopaths, stupidly imitating American cowboys of the American "wild west" of the commercial movies! A total of 21 bullets were fired at him and the car, some piercing his seat and hitting him from the back!

The man, Jim. This photo is now a permanent reminder of the pain that extra-judicial killings can cause.

This whole shameful, inhuman, unprofessional and scandalous police-precipitated saga took place while Jim's mother, Penina, was in London for a conference. Together with other relatives, we strategized on how to break the news to her to avoid the possible lethal shock, including going round through her cousin, Rosemary Okwirry, who was hosting her in London. In the end, she cut short her trip and returned home a devastated mother. Jim's stepsister, Jackline, had been working with the World Health Organization in Geneva and had to travel abruptly to Kenya as well.

The court case that followed took a long time. None of the stories from the police corroborated each other, including a confession of mistaken identity, alleging that it was a prominent politician, John Harun Mwau, who had a similar car and was the one police allegedly wanted. They never said whether and why he was wanted dead by the police and why they never went on to look for him after that. The ominous question here, again, was: were they looking for my son to shoot him dead, like a 'police death squad' on hire? Unthinkably, another [unpopular] version of the killing was that Jim had been romantically involved with someone else's wife, giving him a desperate reason to hire a firing squad, to undertake for him, if at all, the pattern of that operation! So, therefore, the police were hired! That raised its own question: were these policemen hired individually, or was the Police Force hired as a Department?

The three policemen involved were convicted of manslaughter and jailed for fifteen years. We had told the prosecuting counsel from the Attorney General's Chambers that on our part, we did not want any more blood spilled through capital punishment, which a murder charge would incur. We also took the stand that there was an urgent need to transform and even reform the police force through training and motivation! We were ready to sponsor a *Best Policeman of the Year* award. But as we prepared the ground for implementation, the police themselves did not show any interest at all. At the same time, there followed repeated extra-judicial police killings, almost nonstop, starting with young Allan Mbito, a medic-to-be, then another, another, and another. The intervals between them were not reassuring at all.

One of the three convicted policemen reportedly died in prison before the expiry of his term. Their names shall remain outside this book because it would be a further assault on Jim to parade the names of criminally bent agents of Kenya's official security system. Somebody needed to and still needs to *clean* – not simply sanitize – the entire system, much like a surgeon scrubs before an operation; it is not just a smear of disinfectant or a simple rinse that still leaves dirt on the fingers!

We decided to focus on the civil side of the case for ourselves and call it a day. At a later date in the *MEDICOM* Journal, I wrote a poetic rendition on the **"Epidemiology of Death"** in Kenya. In one year, during the month of January, I counted 30 extrajudicial killings – meaning one a day! – and still counting! The same pattern repeated itself over several of the ensuing years! We lost count!

Jim was the only child of mine who ever gave serious thought to studying medicine, but as he headed to clear his Form IV class at Mbeji Academy, he was diverted by his mother and a friend because I had missed a family outing for dinner, having been caught up at work. The strategy for the diversion was to dramatize that a doctor's life was too busy for such family outings! At Mbeji Academy, he had been very serious with Biology and Mathematics, just so as to make it to Medical School! He was deflected that easily from pursuing his father's calling!

The other bits of this story were miraculous – literally! We needed scriptural words from the Bible to accompany the funeral programme. Jim's mother asked me to find some. I closed my eyes and said whatever page came out, that would be it. As I allowed the Bible to open 'by itself' in my hands, it did – at 1 Corinthians 15:51. That was it! We took just that one verse! In fact, I did not even see, leave alone read, the verses that followed! The words are etched onto the marble slab of his grave inside his mausoleum.*

One unforgettable heroine of Jim's story was my 'borrowed' niece, the late Ms. Caroline Ger Onyango, a very smart, sharp and courageous journalist who worked at *The Standard*, one of Kenya's largest and oldest dailies, and KTN's 'elder sister' media house. She recruited another journalist friend of hers, Ms. Nguku, to help with the coverage of this story. They reported the truth, even when other media houses still published contradicting stories. They remain in our hearts as true family friends. We also became very close family friends with the family of Peter (now deceased) and Elizabeth Onyango Asin.

As I go to the press with this manuscript, Jim's girlfriend at the time, Julie Kabinu, has remained in touch with his mother, as far as time and occasion permit!

It would be difficult to list in this book my sincere gratitude to every single one of the 'Friends of Jordo' and their families, as well as all who supported and encouraged us in that tough season. It would take a chapter of its own, and even if I wrote it, I would likely not list all of you to whom we are so very grateful. We remember Benjamin Gakuiya, the Odongos (especially son Paul and his father), Mike and Evelyn Eldon, Bob Okoko and the Okoko family, Sheila Gatu, Long Ngatia, and others. The then Member of Parliament for Dagoretti Constituency, Hon. Beth Mugo, (in whose campaign team Jim had participated from Ngumo Estate), as well as the Hon. Dr. Phoebe Asiyo, Hon. Shem Ochuodho, Hon. James Orengo, Hon. Dr. Kituyi and his wife Dr. (Mrs.) Lynn Mukhisa Kituyi, and many others, gave us all kinds of much-needed and much-appreciated support. We shall always remember! We shall always remain grateful!

*The four verses that follow, verses 52 to 55 were the familiar words that many funeral sermons and preachers frequently quote! "...Oh death where is thy sting..." Our miraculously opened verse 51 read, "BEHOLD I SHOW YOU A MYSTERY. WE SHALL NOT ALL SLEEP, BUT WE SHALL ALL BE CHANGED..."

My own heart patient, Ms. Njoki Gichia, mobilised her sister's family and brought lots of edible supplies for the kind crowd that came and camped with us. Her sister's family empathized with us way beyond the "call of duty!" Njoki was one of the pioneer and founder members of the **Kenya Heart Patients Association** (see Chapter 19).

Finally, I want dedicate photo album that is on my website gallery to all those who stood with us during and after the ordeal of Jim's exit – as family, friends, colleagues, sympathizers and well-wishers, departed or still with us on this earth!

Thank you! Thank you!! Thank you!!!
And may you all *always* be blessed abundantly!

26

TIES THAT BIND

BECAUSE THIS CHAPTER is not a direct historical account, I shall just highlight some of the ties in quick succession. It peeps into my relationship with just a few of my patients. It also highlights, however minimally, the virtually neglected opportunity for inward medical tourism in Kenya – patients coming here for treatment, not Kenyan patients always going (even dying) overseas! Then there is the dimension that is not yet fully exploited locally: that a number of Kenyan regions should aspire to have thriving open heart centres, very much in spite of the largely lopsided rationing of specialties among East African countries, even with such gross wastage of resources (financial, material, human) and a lack of the power to innovate! Things are very different from what they were when I started specializing nearly fifty years ago! Most of our curses on this continent are of our own making!

We are over-politicized, over-tribalized, 'money-mad' and inwardly selfish to a point of self-destruction, even to a point of being vulnerable to another wave of enslavement, as we abuse the politics of ***"nostalgic independence,"*** as if it was ever there! The greatest saboteurs are the contemporary political class with their brand of "FREEDOM OF SPEECH" and their knack for converting big legal, ethical and moral issues into cheap political rhetoric, unashamedly betraying paucity, or serious a lack of, the capacity to represent and stand up to be counted for their countries internationally, leave alone to add value to human development! Our future generations might not have a foothold to stand on, or "ancestors" to be proud of!

Below, however, is my celebration of human contact and interaction, this time at work; if only I had another 200 years to live and watch this continent 'grow,' thrive, and see humanity intertwine!

All said and done, we created and nurtured a homely ward. There was no "bed number 'so and so'" for treatment, although the tradition of ranks prevailed most of the time. But there was a team, indeed a family! The 'long' queues of inpatients waiting for their turns to go to theatre and their long stays in the ward, occasioned by shortages in the hospital, turned into a rare community medical phenomenon! Patients already discharged nearly always went back to the ward to say "Hi!", "Jambo!" to the nurses, especially on the days they returned to outpatient clinics for review – always Fridays. Many of them who were considered as cured and discharged from the clinics and lived far away did not return, except in the days when the "KENYA HEART PATIENTS' ASSOCIATION' thrived and held meetings in Nairobi; but the distinct human face of the ward was known far and wide, from the days when we were on the ground floor of Rahimtullah Wing of KNH (RW,GF) in the seventies and early-to-mid eighties in the 'Tower Block' as Ward 12, and later when it was re-named Ward 4-B, I dare say, to date!

HERE ARE SOME OF THEM: The list below includes my personal private patients in various other hospitals, along with mainstream KNH.

1. Francis Kiiyo

I inherited him from an earlier surgeon at the age of about thirteen years. He had oesophageal stricture. He was treated in many stages, with reconstructions, drainage and pleurectomy for empyema thoracis, and serial bouginage (oesophagoscopy and dilation). My wife and I ended up attending his wedding in Machakos on 20th August 1986. We are still family friends: he attended the funerals of both Jim in 1998 and my own father in 2003, travelling all the way from Machakos!

ABOVE: Florence and I (second row) at Francis Kiiyo's wedding.

LEFT: August 2003. Francis and I at my father's funeral in Ong'eche.

2. Mama Elizabeth Gitau

Mama was referred to me with "heart block" very early in the nineteen-eighties, days when our cardiologists could not insert and guide pacing wires into the heart transvenously. We had to perform a minor operation and implant a pacing wire epicardially on the surface of the heart. She lived with it for decades; we might have changed the pulse generator more than twice!

In later years, she invited me to be a guest of honour at a fund-raiser to build a church in memory of her late husband, Reverend Musa Gitau. A grandchild named after him is now a medical doctor. She visited us at our home in Spring Valley, Nairobi.

With Penina at the fundraiser for the church to be built in honour of Elizabeth Gitau's late husband. Mrs. Gitau (in blue scarf) stands between us in the lower photo.

3. Prof. Charles Nyamiti

Professor Father Charles Nyamiti from Tabora, Tanzania was Professor of Theology at the Catholic University of Eastern Africa, a musician and an author of several books. After his retirement, he stayed at the Seminary of the University for more than a decade and completed five volumes of on "AFRICAN CHRISTIANITY."

He was in effect a miraculous oesophageal patient of mine! He survived his cancer treatment doctor in the early nineteen-nineties!

Miraculous? YES!

In 1989, at 59 years of age, Professor Father Charles Nyamiti was a dying man! He had florid infection in the cavity of his chest (mediastinum and pleural space), which had resulted from a perforated oesophagus (gullet) after a botched surgical procedure by another doctor!

His oesophagus had been torn in the course of an endoscopy in the days (1989) when rigid oesophagoscopes and bronchoscopes were still in use, although fibre optic ones were also already widely used! His doctor had used a rigid bronchoscope (itself pretty sharp at its tip), as distinct from an oesophagoscope, to perform an oesophagoscopy. As a result, his oesophagus was perforated and torn widely along a segment of its length.

There followed severe chest contamination and inevitable infection within the mediastinum and pleural space of the right side of his chest. These were actually two very serious lesions – gross mediastinitis with suppuration, and empyema thoracis with super-infection.

I was called in almost at the last minute, but his last minute did not arrive for another 31 years! For those remaining three decades he stayed attached to the Catholic University of Eastern Africa (CUEA) where he returned after his 1989 sick-off break until 2018, when he came to our house in Riara, bade my family farewell and returned to Tanzania. That last minute came on 21st May 2020 back at his hometown, Tabora.

When I arrived to see him for the first time in the private hospital, he was moribund. My spontaneous question was whether they just wanted my **specialist signature** on his death certificate! Why did they not call me earlier, or even refer him to me for the simple but unwittingly delicate procedure!

There followed a very challenging struggle for both patient and doctor at the Nairobi Aga Khan Hospital! When he was able to talk, he told me, in no uncertain terms, that I should remove him from there to any other hospital! I did! But the problem was not with the hospital! It was the surgeon who had dared beyond his specialty.

The priority now was to stabilize him enough for a major chest operation to clean up the inside of his chest and repair his perforated gullet. I was prepared for the possibility of doing the operation in stages on separate occasions over intervals of time. Luckily, in the end, I never needed to defer or stagger any part of that main session of the operation, except for a few subsequent dilations or stretches of the oesophagus endoscopically from inside, under light and short general anaesthesia, in the months that followed.

During that main operation, I encountered a small (3mm) solitary, pale-coloured lymph node, like a 'by-the-way' gland, near the hilum (root) of the lung but very much within the operating field! I dissected the lymph node out, jocularly commenting that that was not the place for such a lymph node or gland, even with the gross inflammation of mediastinitis he had just weathered. Mandatorily, I sent it for histo-pathological examination.*

My teaching dictum was and is that *DURING ANY OPERATION:

(a). All (removed) tissues belong to the pathologist *who shall examine and report on its nature for diagnosis and management of the patient's condition.*

(b). All operating instruments belong to the scrub nurse: *he or she is the one who knows what the surgeon <u>needs, not</u>*

necessarily what he asks for.

(c). All the bleeding belongs to the anaesthetist***; he or she is the one who shall check the correctness of the donated blood and take charge of its transfusion, ensuring no mismatch.***

(d). THE SURGEON JUST OPERATES***, it being understood that he is not operating on RBCs (red blood cells), causing unnecessary bleeding! He or she needs to focus and concentrate on the actual operation.***

Said with mock light touch, any flippant joking about any of these adages could land one into a lot of trouble from me! No surgical operation, however minor, is a 'walk in the park.' It is all about ultimate precision in diagnosis, definitive safe operation/treatment and over-all welfare of the patient! Last but not least, it was both a plea and an order for all to be serious; by creating a mnemonic to shape the frame of mind of the entire team, people tended to think alike and act together in unison!

It was reported as "LYMPHOMA", a form of cancer!

I said "NO!" Immediately I ordered for a second opinion! I specifically requested the late Professor Edward George Kasili, as a haemato-oncologist, to review the specimen for me and report accordingly!

He assembled a group of his colleagues, and they examined it together!

SECOND REPORT: **LYMPHOMA!**

There was no option but to start appropriate treatment!
NEVER WERE A PATIENT AND HIS DOCTOR EVER SO LUCKY TO FIND A CANCER WHOSE 'SEED' HAD NOT EVEN 'GERMINATED!'

WHY DID A PATIENT HAVE TO GO THROUGH A BOTCHED PROCEDURE, ENDURE SEVERE INFECTION AND A MAJOR OPERATION TO ARRIVE AT AN UNBELIEVABLY EARLY

DIAGNOSIS OF CANCER, AND WHAT KIND OF SURGEON WAS THIS, PICKING ON TISSUE 'DEBRIS' AND ENDING UP WITH A VIRTUALLY EARTH-SHAKING DIAGNOSIS?

To the reader, especially health professional readers, I must say and repeat, and repeat the repeat: NEVER EVER IGNORE A CLINICAL FINDING, EVEN A HUNCH, HOWEVER 'FLIMSY!'

If that story of the late Professor and (Catholic) Father was not a miracle, one should wake me up violently from too much slumber on BASICS AND BASIC PRINCIPLES! **And where basics and basic principles are accommodated, adopted and applied, real miracles will always happen!**

Doctors pray and plead for early referral and prompt diagnosis and are never that lucky! So, as far as I was concerned, in this case, on this occasion, any medico-legal rhetoric about the 'original' oesophageal mishap was not my inclination or destination! We needed to do more teaching, even of colleagues, without paranoia, or chasing an ambulance which is already heading to hospital anyway! If anybody hears me, then let us always be very serious with our patients, and let those others (Americans?) chase as many ambulances as they wish!

Before Father Nyamiti's discharge from the serial follow-ups, his oncologist, Professor Edward George Kasili (a rare and exceptional blend of pathologist, haematologist, oncologist and clinician), contracted hepato-cellular carcinoma (liver cancer)! He succumbed surprisingly quickly!

By that time, I was Dean, School of Medicine. We had engineered a re-visit of the "Memorandum of Understanding" between the University of Nairobi and KNH. He was the Chairman of the joint committee. He died before his committee finished its work. When the job was finally completed after his demise, the report was dedicated to him by a resolution of the assembled Faculty at the School of Medicine. The Vice-Chancellor, Professor Francis Gechaga, sent me to Bungoma to represent him at the funeral. I went, alone! What a drive!

Back in Nairobi, his surviving patient got through different medical and clinical problems: prostate, treated by Mr. Robin Mogere, and orthopaedics (the hip and knees), treated by "Mzee wa Kazi," Mr. Joab Bodo! Nevertheless, the doctor-patient relationship between him and I was so solid that he always came back to consult and verify anything new, whatever the specialty and whoever the specialist! It was now beyond "Medicine" – we were very well bonded friends!

In 2012, the grand old man travelled with me and my family to visit us in our rural home at Ong'eche-2 in Kanyaluo, Karachuonyo, Homa Bay County!

Then fathom this:

In 1993, four years after the miraculous diagnosis, an eight year old boy with a hole in his heart was brought in from Tanzania by missionaries in Tabora.

One day, many years after the successful open heart operation, in around 2014, the Professor asked me if I knew or remembered a young male patient called Gerald Kabogota!

That was an unforgettable name to me and the entire team, even without talking of successful medical tourism within the Eastern Africa region! Gerald Kabogota was just as unforgettable as Nko Nkirwa who had rheumatic aortic valve disease that required replacement. After returning home, Nkirwa came back after some time with large clots in his metallic artificial valve. He underwent another open-heart operation for a second aortic valve replacement, and then went back to Arusha, quite uneventfully, in around 1980.

It turned out that Kabogota was the son of Professor's nephew back home in Tanzania, Mr. Thaddeus Shigela! By African 'genealogy,' Gerald Kabogota was his grandson.

Eventually, in 2017, when Mr. Gerald Kabogota was already head of a school in Mwanza, he and his father came to visit his granduncle and to sort out some immigration issues in Nairobi! The celebrated

Professor found time and brought them to my office, at Arrow House, Koinange Street, in Nairobi! That was truly memorable, like a triple reunion!

A note on the photo below:

Medical Tourism in Kenya Yesterday.

6th January, 2017: Standing with me: Gerald Kabogota (middle) and his father, Thaddeus Shigela. Seated: Prof. Father Charles Nyamiti, scholar, author, musician and Professor of Theology at the Catholic University of Eastern Africa (Church rank equivalent to Bishop).

Here are two Tanzanians from Tabora, whom I operated on in Nairobi in 1989 and 1993, respectively. Only later did I learn that they were close relatives! Prof. Nyamiti was on his would-have-been deathbed at the Nairobi's Aga Khan Hospital after sustaining a traumatic perforation of his oesophagus in 1989 at 59 years of age. Now (2017), at 85, he was about to complete the 5th volume of a series of books on Christianity from the African perspective. Gerald Kabogota, his grand-nephew, now in his thirties and a teacher, was sponsored by missionaries because he had a heart problem. He was then 8 years old. I had only the late Mr. Hasmukh Kamdar to assist me, as local brain drain had robbed us of two trained colleagues, one of whom went into full-time private practice as the other transferred to another University. Two in the next generation of my trainees were Dr. Yashwant Sonigra and Dr. Stephen Oduor Ogendo.

Kenya once received patients from Zambia, Ethiopia, Sudan and the DRC, among them thoracic and cardiovascular patients! Somehow, somewhere, something snapped! First, some international crosscurrents and conflicts with Kenya's Nyayo regime. That ended up in blockage of foreign exchange. That prompted doctors who wanted to attend international conferences to keep foreign exchange abroad by referring their patients for treatment and being paid in foreign currency into their 'survival' accounts out there and pay their conference dues, even journal subscriptions, using those accounts! It almost became a culture, quite silently! Secondly, there came aggressive marketing from abroad, notably India, actually shopping for patients! Things changed! The two dynamics melted into each other! What a pity! The consequences persist and now treated as normal! Almost strategically, people just blinded themselves, as local potentials got thwarted almost irredeemably!

We can and must return to excellence! Kenya is still qualified and equipped enough to be a destination for medical tourism!

2017: With Gerald Kabogota (standing centre), his father Thaddeus Shigella (standing right) and Prof. Charles Nyamiti at my office. See note above.

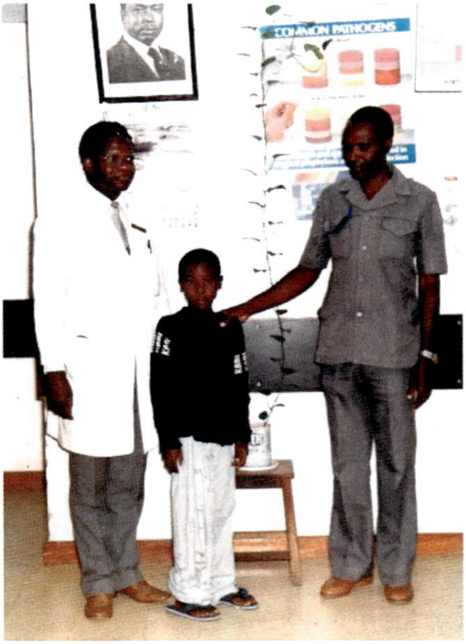

LEFT: With Gerald Kabogota from Tabora, Tanzania in 1993. He was escorted by his father Mr. Shigela (right) and Catholic nuns for an open-heart operation.

BELOW: Gerald Kabogota holds hands with a nun after his operation. I am standing to his right. His father stands to his left behind the nun.

2010, when Prof. Nyamiti visited us in Spring Valley, Nairobi. Standing, from left to right: my son Michael, Steven Lombo, Micah Atang'a Okello, myself and George Anyango. Seated, from left to right: Mrs. Pamela Anyango (wife to George), my uncle Johnson Ng'oma Aneya, Prof. Charles Nyamiti and Dr. Florence Odhiambo.

With December 2012 visitors at my Ong'eche home. From left to right: my cousin Samuel Ogola Mboya, granduncle Peterlis Oloo Ojung'a, myself and grandaunt Mrs. Rebecca Ochogo at centre, Michael and Loi (my children) and Prof. Nyamiti.

4. Mzee Naftally Matoke Matagaro: The Patriarch

This very dignified, smooth and suave old man was referred to me at seventy-five (75) years of age by a colleague of mine, Professor Elly Ogutu, with a diagnosis of (confirmed and proven) squamous cell carcinoma of the oesophagus – his presenting symptoms and signs, imaging, oesophagoscopy with biopsy and the histology of that biopsy specimen.

The best way of treating the disease so far was to operate and remove the tumour (oesophagectomy) if and when possible, then join the remaining ends of the alimentary tract – stomach or colon to whatever is left of the oesophagus on the upper side!

Unfortunately, dysphagia (the technical term for difficulty in swallowing) is a very deceptive and slippery symptom! Many people, (the patients to be) take it easy until it is too late! They escort "sticky" food with water and manage to feed for some time, even months! Quite often, clinicians also miss opportune diagnostic moments by relying on the report by patients that they "can still swallow!" Again, until it is too late! And yet it is one disease for which doctors are allowed to ask "leading questions," and must work with very high indices of suspicion.

The health worker (any health worker) who gets a description of any problem with swallowing must take it very seriously and advise the person to see a specialist or refer him or her to one!

As for healthcare students, nurses and paramedicals, and even doctors, what I term as the **"Rule of Six"** applies:

1. Epidemiologically, it is a **very common** disease in Kenya. Common things must be thought of more commonly! That is common sense medical intelligence.

2. The difficulty in swallowing is **progressive** (increases with time), starting with mild consciousness of food not going down freely, followed by different degrees of 'blockage' of the food path, through a stage when solid foods cannot go down,

but might be escorted with water or other liquid, even wine (of course not therapeutically for the treatment but just as a makeshift 'lubricant' that makes the bolus of food thin enough to pass down)! The final stage four (4) is when the person cannot swallow even his or her own saliva.

(The other main type of dysphagia that comes at a much younger age, from the late teen-age years to early adulthood of the thirties, occurs episodically and is non-progressive, rarely presenting after 40 years of age, unless complicated with malignant transformation! It is termed "Achalasia of the cardia." It is also treated surgically, to open the affected segment by actual operation, or stretched from inside the oesophagus with a special balloon. It is actually a congenital abnormality related to the nervous system that manifests long after birth).

On such an occasion, **the patient** would have **spoken**. The description of the symptoms, or the 'history,' is usually straightforward. The clinician must always ***listen very carefully, very attentively*** – "He or she (the patient) is telling and giving you the diagnosis!"

3. The special images **(x-rays, contrast "swallows," scans and MRI)** tell their story of typical appearances, extent and stage of the disease. The type of staging using these modalities is mainly technical, and lay readers should not struggle to understand without the help of the attending doctor.

4. The endoscopist will **actually see** the tumour and take a piece (biopsy) from it for further elucidation (under the microscope) as to the nature of the tissue from the oesophagus.

5. The **histology of the biopsy** will "prove beyond any reasonable doubt" what the diagnosis is for that patient! Several samples of biopsies are usually taken from different

sites at the same sitting of the procedure to minimize the chance of missing the real diseased tissue! Where there is disease, it is extremely exceptional that all taken samples would turn out to be negative!

6. When **the teacher/consultant/specialist/'boss'/senior says so,** from knowledge and experience, please listen, take it and proceed with plans to **assess** and treat the patient, accordingly, or systematically disprove the diagnosis! You may save the patient, the teacher and the medical profession!

Simply to say: **All of the above!**

The 'small' difference is that computerized tomographic scanning (CT Scan) and magnetic resonance imaging (MRI) can give more detailed information to aid in the decision to operate or not to operate! Nevertheless, a final decision is best made from all parameters, including the patient's own clinical condition. The surgeon's **experience on the operating table** must be tempered with **humility, ethics and professional clinical acumen!** The surgeon will not necessarily always succeed in removing the tumour. What he encounters on the operating table in the given patient and the actual growth in that patient often prove to be the final determinant.

Back to the Patriarch:

I operated on him in 1993. That restored his swallowing! About three years later, he developed a swelling on the outer part of his right forearm (lower arm, between elbow and wrist). It had come and grown rather fast, unlike another large mass in his opposite (left) axilla (arm-pit), which had remained more or less the same size (approximately 40mmx40mmx30mm), and I had even ignored it at the first operation! Now both had to be removed!

I did so at one sitting (under the same anaesthesia) and requested for a microscopic, histological, examination of both, to be reported separately.

The older larger swelling from the left armpit was found to be a simple reactive lymph gland. The one from the right forearm was a cancerous spread (metastasis) from the original oesophageal lesion!

Both wounds healed primarily with no problem. After a short while, he was given low-dose irradiation with short-wave diathermy locally on to the right forearm scar. That scar and surrounding skin of that arm stayed healthy for the additional ten-plus years of his life. He passed away at the very ripe age of 92 years from unrelated causes, seventeen 17 years after his operation!

This was an exceptionally good outcome! Many patients present to health institutions and health workers very late! My policy, aim and teaching is to give them at least two years of good quality life and tolerable swallowing. Within that time, with due counselling, they should manage to organize themselves, their families and their estates in readiness for the eventual outcome!

Over all those years, Mzee Matagaro admonished and encouraged his grandchildren to study medicine and do good for humanity (people like him), as he had been a beneficiary of the medical profession! His son, Mr. Jeremiah Matagaro (retired Police Commissioner, also a great friend – 'An Officer and a Gentleman'), confirmed to me that because of that encouragement and, indeed a good dose of insistence, there are now five health workers in the family complex – three doctors, one pharmacist and one nurse! Bravo! From another angle, one may say that here is a family of brilliant people! Cheers!

Mzee Naftally Matoke Matagaro.

Some members of Mzee Matagaro's family.

5. Saradindu Ghosh
Kolkata(Calcutta), West Bengal, India, 1970.

My association with Saradindu Ghosh must have been the beginning of my open and gratifying relationship with my patients. I had just completed my internship in mid-1969 at my alma mater, Calcutta Medical College in India. Almost seamlessly, I had been absorbed into the Institute of Post-graduate Medical Education and Research (IPGMER) at the Sheth Shuklal Memorial Hospital (SSKM) Hospital, courtesy Professor and Mrs. A.K. Basu, my thoracic and cardiovascular surgical mentor-family.

Saradindu was in his forties when he was referred to the chest surgical team under Professor A. K. Basu. He had chronic empyema thoracis (internal abscess with pus in the chest cavity). His right lung had been destroyed by tuberculosis.

He underwent a lobectomy (removal of one lobe) of his right lung, which left him with two viable lobes. The left lung was not affected. Because of the persistence of the chest infection, with communication between the pleural space and the exterior, and with an open wound along part of the original thoracotomy area (technically a pleura-cutaneous fistula), I was given the responsibility of dressing that wound, as opposed to the team leaving it simply for the nurses to do.

Over and above my other responsibilities, including operating theatre, ward rounds, outpatient clinics and intensive care unit (ICU) rotations, this became a job for no one else, but me.

It took several months. The patient stayed in the ward all the time he required those dressings. At first, the wound needed at least two dressings a day. With time, the dressings were reduced to once a day. Much later, with full control of the infection, they were punctuated to alternate days; then finally to one dressing every three days, to allow granulation tissue (clean healing cells) to consolidate itself and get to mature in the process of lining that part of the surface of the chest, instead of being rubbed off at every (frequent) dressing!

Sometime after his discharge, Saradindu reappeared in the unit with a package. That package was for me. As an artist, he had decided to celebrate our connection by highlighting our Indo-African friendship with a ribbon binding Africa and the Asian subcontinent inseparably! The artistic drawing, complete with his and my photograph are printed here for the eyes of the reader. Even if only with that, how would I, or could I, forget India?

Saradindu Ghosh

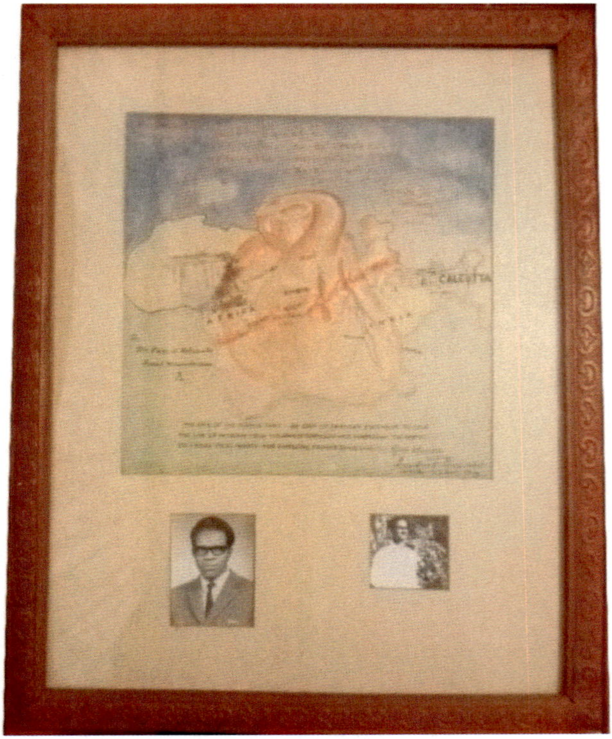

Saradindu Ghosh's gift to me. It now hangs on my office wall.

6. Roslida Obura (85 Years at presentation in January, 2015): The Matriarch

The year was 2015, the month January. The patient was the mother of a colleague and friend (a former student of mine years back) in the Department of Surgery; his brothers and sisters were also well known to me, just like friends!

She had a calcific atherosclerotic abdominal aortic aneurysm, the kind of **geriatric** condition I had encountered in the western world; in this case, the mark of emerging unmoderated affluence in Africa! Her age was registered all over her body.

Intra-operatively, I found a very friable abdominal aortic wall, with extensive atherosclerosis. Repairing the aneurysm with a vascular graft was rendered all the more delicate by an arterial wall that shredded with every bite of a suture needle and the running through of suture material. With that was the challenge of possible uncontrollable bleeding! While the distal (lower) anastomosis held well, the proximal (upper) one proved more challenging! Eventually, I called in a vascular surgical colleague (a younger generation trainee of mine) to come and join me in the theatre to complete the operation, taking over from the nurse assistant! Basically, I wanted somebody with whom I could discuss and strategize. Dr. Maurice Muhinga responded immediately and arrived in the operating room in no time!

We quickly made the decision to trim the aorta further back proximally into the rather intact (fresh) upper segment.

It worked! She made uneventful recovery!

Frail from age, she lived with the graft in her abdomen, plus other gadgets to aid her movements, vision and hearing – a very notable example of the feat of 'spare-part' surgery, and a pointer to delicate, critical decision-making in surgery, and, with it, surgical salvage even in old age! She clocked 90 years and died of causes unrelated to her surgical diagnosis and operation in early 2020.

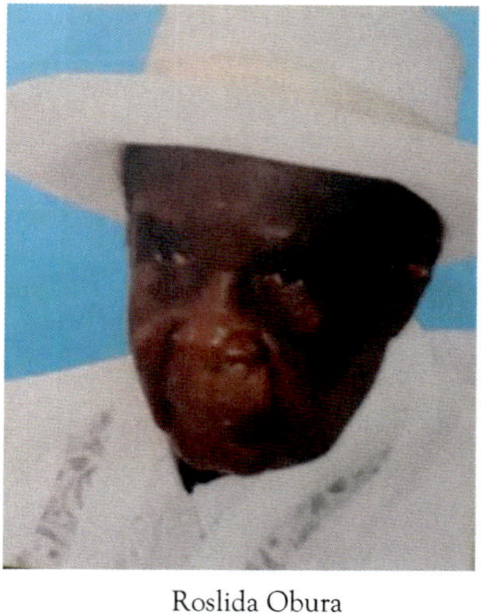

Roslida Obura

7. Kenneth Juma Mashaka, 45 Years (2013-2014).

Forty-five year old Kenneth Juma Mashaka was a very pleasant, fairly young man, gainfully employed not far away from his birthplace, Kilifi, on the coastal strip of Kenya.

He was referred to me by a chest physician in early December 2013, with a proven diagnosis of cancer of the "middle third" of the oesophagus, or gullet. In lay circles, this is loosely and erroneously called "cancer of the throat," particularly in Kenya! The patient presents with difficulty in swallowing, at various stages of severity. The final stage (Stage V) includes inability to swallow liquids , even one's own saliva! Kenneth was still able to swallow liquids at the tail end of 'Stage III', and still amenable to an operation to resect the obstructing tumour. Other aspects of this diagnosis have been discussed above.

He needed to organize his finances through consultations with his employer and insurance. He returned in time enough for me to operate on him on 15th January 2014.

The operation went very well. I was able to resect (remove) the tumour with the nearby (presumably tumour-free) segment of the oesophagus.

The recovery was straight forward and uneventful. His wife, equally pleasant, stayed by his side throughout. His doctor, the chest physician who had referred him to me, and coincidentally a clansman back at home, visited him in the hospital.

He regained his swallowing well and, upon discharge, left the hospital in very good physical condition and high spirits. He had not lost too much weight before the operation. As advised, he returned for outpatient reviews regularly.

Three years down the line, in 2017, he was keen and ready to demonstrate to me how well he could swallow! For that, we had a lunch of roasted chicken (his choice) and maize meal ('*ugali*') together.

He remained symptom-free until late October 2018, when he complained of a cough. In November, he noticed blood streaks in his sputum! The swallowing remained unaffected. He confirmed that there was no problem with breathing, but the cough persisted. Laboratory reports on the sputum did not reveal any infection. Plain chest x-rays were also unremarkable! They only showed the stomach inside the chest cavity where I had placed it to replace the resected oesophagus during the operation some four years and eight months earlier. His finances were now threatened, so I avoided subjecting him to more sophisticated evaluation.

While the 'ordinary' tests were being carried out, I put him on empirical trial anti-TB chemotherapy, just so as not to miss something tropical while concentrating on the cancer. Most likely as a result of that **trial treatment** (which is recognized and allowed), the blood in his sputum disappeared, or stopped!

Clearly, there was no more surgical operation to be contemplated, anticipated or undertaken on Kenneth. From there on, his further management would be mainly medical and non-surgical. Because of that, I referred him back to his chest physician who had referred him to me. **Surgical oncology** had already bought him close to five years, nearly all without debilitating symptoms, until that tail end! The anti-TB medication was immediately stopped by the chest physician.

In the ensuing period, he suffered a lot of depression. Further tests revealed seeds of the original tumour had now spread into parts of the lungs, five years down the line. The chest physician, a private practitioner, referred him to an oncologist working in a public hospital.

He was admitted into the ward under that physician for about one month. He succumbed on 15th February 2019, exactly five years and one month after his operation at the beginning of 2014 in a private hospital.

That is the usual frustration with cancer – microscopic seeds of the tumour can remain behind in the body at the time of the operation and continue to spread and grow in different parts of the body!

The World Health Organization (WHO) recognizes that, five years of survival after treatment of cancer without debilitating symptoms, is an acceptable outcome, if not a cure.

But what stressed the late Kenneth the most was the atmosphere in what was clearly demarcated as an "Oncology Ward" under physician oncologists! There was too much loose (almost scary) talk about cancer around him, including his own! Even subordinate staff talked to him about how advanced and irredeemable his cancer was! That overwhelmed him, even though he had all along known his condition and possible outcome from my detailed discussion with him before the operation. At one point, he even telephoned me pleading that I go and discharge him from hospital! The wife also telephoned me from the Coast where presumably she had gone to look for more money! It forced me to talk to his new doctors, but the damage was done! He went downhill very fast thereafter!

A few basics were missed completely. Cancer care incorporates astute clinical bearings, unfaltering and humane communication skills, public health, counselling and psychotherapy, even anthropology, all seamlessly wrapped in one, over and above chemotherapy, radiotherapy and any other technological interventions, surgery or no surgery!

The specific overriding principle and priority in treating cancer of the oesophagus is to help the patients regain their ability to swallow. They should also get back enough health and strength for their day-to-day activities, if still possible; more so to buy them enough time to organize, or re-organize, their estates as mentioned above. In addition, the employer and the family should be counselled enough to cope with the progressions and final outcome.

As a routine, we recommend retirement "on medical grounds," with all due benefits, if employed, while he or she is still alive, however good the recovery status may be! But I have a youngish teacher (Odima Ja-Uholo) who resumed his teaching career in Uholo in Ugenya after his operation, continuing as I go to the press with this story in 2023. It was his express personal interest and decision. It was also good for his convalescence and psyche with hardly any demand on rehabilitation or counselling! These are important aspects and necessary considerations in post-operative care and follow up.

Kenneth became a friend and was more comfortable that way, than to tolerate a 'patient-doctor relationship' tag! That fitted in well with my follow-up rehabilitation style!

This is my tribute to a brave patient, and a wonderful friend!

Rest in peace, Kenneth!

It is high time surgeons appreciated their professional scenarios as their unique, if not ultimate, opportunities to contribute to health care delivery, right from the primary health level, up to and including super-specialization levels. Surgery is not complete without a human touch! The human touch must be just as "hands-on" as the branch of medicine called "SURGERY," with no dramatics or unduly personalised emotions! Surgeons must not permit themselves to deteriorate (or degrade themselves) into simple technicians, at that unfeeling level! All must aspire to become and be the definition of 'Surgery.'

That is my challenge to fellow surgeons of today and tomorrow, with all the technology, even after the best robots 'take over' from us! (I need not add that all health workers must aspire to *become and be* the definitions of their respective callings – 'Doctor,' 'Nurse,' 'Physiotherapist,' etc)! Let us tie and bind ourselves wholly and holistically to our professions and to our patients! Thank you!

From left to right: ward doctor at Mater Hospital, ward nurse, myself, Kenneth Juma Mashaka and his wife.

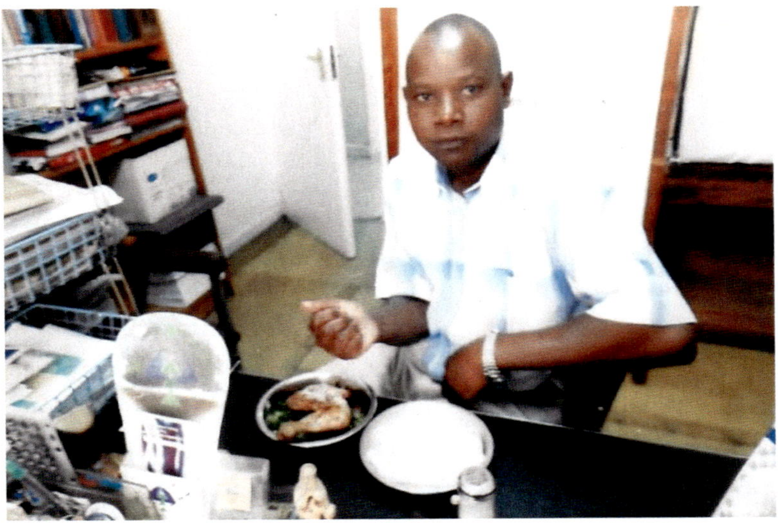

17th January 2017. Kenneth Juma Mashaka demonstrating his ability to swallow by enjoying a meal of ugali and chicken with me. Here is a fulfilment that should be the aim of the doctors: ability to swallow AGAIN!

17th January 2017. Kenneth Juma Mashaka and I. Meal complete!

8. Professor Richard Samson Odingo (Nobel Laureate):

Humble to the core and brilliant to the peak, Professor Richard Odingo (my senior by far and later to be a Nobel Peace prize laureate) fell into my humble hands in the mid-nineteen eighties when he was wheeled in straight into my operating theatre from the Flying Doctors' plane with an incompletely closed abdominal surgical wound all the way from Kisumu, otherwise some 350 kilometres by road to Nairobi, when my very good and able student, the late Dr. John Opar (whom we had already enlisted for thoracic and cardiovascular surgical specialization but was yet to be released by the Ministry of Health because of shortages in public hospitals), explored a painful abdomen and encountered a large abdominal aortic aneurysm. He quickly closed Professor's abdomen, mobilized the Flying Doctors, and got him onto their plane which transferred him to Nairobi. Where there is an abdominal aortic aneurysm, diagnosed or not diagnosed, ***any pain*** is a sure sign of impending leakage and rupture. Rupture of an abdominal aneurysm results in instant collapse of the patient. Without real prompt surgical intervention (in its totality), that results in definite death of the patient!

With prior communication from Kisumu from my student and friend, as the plane left the clouds behind, we mobilized the operating theatre. When he arrived from Wilson Airport in an ambulance, we were ready.

We fought for his life and thank God, again and again, we won! But it was not me alone! It was his God, the Kisumu team the Flying Doctors and the Nairobi team!

From there on, we became very good friends, with full respect between us, way beyond patient-doctor/doctor-patient relationships! So much unspoken love; so much mutual respect!

When he finally bowed out on 12th June, 2021, I felt fully consoled that he had lived the rest of his life fully thereafter! Both his Nobel Peace Prize and second marriage to Alice (whom he introduced to me while she was still 'his' student but followed suit and soon became a Professor herself) came after his conquest of a leaking abdominal aortic aneurysm –a fairly great chain of events in medical history!

But he was not alone for such miracle blessings in my career. Another patient with an actual partial intra-abdominal extravasation of blood from another abdominal aortic aneurysm, was actually put on an overnight train from Mombasa with much less communication, but arrived alive and left theatre alive. We lost touch when he returned to Mombasa.

I thank the Almighty God for having given me the courage and token skill to touch some of these lives listed above and many others I have not included!

Finally, I must not forget to record my brief encounter with the (then) future President of Southern Sudan, **H.E. Salva Kiir,** long before he ascended to that office. I shall not go into any details, except to say that sometime in the nineteen-eighties he and other five freedom-fighter comrades crash-landed their light aircraft in the area of Iten in Kenya's Rift Valley. They were all transported by the Flying Doctors and admitted into Nairobi Hospital. I took part in their management. None of them was seriously injured. There were some manageable chest injuries, which I took care of. All ended well and they all left hospital within a few days! It was left to me to summarize medical reports about every one of them. Little did I, or anybody, know that we were treating a future President within the group! (Dr. Garang' was still very much alive, and very strong, heading this wing of their freedom struggle). Although the accident occurred very much within Kenya, I must observe that ***those were the days when medical care and service came to Kenya.*** In a preceding historical setting, some untutored adviser or authority might have forced a decision to fly them "abroad" somewhere! And yet such came to pass, long after Kenya found herself on the map as a destination of 'medical tourism!'

It so happened that the second son of a senior colleague of mine, the late Dr. Karuga Koinange (himself a chest physician), fell into my hands after an unfortunate road accident near the Kyuna area of Nairobi. Because his thoracic aorta was torn in the accident, serious thoughts were entertained to fly him to South Africa, but the father's trust and confidence in us prevailed, especially also against the risk of the long flight. With Kenya's first 'indigenous' cardiac anaesthetist, Dr. Allan Kagasi Kisia, we operated on him right here in Kenya. Professor Emmanuel Ayim, a senior cardiac anaesthetist was not in theatre that day. A naturalized Kenyan from Ghana, he is the one with whom we flew to Mogadishu and, on a different day, with the Flying Doctor plane to Wamba Hospital in Samburu.

27

PENDING AND SUSPENDED DREAMS

I.
The Birth of "Kanyaluo Manyien" (KAMA)

WHEN PRESIDENT Mwai Kibaki went to open the newly tarmacked Kendu Bay-Homa Bay road on 9th August 2009, there was a good representation of home (rural-based) and town-based people from the entire region, including Kanyaluo – the large clan from the household of the first wife of Rachuonyo, Owaga Nyaluo. I was there together with my clansmen from Kanyaluo.

There came a bombshell from the President: vintage Kibaki! He would not deny you point blank! He would challenge you to think for yourself beyond a certain point, in this case beyond his indirectly very challenging words!

He said, seemingly in jest: "Haya! Tumewapatia njia. Fanyeni nayo vile mnapenda!" ***("Ok! We have now given you people a road. Do whatever you like with it!")***

His Kiswahili intonation was like he was handing over the road with only partial trust that we might be able to do anything at all with it!

For sure, it was not abandonment! Some of us saw it as a provocative but positive challenge: a clean slate, a virgin ground pronouncement, ready-made for exploitation by able-bodied and able-minded citizens of the place!

Again, for sure: he was not just about to come from Othaya to exploit it for us, or to hold our hands for any connected undertaking, exploitation or development, other than facilitation!

His government, like a good 'polygamist' system, had thus far given our 'household' the one big basic provision for prosperity in the form of a key piece of infrastructure. In a land of brains, it was now up to us to make sense of his words, and make good use of them!

I attended that ceremony as a double representative of Karachuonyo Development Society (KDS) and the much older Kanyaluo Progressive Association (KPA), both based in Nairobi.

The sitting MP for Karachuonyo had a very 'oblique' perception of KDS; KPA was completely outside his radar! On my part, I was ready with a word or two, if called upon, but the opportunity never presented itself. That was alright with me; protocol did not allow, and I was not on the programme. The MP was not one who might have introduced some of his (unofficial) people! For a more practical way forward, I leaned more on KPA.

Immediately the ceremony ended, those of us from Kanyaluo quickly agreed that the president's challenge warranted and compelled a prompt "post-mortem!" We mobilized and assembled in the lounge of Hotel Maryland within the 'New Kendu Bay,' along the Kendu Bay-Oyugis road near its junction with the newly officially opened highway.

Those present at the meeting included elders from different parts of Kanyaluo and those who turned out to be representatives from towns around the country – Rongo, Migori, Homa Bay, Kisumu, Kericho, Eldoret, Nakuru, Nairobi and (most likely) Mombasa. The sitting Councillor (as they were called before the devolved form of government) did not join us and forever missed the whole spirit of the occasion and its aftermath!

The bottom-line was that we had been given a very positive challenge. What would we do with the highway for ourselves, as well as the murram road from Oyugis, via Karabok, through Oyombe, to Adiedo and beyond? The 'new' road did not run directly through Kanyaluo, but was close enough for all practical purposes! It was now time for action!

But not yet! There were hardly fifteen of us!

We agreed that more people should join. Each and every one of us was to return to their bases, or places of work, spread the word and mobilize others. The best calendar date for the true inaugural meeting of the mobilized 'crowd' was 27th December 2009. Kanyaluo had to be reborn for a new horizon and to tackle the challenges of the moment and all other matters of self-help and development, including education, water, health, food and food security, as well as environmental conservation.

I was appointed interim convenor. Automatically, I was also the messenger to, and mobilizer of, Nairobians not present thereat.

Come 27th December 2009, some sixty-five delegates converged on the grounds of Omboga Mixed Secondary School, a central and popular venue used for such occasions only when students are not in session.

This was a very inspiring, stimulating and successful meeting, complete with minutes! Pending a future election, an *ad hoc* and interim committee was formed. I was formally appointed interim Chairman. Mr. Yoga Okumu, a senior schoolteacher among us, was appointed interim Secretary-General.

The interim committee held its first meeting on 14th January 2010 in a little cottage at my homestead, Ong'eche-2. We needed a constitution, official registration and membership drive.

There followed a flurry of meetings in the ensuing weeks and months of the first half of that year, 2010, until a mid-year general meeting was held in June to brief the main group about progress made that far. The next general meeting was held in December 2010.

In due course, we were registered as a **"Community-Based Organization"** (CBO). The registered name, **"Kanyaluo Manyien" ("The New Kanyaluo" - KAMA),** was meant to reflect the dream or vision of, and for, a new Kanyaluo. At that point, there came a whole line of possible projects, to be duly prioritized and punctuated, one after another. The range included health and education. Special tribute here goes to the medical students from the University of Nairobi's Medical School (call them my students) who, on our special request and invitation addressed to their Association of Medical Students of the University of Nairobi (AMSUN), travelled all the way from Nairobi and held a day-long free medical camp under the leadership of Professor Erastus Amayo and myself. The students themselves were led by the Vice-Chairman, Mr. (now Dr.) Jackson Njenga. The Chairman, Mr. (now Dr.) Njihia was unable to join the trip! Several medical students from my home area, Kanyaluo, who attended the same medical school were among the twenty-seven (27) of them, with Ms. Faith Bob (then 4th year medical student) hosting all the ladies in the team at the home of her father, retired Brigadier Bob Yugi near Adiedo, in Komwoyo, within Kanyaluo. The boys were hosted within the secondary school, while the free medical camp was held at the Omboga dispensary. One student, Jonathan Katana, rode his bicycle from Nairobi to Omboga, with an overnight rest in Kisumu: a total distance of more than 400 kilometres!

Notable also were the following highlights and occasions under my chairmanship of KAMA – cheers and congratulations to the executive committee and team that worked so selflessly with me for each and every one of those achievements:

(a) Solicitation and presentation of schoolbooks donated by the Jomo Kenyatta Foundation to every school library in Kanyaluo in response to our plea from KAMA.

(b) A successful football tournament, complete with trophies and presents for all teams in Kanyaluo, which saw the locally famous Otada Club win.

(c) Promotion of a short-races sprint athlete, Ms. Immaculate Akoth, who competed up to national level. We presented her with a pair of running shoes and a kit.

(d) Promotion of under-18 youths by giving a boy and a girl a cockerel and a hen each, to breed and graduate on to goats or sheep, then to cows, to inculcate the attitude and spirit of self-help and all that it entails! When we checked later, the boy had a sheep. The young lady turned out to be the same Immaculate. She went for goats! Parents of both youngsters were very supportive of them!

(e) A very successful day-long workshop for support, encouragement and promotion of the Kanyaluo girl-child in upper primary classes (Standards 6, 7 and 8) from all the primary schools in Kanyaluo, held at Adiedo Secondary School in April 2012. Facilitators comprised senior lady teachers and headteachers in the entire neighbourhood beyond Kanyaluo, including Asumbi Girls, Olare Mixed, Nyabola Girls and, of course, those within Kanyaluo itself. The plan was to follow up with a similar catchment of participants and facilitators for the boy-child. That is yet to come to pass!

(f) A brave attempt at affirmation and establishment of cultural pride of place by initiating and constructing the home of the eponymous Rachuonyo at the homestead of his eldest wife Owaga Nyaluo, as a cultural and resource centre, an IT complex and a tourist attraction to be included in Kenya's "Western Tourist Circuit," along with Simbi Nyaima, Bala Hot Springs, both also in Karachuonyo, linking up with the Tom Mboya Mausoleum, Nyamgondho Wuod Ombare, Thim Lich Ohinga, on to, or from, Maasai Mara! We went as far as communicating with the Social and Cultural Services desk of the Nyanza Provincial Commissioners' Office. We also proceeded to fence the one acre space given by the chief and clan elders for this project and put up a temporary structure as the beginning of implementation of the vision. For reasons beyond this narrative, the project came a cropper, but has the potential to be redeemed! The signpost still stands on the same parcel of land as I move this manuscript to the printers.

(g) Finally, there was our dream of a University in Kanyaluo, for which we consulted quite widely – locally with the community, Sub-County (then Sub-District) and Ministry headquarters levels. We sought affiliation with and mentorship from Maseno University, which prompted the then Vice-Chancellor to make a quiet semi-official inspection visit to the proposed venue at Omboga Secondary School. He had sent a representative in the previous year to establish contact and even make Omboga a Maseno "Learning Centre", to be moved from Homa Bay town.

(h) When Omboga won county soccer matches and qualified to proceed to the regional tournament in Kisumu, we procured and appropriated a bull, 'invaded' the school and slaughtered it in celebration with the team and entire school!

(i) We planted trees in several Kanyaluo localities, mainly schools: notably Omboga, Kowuor, and Adiedo Secondary Schools (last one on the occasion of the 'Girl-Child Day'), and Kobila Primary School. This was to go on.

Literally true to Luo Nyanza characteristics, amidst all the above, there was no shortage of purportedly clever, but merely 'simplistic' busybodies who relish anything but unity or joint effort! For that, the less said the better! We did not simply sense or feel, but actually encountered, contrary manoeuvres and machinations from both within and without Kanyaluo, including scores of e-mails and delegations! This happened a good half-century after Kenya's "independence" from and by the area's intellectually 'endowed' elite!

27th Decemember 2009: First meeting of the proposed Kanyaluo Manyien at Omboga High School.

27th December 2009: Display of Kanyaluo Manyien registration certificate.

14th February 2010: Interim committee of the newly formed Kanyaluo Manyien before registration.

Second KAMA meeting in early 2010 at Omboga Mixed Secondary School.

17th January 2017. Presenting books to Kanyaluo schools from the Jomo Kenyatta Foundation.

Successful chicken rearing: Immaculate (left) with her father, mother and younger siblings.

Planting a tree at Kobila Primary School as was KAMA's annual practice every rainy season.

At the proposed Dala Rachuonyo site with James Besalel Owiti Koyo, Vice Chairman of KAMA and Mr. Yoga Okumu, Secretary-General. The land was donated by Chief John Ounda Aol and his clan elders and was parcelled out of the spacious compound of the Ayier Chief's camp.

TOP AND BOTTOM: 'Phase 0' of ongoing works at the proposed site of the Dala Rachuonyo homestead.

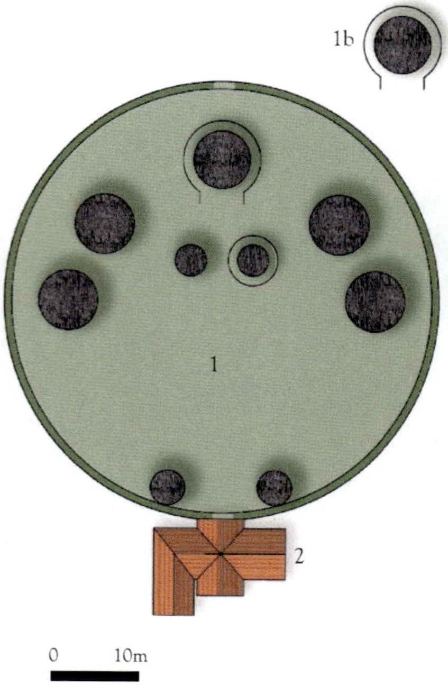

LEFT: Conceptual site plan for the Dala Rachuonyo and Karierio Educational and Cultural Centre.
1. Dala Rachuonyo homestead with huts and cowshed
2. Office block
3. Amphitheatre hall
4. Administration block
5. Oyugis-Omboga road

TOP: 1.Dala Rachuonyo homestead (enlarged).
1b.Omweri's hut outside the main compound.
3. Office block attached to compound.

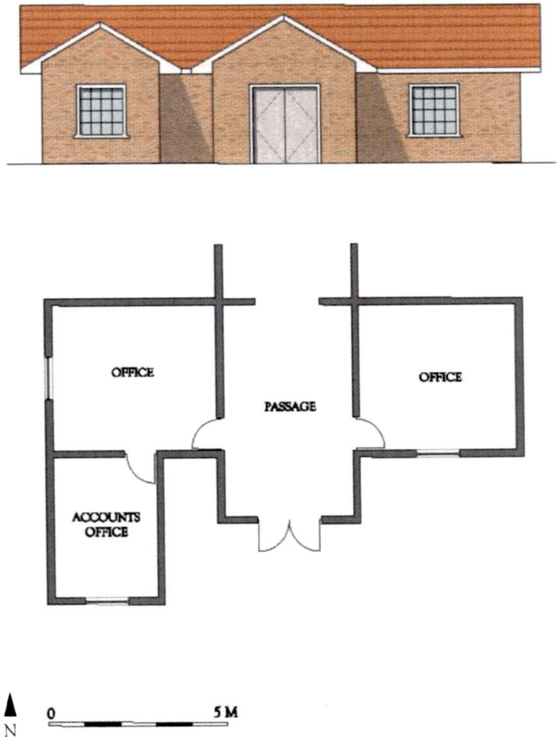

Dala Rachuonyo and Karierio Educational and Cultural Centre: Conceptual drawings of office block.

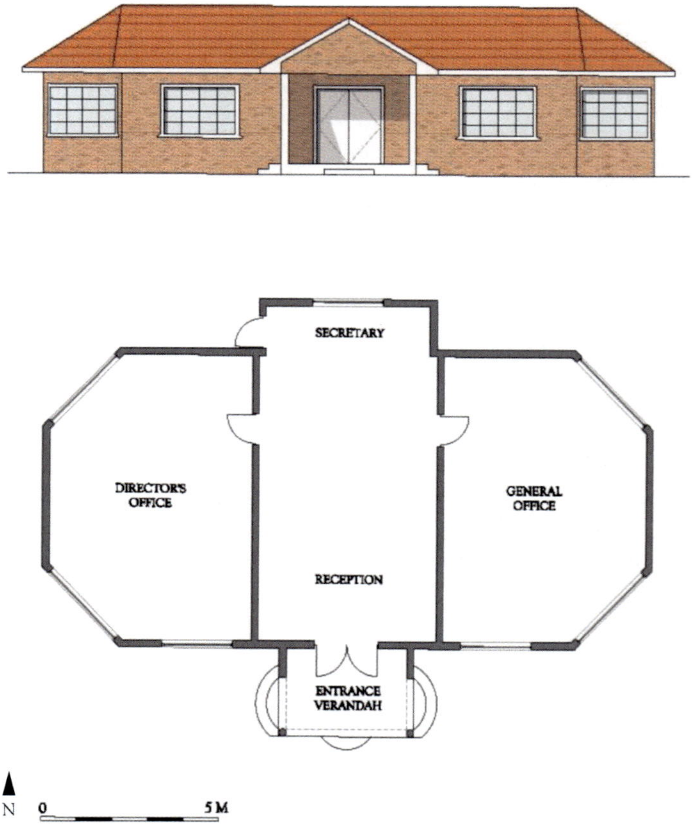

Dala Rachuonyo and Karierio Educational and Cultural Centre: Conceptual drawings of administration block.

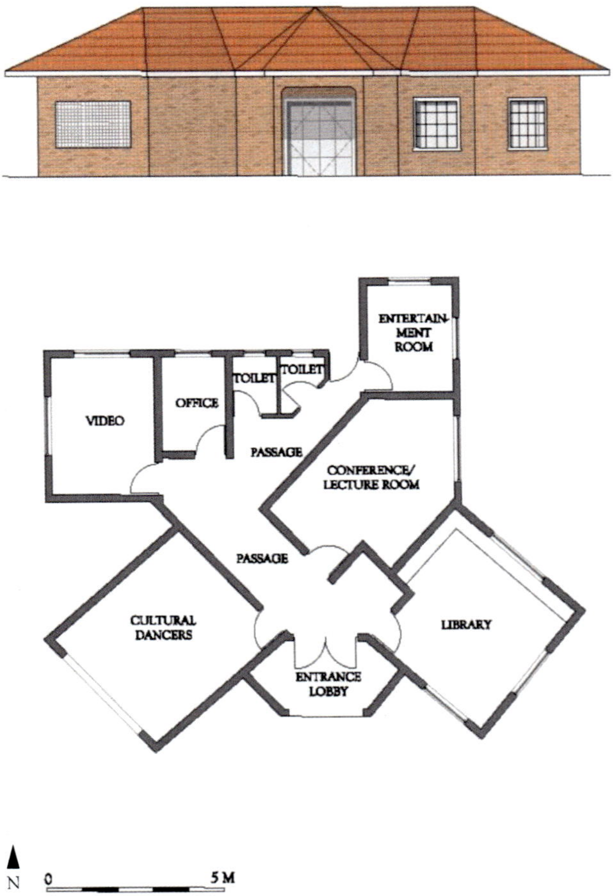

Dala Rachuonyo and Karierio Educational and Cultural Centre: Conceptual drawings of amphitheatre hall.

AMSUN team. Senior medical students who travelled from Nairobi to Omboga and ran a very successful free medical camp. Prof. Erastus Amayo stands far right. I am standing in the centre.

Free medical camp day. Prof. Erastus Amayo, myself, Dr. Ojwang' Lusi, the Provincial Medical Officer (Nyanza), Mr. Tom M. Aros (area Assistant Chief) and Mr. Nathaniel Swaya (chairman, dispensary committee).

LEFT: Jonathan Katana, who rode his bike from Nairobi to Omboga.

BELOW: Taking over chairmanship of the Kanyaluo Progressive Association in Nairobi on 30th June 1990. The outgoing chairman, Mr. Robert Ngao Swaya, shakes my hand. KPA was the forerunner of KAMA.

Farewell photo with Philip Asiyo Majiwa (in the white jacket) before he proceeded to India for further studies. At the extreme left is his father, Mr. Daniel Majiwa Amenya. Next to him is Mr. Robert Ngao Swaya, former chairman of Kanyaluo Progressive Association. I am on the extreme right.

II.
Karachuonyo Development Society (KDS)

In a letter dated 13th February 1998 I congratulated, in writing, the newly elected Member of Parliament for Karachuonyo Constituency, Dr. Paul Adhu Awiti (now deceased), in the aftermath of the general elections of December 1997. As someone I knew, my letter was at a personal level, but I also wrote it in my capacity as chairman of the Kanyaluo Progressive Association (KPA) which was based in Nairobi. We participated in welfare and development activities for our rural home community. We were his constituents.

In that same letter, I took the liberty to talk about Karachuonyo constituency as a whole. The wave that ushered him into that victory was like a breath of fresh air. People were happy!

I assured him that, from my observation, all sectors within the constituency, including and especially the professionals and entire fraternity of the elite, were eager and ready to support and work with him. I proposed that he should endeavour to bring us together under his umbrella for the sake of the welfare and development of our people 'back home.'

He did not even acknowledge receipt of my letter, then or later!

Nine months later though, around November 1998, I heard an announcement on the radio that there was going to be a meeting of all people from Karachuonyo on a Sunday at the Kenyatta International Conference (now *Convention*) Centre, KICC. It tickled my curiosity and of course my interest. A radio announcement meant all were welcome. I decided to attend.

Come that Sunday, the appointed day, I arrived in time before the meeting started. There was already a "committee" in place, seated on the 'high table' in front. I do not remember hearing the word "interim!" These were the MP's chosen people, a hand-picked 'dream team!' But as I had declared in my letter nine months earlier, I was willing and ready to join the rank and file assembled, and those yet to be mobilized! There was a good attendance.

I kept my cool, with no so-called body language. For well over one hour, I listened to what one would have hoped to be a fruition of my proposal for the MP to bring us 'Karachuonyoans' together into a culturally entrenched and development-appetized 'one-and-all!' Something was not happening or adding up! The day was literally going. The sun was fast toning down both its heat and brightness! It was not going to happen, whatever 'it' was! It was like a workshop with no mood set, and no direction!

With some impatience and frustration on my face now, I raised my hand to make a contribution.

In the end, those who knew me were not surprised; those who did not know me sat up alert. There were three of my former high school classmates in the audience who were members of Rachuonyo Students Association (RSA) under my Chairmanship at Kisii High School as "finalists" in 1960.

Did we as Jo-Karachuonyo need to unite? What were our aspirations? What were our challenges and problems? What would be our priorities? Were we in any position, and did we have any capacity, to offer (or conjure up) any solutions for development of Karachuonyo? ~ PERIOD!

That was my preamble. Then I went into some details to try and spell out and outline possible answers to those questions, as a more practical, rewarding and implementable way of addressing the issues in Karachuonyo.

The long and short of it was that an interim committee was formed. I was readily and popularly included in the group and nominated a co-chairman with the earlier appointee of the MP, who was a namesake of my surname. Surprisingly, soon after that day, after some time along the way, he stopped attending committee meetings and just fizzled out and away! But the rest of the committee and general membership forged on:

1. We put a constitution in place and got the society registered with the Registrar of Societies under the name "Karachuonyo Development Society" (KDS).
2. We consolidated our agenda and published a brochure-like pamphlet, with a good run of who and what we were (and still are), as well as relevant issues and a template for a plan of action. We created sub-committees for different sectors of our socio-economic complex. We had the capacity within our membership, especially in education: like Dr. (later Professor) Tom Konditi chairing the Education sub-committee where we had Professor Shem Wandiga (Ja-Kendu, as I have always called him) and Jeckoniah Ogeda Odumbe, once in my committee at Kisii High School. This was a powerhouse, par excellence.

3. We participated in as many educational and development activities back home as they happened. Almost as a rule, we were represented by the indefatigable, highly committed Treasurer, Mrs. Dorothy Martha Atieno Deya, otherwise herself a business lady with a small stationery-cum-printing shop in Nairobi's Central Business District (CBD) on Tom Mboya Street. The educational activities included donating books to schools and attending zonal and District Education Days, with KDS trophies and prizes for winners.
4. KDS was almost becoming a household name. We swore not to talk or engage in rhetorical politics; but 'that kind' of politics caught up with us anyway!

In our constitution, we undertook to work with any and all (present and future) elected politicians of the area. The given incumbent Member of Parliament was automatically to be the Society's Patron, whoever he or she was, always.

So, when the Honourable James Kwanya Rege succeeded Dr. Awiti at the expiry of the latter's second term, another breath of what was (abortively) touted as fresh air swept across the land of Rachuonyo, the son of Jok. We quickly changed our letterheads with his name as the new Patron.

We organized a mammoth reception for him at the Kenya Polytechnic, (now Technical University of Kenya) for Karachuonyo people in Nairobi to meet and congratulate him. The crowd was so big that we ended up being moved twice to other halls; but even the largest hall on that campus still left many people standing in the aisles!

The programme included keynote speeches, starting with a welcome address by myself. I covered the history of KDS. The other speakers were:

1. **Education** – Professor Shem Oyoo Wandiga;
2. **Entrepreneurship** – Dr .William "Major" Onyango
3. **Economics of Fishing and Fishery in Karachuonyo and Beyond** – Dr. Seth Gor.

Dr. Gor (deceased 2020) nearly moved the audience to tears with his rendition of the miserable state and dynamics around the lake, fish in that lake, the plight of the destitute lake-side dwellers, not to talk of the fishermen!

That was the evening and night when the whole of Kenya went into darkness due to a total power failure. As a newly appointed Minister for Energy, our brand-new MP took the matter up immediately, as the black-out had occurred right in the middle of our reception - his 'inauguration' function as it were. We were all impressed by his rush to attempt to solve the problem, but there was nothing he could do immediately: it was massive and widespread over the whole country.

On that occasion, we undertook to hold a bigger reception for the MP back home, upcountry, within the Constituency; but this time round he was to help mobilize people back there as an opportunity for his own additional familiarization with them for future interactions. That was never to be! He chose what finally became his lacklustre legacy!

In late August 2008, I attended the regional meeting of the World Health Organization (WHO) in Yaoundé, Cameroon, both on invitation to receive a WHO award for tobacco control in Kenya and as Chairman of Kenya's Tobacco Control Board (the TCB, previously called the National Tobacco-Free Initiative Committee (NTFIC)). I was together with the team from the Ministry of Health. I arrived back in Nairobi on or around 5th September 2008 and later in the evening went for messages in my office within Nairobi's Central Business District (CBD).

That same evening, a youth winger of the MP knocked at my office door with two letters inviting me to attend a meeting of **"Karachuonyo Development Forum (KDF)"** on 7th September 2008 at what was our usual venue. The youth winger could not explain anything intelligible! Was that a new body, or was it a misspelling of KDS? Who was to chair that particular meeting?

The meeting was one; the letters were two (both for me), not even one for my wife or any other member of KPA! In one I was addressed purely and exclusively in my personal and individual capacity. In the second one, I was addressed officially as Chairman of the smaller Kanyaluo Progressive Association (KPA), based in Nairobi; indeed, I was, so the second letter was officially correct by protocol.

At KDS level, I told the youth winger to convey the message that I saw it as insubordination, or a political miscalculation by a whole Patron, politically misdirected, with some degree of political illiteracy if not also political immaturity, and an unwarranted sabotage. If I wanted to join career politics, I could have done so immediately after my high school. All I was doing now was trying to join hands in giving back to the society that had helped me: what with my fundraiser of August 1961 at Omboga and commitment with heart patients! There was absolutely no reason for anybody to fight me, even with medically diagnosable paranoia! I would not attend that particular meeting! We had just given ourselves a leadership vacuum at parliamentary elections, and it had progressively gotten worse! Strangely enough, I was intimated later that he had been warned not to give me a chance, otherwise I would (in the pet language of my good friend Joseph Kaguthi, first Director of NACADA), "dwarf" him! To say that that was very strange would be an unforgivable euphemism, a gross understatement!

To my recollection, that meeting never took off, never took place! It was rescheduled for the following week; again, it flopped. This happened nearly four times! In a similar manner as I had been approached, the MP tried to engage four different people at the core of KDS to chair for him his toy forum and the wishful abortive meetings! That body was never registered!

About two years later, I received a circular-like letter from the same MP stating that so many groups were calling upon him for help in various development matters in different parts of the Constituency, and he was overwhelmed. He felt the urge to unite Karachuonyo, or some such! Could I attend a meeting to form a body to forge the way forward for Karachuonyo?

This time I replied in writing. I gave him a chronology of events and group dynamics of Karachuonyo (and his leadership in it) from February 1998 up to the date of his circular under reply. He did not reply. The meeting never took place! What I heard later is that he told some other Karachuonyo people around him that I wrote him 'an impossible, incomprehensible, even unfathomable," letter, in a language he could not himself grasp! I am not sure if he shared the contents of that letter with anyone else, whether inside or outside his toy committees!

A few years later, I bumped into the same old-time youth winger on the streets of Nairobi. Without wasting time or mincing words, he pleaded with me, in his own words:

"PLEASE BRING BACK KDS FOR US!"

I would not say that the rest is history, as some story-telling orators might say, because I have a disclaimer:

THIS IS NOT HEARSAY OR GOSSIP! IT IS NOT ANY FORM OF AGGRANDISEMENT! FAR FROM IT: IT IS NOT THAT SIMPLISTICALLY PERSONAL! I HAPPEN TO HAVE HEADED AN INSTITUTION TO WHICH I WAS DEEPLY COMMITTED AND WHICH I SAW AS A GROUNDING FOR POSITIVE CONTINUITY OF DEVELOPMENT OF MY HOME COMMUNITY, COME NEW OFFICERS! I HAD SO MUCH ON MY HANDS AND STILL SACRIFICED MY TIME AND ENERGY TO HELP CREATE A PROGRESSIVE ENABLING ENVIRONMENT FOR ALL OF US BY PRESIDING OVER AN ORGANIZATION FOR WHICH ALL WE NEEDED TO DO WAS TO OWN AND BUILD!

I HAVE INCLUDED IT HERE AS OUR COLLECTIVE STORY ON THIS CONTINENT, BUT PARTICULARLY FOR MY

FELLOW LAKE-SIDE DWELLERS WHO ARE SO CLEVER BUT JUST CANNOT UNITE OR WORK TOGETHER FOR THE COLLECTIVE GOOD OF ALL, FOR DESTINY, POSTERITY AND FOR HUMANITY! IT IS A BLOT ON OUR COLLECTIVE HISTORY!

ONE DARES TO RECOMMEND THAT WE SHOULD LET POLITICIANS DO THEIR DIRTY POLITICS, WHILE INDIVIDUALS AND GROUPS IN VARIOUS SECTORS SHOULD CONSOLIDATE THEIR COLLECTIVE WISDOM AND ENERGIES TO COORDINATE AND UNDERTAKE THEIR DEVELOPMENT AND SURVIVALIST ACTIVITIIES TO ENHANCE PRIVATE SECTOR LEADERSHIP. CAREER POLITICIANS ARE JUST TOO NOISY FOR THE GOOD OF THIS CONTINENT!

Then there was the parallel occasion imitating the inauguration of Barack Obama Jr. on 20th January 2009. On that occasion, facilitated and assisted by a local member of the Obama Opiyo family (Mr. Wilfred Obama Kobilo, who had remained in Karachuonyo, barely 4 – 5 kilometres from Kendu Bay town), we marked the day in style, many hours before the official inauguration at the White House, which was bound to happen during Kenya's night-time. There were even a few foreign visitors at that function.

As KDS we proposed, actually resolved, that the road leading to the home complex of the first Obama, son of Opiyo, and father of Onyango Hussein, where Barrack Obama Sr. was born, be named "Obama Road." We prepared two metallic road signs, written and marked with the same. I delivered them from Nairobi in my famous pick-up van in time to coincide with the tour of the Minister for Culture and Social Services, Hon. Esther Murugi and her Principal Secretary, Dr. James Nyikal to inspect development projects in Karachuonyo. The Minister graciously officially opened the road by unveiling the new road signs, one at the junction of the highway from Kendu Bay, the other at the entrance to the local Obama homestead. Former president Barack Obama had actually visited this homestead in his youth around 1980.

The launch of the Obama Opiyo mausoleum was yet another KDS-patronized occasion at the place!

A WORD ABOUT CIVIC EDUCATION:

Civic education is not a classroom affair, or any of those "runaway" curriculum technicalities. It is a subtle combination and culmination of several things in one complexity. In short, it is an experiential quantum. Within it, there is 'role modelling,' 'mentoring,' counselling,' 'advice,' various exposures and direct interactions, as well as some forms of arbitration and even aspects of body language. These are the common dynamics or currencies of civic education, especially as an educational, developmental and maturation platform including emotional and social intelligence and maturity. As an observable qualitative trait, it tends to be diffusely engulfed and overshadowed by academic portfolios in the forms of certificates, diplomas, degrees and awards. Therein lies the basis of incongruity and even contradiction between mesmerising qualifications on paper, on the one hand, and meritorious performance, integrity and a legacy-bound display of one's level and image, on the other. Therein also lies the virtual secret of smooth interphase between one and his/her environment, his/her neighbour and posterity.

Although there are both pleasant and unpleasant experiences in life, every encounter in life is full of lessons of what to do and what not do, what to say and what not to say, what to copy and what to avoid, and a general and broad expansion of what is learnt at home and at school.

Sometimes it manifests as a "me-too" or "copy-cat" phenomenon and adaptation. Once again, therein lies some of the secrets of interpersonal and social maturity, different attitudes, invention beyond innovation, and overall creativity.

Very selfish people run away with borrowed ideas without acknowledgement of source, and then purpose to display, even claim, ownership and originality for self-glorification. These are aspects and dimensions of intellectual dishonesty, trickery and, to some extent, immaturity, which hinder social and cultural cohesion, not to talk of development! They end up disrupting positive visions and thwart progressive dreams. Finally, messages and lessons are lost, and nobody gains or benefits, including themselves!

I have spent a fair amount of my time in formal and informal engagements and have often wondered why many groups start well but lack the staying power to survive, thrive and blossom, or even create an impact!

"Welfare" and "development" bodies were particularly vulnerable in such connections. Much as their constitutions stated that they were non-political, there were almost always 'semi-political' betrayals, blockages, sabotage and gross indiscipline, with no effective avenues for streamlining errant and retrogressive behaviour!

My take, in evolutionary terms, if you will, is that such communities have not matured enough on the learning ladder of positive collective group survival, either as clans or nations. The sad part is that their mob psychology is more developed and crowds swarm like locusts when time comes (or is created) to react and destroy!

The political dynamics of a whole half of a century since Kenya's independence has taken its toll on the entire landscape. However, the sadder picture is that our public leadership has failed to offer any meaningful or remedial civic education, as "EXOTISM" (worship of the exotic; my coinage) takes centre stage!

The political divide overlooks one thing: that there are several different workable political systems, so well documented in history and contemporary times. Cut-throat polarities and polarizations are a form of foolishness and immaturity. That makes it necessary and very important to ease apart "politics" and "political career" away from what I would stratify as *"political intelligence," "career politics" and "political stupidity."* Street wisdom is a learnt or experiential attribute that goes beyond politics in the sense highlighted here.

At the height of the Cold War, Russia and United States of America still had their levels of communication, and still delivered to their respective peoples.

Tanzania and Kenya are almost worlds apart – one is over-tribalized and over-politicized, the other exudes fertile seeds of 'high thinking and simple living,' but sometimes seems radar-less!

What did the war between Kwame Nkrumah of Ghana and Obafemi Tafawa Balewa of Nigeria do to positively contribute to the African continent?

The rot with our thinkers, our leaders and our institutions in Africa causes us to rush to adopt, nay, imbibe like sponges, the "new," even untested experimental innovations, before being ready, and without demonstrable capacity to mould, modify and assimilate them meaningfully and beneficially! The term "domestication" is like a loose missile of political imagery, essentially escapist!

Somersaulting over the basics that way keeps us looking up to venturesome thinkers who themselves also feed and borrow from our naivety, read uncircumspect, unguarded and non-strategic openness!

Look around and fathom the abyss of the mutated gene of dependence. Bad politics, based on undigested hyperbole, is the virus propelling that mutation! When profit dips, but still figures well within the profit margin, is there real loss for the profiteer? The larger nation might lose in tax, but, otherwise what? When individuals break away from that kind of a herded mass, things seem to change and roll better. Results, achievements and outcomes start showing a more encouraging trend. At the end of the day, strong individual personas show up, but theirs are not the faces of the communities in which they live! They are more of entrepreneurs than social or cultural identities, even if inertia drivers and role models to some extent. They might be compelled to go the charity way, to forestall insecurity, including and especially for themselves, by chipping in to alleviate the engulfing poverty that always accompanies the class dichotomy of the haves and the have-nots. All will have failed, nonetheless - the community, the county and the State!

As part of my observation and experience, I decided to add some of these comments on civic education here just as such - there is a bitter failure in succumbing to the fate of those who have eyes ***and can see***, but are being led by the blind with ***plastic make-believe eyesight***!

I do not encourage lamentations. In fact, I hate and usually do not entertain them; because one needs to use the space and time to offer solutions and direction. The intention of inserting it here is to alert all my readers to stay awake and vigilant, and not only wait to learn from the torrential flood of life, gliding and sliding past, but also to see human drudgery as a challenge, so as to do better by reaching and helping others.

Like the Greeks said ages ago:

"The eyes do not see what the mind does not know!"! **(So put something up there, in the mind!)**

My plea and appeal is that we learn from our surroundings, our environment, our interactions and our challenges!

"Fore-warned is fore-armed!"
"Prevention is better than cure!"
"A stitch in time saves nine!"
"Hard work pays!"
"Time is money!"
"Take care!"
"Experience is the best teacher!"
"Live and let live!"
"Mind your neighbour!"

"United we stand; divided we fall!"
"Unity is strength"
and for sure,
"Knowledge is power"...and more!
Learn and Live!

It is important to note that even those who colonized this continent came and learnt lots, but behaved inherently selfishly by appropriating what they learnt and parading it after revising it as their own superior culture and ownership! When peoples meet and interact, knowledge, behaviour and world views criss-cross bilaterally, even multilaterally. It is never a unilateral one-way "civilizing mission."

The unfortunate part is that a similar pattern is ongoing in our contemporary midst under what could and should be our own 'enlightened' and forewarned watch! This continent's own raw materials are exported raw and returned as finished products, with so-called **"added value,"** very much as if provenly better, like we couldn't do it! No foreigner will ever sit in your civic education class, but they will strategize to control you, using your own basics and innovating what you already own, all the while making nonsense of "copyright" and "intellectual property rights!"

One lifetime is hardly enough to correct the mess, but contemporary generations should set the stage for continued and progressively continuous development of the generations that follow, unlike present-day politicians who are attuned to handouts and hand-to-mouth plunder by wasting resources as they entrench perpetual foreign dependency and perpetual vulnerability! With very few exceptions, politicians and political leaders on this continent have largely failed! Their most outstanding legacy is NON-PERFORMANCE and IN-FIGHTING, as they set the stage to betray their own people, who continue to look like children of a lesser god! Inadvertently, present day politics on the African continent is a 'new age' gateway to slavery! The economy, as mismanaged, is a highway for the poor and stricken to 'sustain' and perpetuate their own miserable state and "fate!"

Sociologists, anthropologists, scientists and avowed professionals are the ones to turn to. We owe this continent and our people the ultimate emancipation, starting with their minds and 'no-nonsense' facilitation!

That is why, on my part, I end this autobiography by declaring and acknowledging our big challenge! In the final analysis, civic education and 'street wisdom' might end up helping more than the under-serviced curriculums and career politics in the marketplace! Get the basics right, critically recall and imbibe history, grab technology, use them all, and the case is as complete as the university of life can offer to harmonize universal awareness, across the 'tribes', religions, cultures and races! Never forget history, yours and all! Then count, promote and harness the following four as an essential foursome:

History, Basics, Technology and hard work.

That leads me to highlight the silent threat of what I choose to call here "Technological and Scientific Sheng," particularly for my profession of health science and specifically medicine, clinical medicine. The looming short-cuts in medicine at times tend to preclude basics. The trend may be traced as an unwitting by-product of technology, which, in essence, is not the same thing as 'HUMAN SCIENCE.'

There are those who have no (sound) basics but want to feel that they know! I see this as the genre of mediocrity. Knowing a lot from the internet, for example, but next to nothing about the patient is already a looming pitfall in the medical profession in parts of the world!

There is no greater need for clinical skills than now in the midst of technology. It is very possible to lose both the patient and the person! There is no medicine without clinical skills, which must include communication. There are at least three constants in a health care delivery set-up like the hospital, namely **the patient, the nurse and the doctor. The other constants are the phenomena of health and disease.** The rest are just **supporting categories, services and gadgets,** including technology in all its forms, and the administrators.

To avoid and pre-empt the path along which socio-politics has to date misdirected this continent, the medical profession must step back and reinvent itself in order to inculcate 'educated enthusiasm' as opposed to 'copy-cat enthusiasm.' Educated enthusiasm begets curiosity, science, innovation and invention, and facilitates skills and practicality. Copy-cat enthusiasm, on the other hand, begets mediocrity, with no capacity for even improvisation, let alone innovation.

Tease the two apart and set them aside in their own dimensions for institutional and international relations, interactions and collaboration.

The world is a template in itself! Do not ignore that; but you also do not want to waste time trying to reinvent the wheel, or copy when you cannot paste!

Ivan Illich talked about medicalization of health. I worry about politicization of medicine! Beyond these, tragically for this entire continent and all its sectors, there is highly institutionalized politicization of corruption!

III.
"Tek To Nyalore" (TTN)
or,
"Tough But Doable" (TBD).

On the eve of Kenya's general elections of the year 2002, I earned the dubious distinction of being invited as an assistant guest of honour by my in-law family and community at Onding' village in Gem, Siaya District (now County).

The occasion was a very noble one – to raise funds for the construction of a dispensary in the memory of my late mother-in-law, who had been a very active community worker.

Renowned architect Joel Nyaseme, now deceased, from a neighbouring clan that side, was making his debut into elective (career) politics at the time. He was already enjoying sizeable 'home-ground' support. He was the main (or first) guest of honour. There was excitement in the air!

And here I was – very politically conscious and community compliant, but a typical outsider in the career politics of the constituency and a surgical operating room recluse, if at all!

Nonetheless, I recognized two of my other attributes - a health worker par excellence called upon to spearhead the establishment of a health institution, and the eldest son-in-law in the immediate home of my late mother-in-law.

I could feel the respect accorded to me. It was indeed palpable in the whole place! More challenging was the huge expectation from the community!

For sure, I was not going to compete with the lead guest of honour. Protocol was straight forward. The donation front was clear. At that time, Joel Nyaseme was still very well-endowed financially; he was literally a force to reckon with.

It is still true today, in Kenya's heavy financial presence at political campaigns for elected office, that aspirants use such seemingly "small" functions like that one to reach the grassroots of the masses. His coming to grace the occasion was proof and confirmation that he was financially fit, able and ready. His 'niche' for the day had long been cut out for him.

My platform was my own watch-out. The bottom line was that I must not disappoint my hosts and hostesses! I found myself already armed with three elements:

1. The goodwill and best wishes for the health facility. So, I made sure that I attended.
2. I was not going to help preside over a non-starter – a pre-failed project! It was going to be difficult and challenging for a small

community like that. So, mine was to address the 'mentality' and mental frame for sustained and sustainable commitment. Then popped out the caption **"Tough But Doable!" (TBD)!** But this is the English translation of the magnetic phrase in the vernacular, Dholuo: **"TEK TO NYALORE" (TTN),** conveyed with all the simplicity and humility that I could marshal for a confident son- and brother-in-law!

3. My small cash donation was another humble display! Today, I cannot even remember how much it ever was!

So, after all, I had a three-some for a 'niche!' But "TTN" alone inspired me also! Everybody had to repeat and chorus with me: "TEK TO NYALORE!" Chorus: "TTN!" This was repeated up to three times.

Even today I would ask and urge the reader to repeat the same words, and force themselves to absorb and internalize that simple but forceful and captivating set of only three words! On that occasion, nearly two decades ago back from today, 2023, nearly all else became subsidiary that evening! I could feel it! The 'long-lost' son/brother-in-law had finally reached home!

That same phrase also instantly became my password in many public and community encounters thereafter. Back home in Kanyaluo, part of Karachuonyo, Homa Bay County, it easily evolved into a nickname among some of my clans people:

"Tek to Nyalore, Amollo K'Odhiambo," or simply, "TTN."

The English translation ("TBD") was hardly used! Not surprisingly, immediately after the harambee meeting at Onding' in Gem, Siaya, a football club was formed and duly named **"Professor Odhiambo Tek To Nyalore Football Club."** It went on for quite a while, but they did not reach 'league threshold.'

The dispensary itself grew to become a full health centre with maternity services. It still bears the same memorial name – "St. Elizabeth Owaga Memorial Health Centre." My late mother-in-law had actually helped the local community with the little health advice and care that she knew.

Some twelve to fourteen generations before this time, my own great grandmother, Rachuonyo's first wife, was also called Owaga "Nyaluo." She had come into that marriage from her paternal home in Alego clan of Kaluo, where she had been born and bred. Her second name "Nyaluo" is also associated with her championing her 'Luo-ness' by spearheading the ceremony of initiating young Rachuonyo (her husband) by removing his six lower teeth, according to the Luo culture, custom and tradition.

With my mother-in-law 'namesaking' my great-grandmother, I was squeezed into a 'small world,' of course with no in-breeding!

Much later we woke up to the fact that Mwalimu Julius Kambarage Nyerere, Tanzania's Prime Minister and later its first President, had actually coined a powerful, even better, slogan for his people long before me, even if in different words:

"IT CAN BE DONE!"

It rang sweet and I felt historically vindicated when I soon also heard the K'Ogelo-blooded American, ex-president Barack Obama, sway a whole continent with corresponding echoes of

"YES WE CAN!"

One interesting connection here is that my senior partner at the Onding' fundraiser never heard me at all! He could have adopted my message as a campaign slogan!

He had arrived at the venue with an entourage of women singing his praise as a possible future "Member of Parliament" (MP) of the place! "Honourable!" "*Mheshimiwa!*" With a good 'political' speech and rather full of himself, he just sat there and enjoyed the evening for all the recognition and support it gave him. And that was it! He later lost in the party nominations. He became just another statistic of prominent professionals who burn their fingers by dabbling in career politics - and African politics at that with a Kenyan flavour! Perhaps endearing his potential voters with the three-worded catchphrase might have made a small difference for him!

28

ANCESTRY AND ROOTS

FATHER'S PATERNAL ROOTS (OMBOGA...K'OLONY)

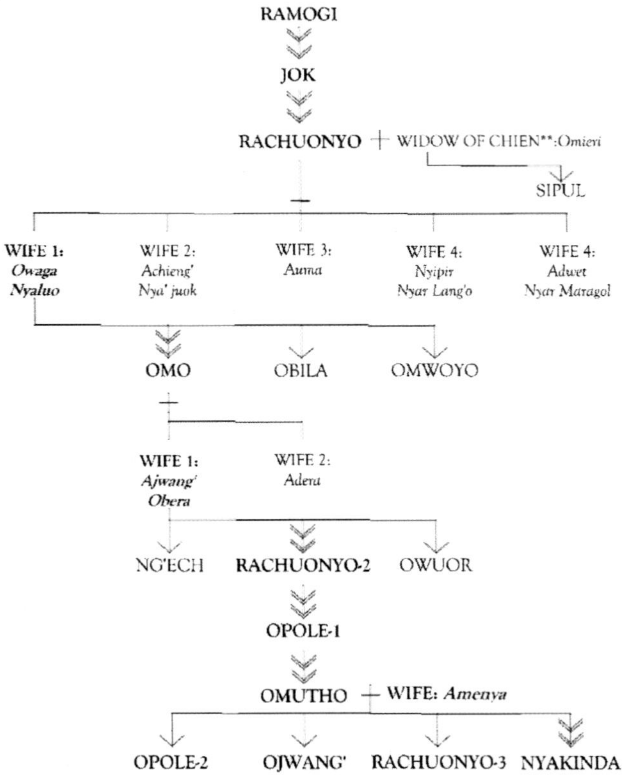

*Wives are indicated in italics. Direct lineage is indicated by a double arrow.
**Chien was host and benefactor of Rachuonyo. Rachuonyo married Chien's young widow, Omieri, and together they had a son, Sipul.

FATHER'S PATERNAL ROOTS (OMBOGA...K'OLONY) cont'd

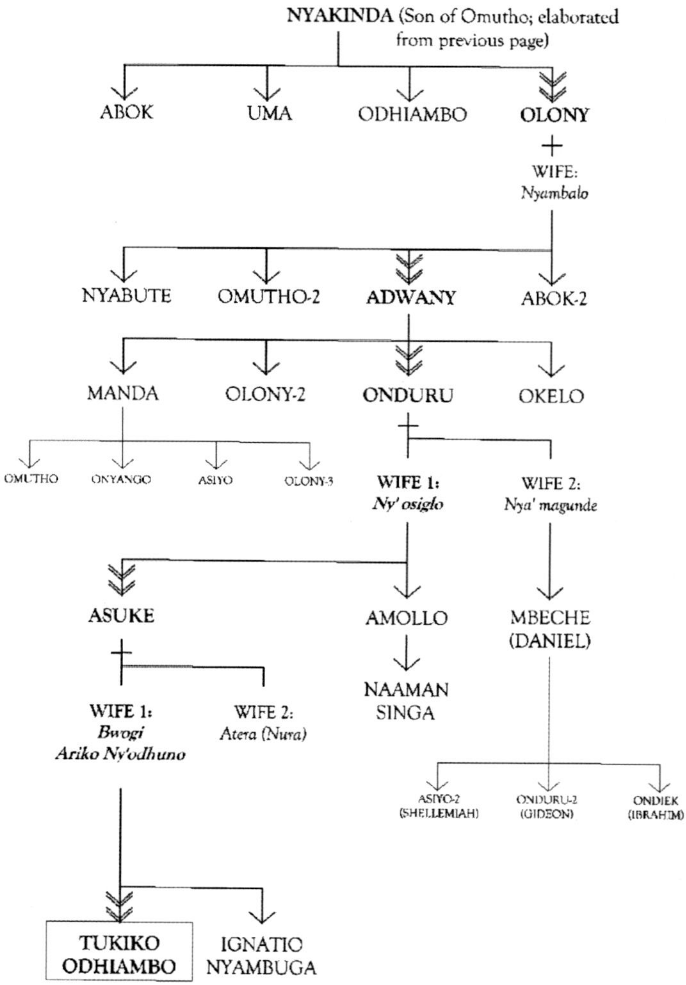

FATHER'S MATERNAL ROOTS
(KANYADA)

?RAMOGI?

↓

↓

NYADA

↓

OMOL KIRAWA

↓

OMOL MBUI

↓

OTHIDHA

↓

ONYANGO

↓

OGUMA

↓

GENGA

↓

ODHUNO**

DAUGHTER: *Bwogi (Wife of Asuke; mother of Tukiko Odhiambo)*	OJUNG'A**

*N.B: OTHIDHA - Owadgi OKWEDHO, with three sons, spread out into large CLANS, namely:

i. KANYADIER,
ii. KALENYA KANYANGO,
iii. KANYABALA,
iv. KATUMA.

**See following pages for additional lineage

FATHER'S MATERNAL ROOTS (KANYADA) cont'd

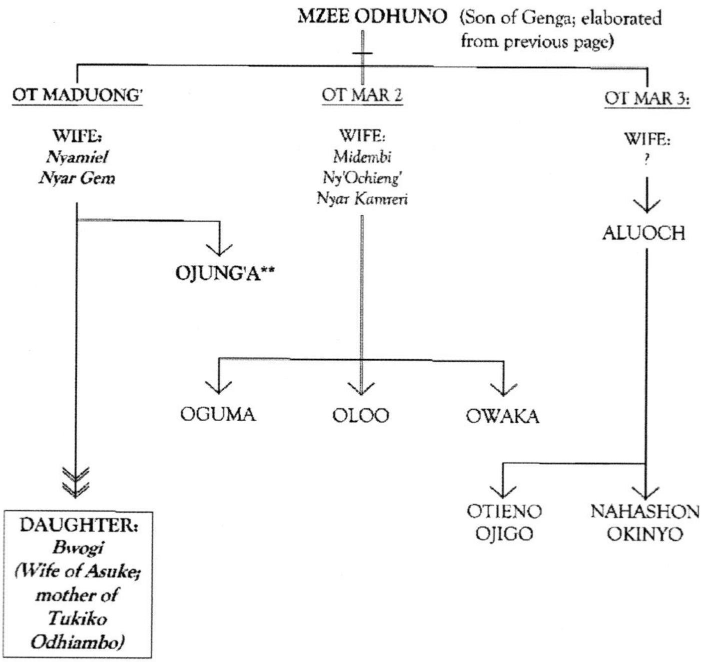

**See following page for additional lineage

FATHER'S MATERNAL ROOTS (KANYADA) cont'd

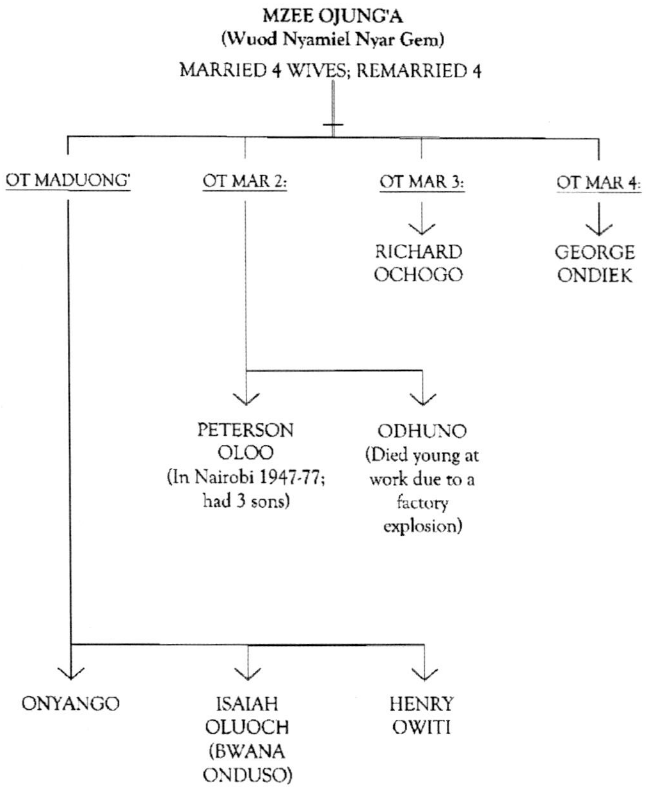

MOTHER'S MAIDEN HOME FAMILY TREE (ANDING'O)

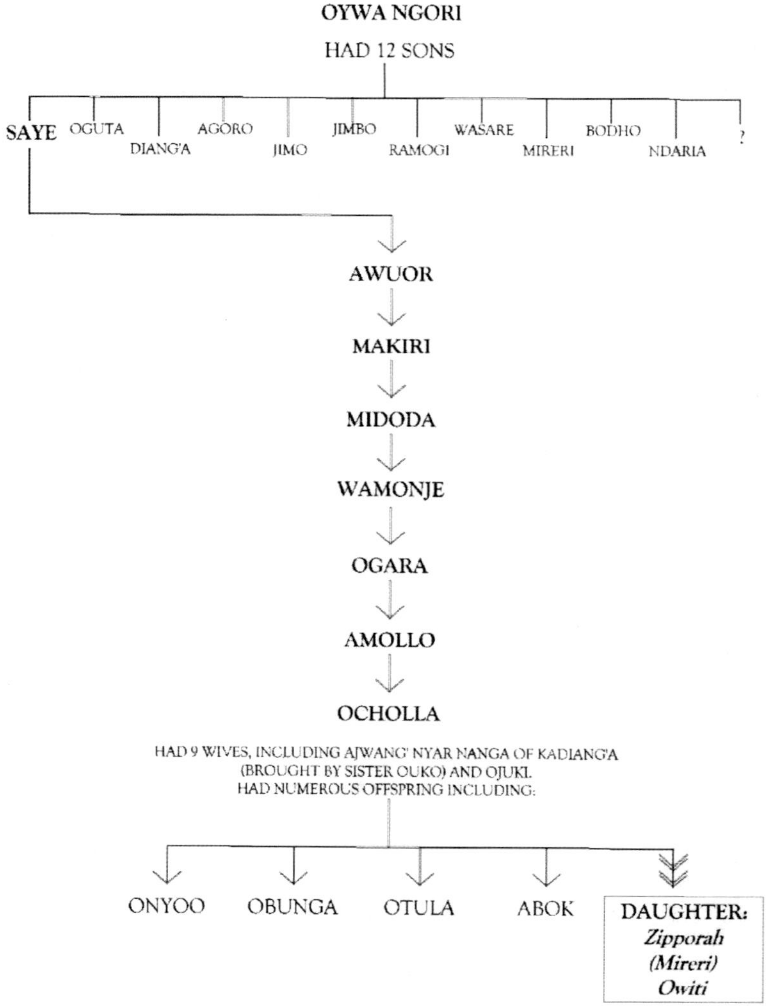

29

THE FINAL MOTION

STRATEGIC INTER-DEPENDENCE: SELECTIVE COLLABORATION, SPONSORSHIP, SOLICITATION, AND WORLD LEADERSHIP FOR PEACE

I HAVE BEEN prompted from within myself to include this chapter in this book because, emanating from too much goodwill in Africa, our singular and collective intelligence seems unable to adequately critique chicanery from outside this continent, as if all so-called new ideas are sacrosanct - ideas with which our people always want to be identified! Such ideas penetrate the continent with help from sleepwalking scholars and intellectuals seeking recognition for seemingly progressing with what is supposedly modern and with the times, only for a different view from 'out there' to re-direct thoughts, with yet another swing of intellectual culpability! Therefore:

1. Given that for all this time, the world knows what riches in the wrong hands can do;
2. Being cognizant of history, one must not forget what certain races have meted out on others that were deemed inferior, even if to be forgiven;
3. Understanding contemporary dynamics and the current interest in and emphasis on hidden motives, tricks and machinations of and for race 'survival' (read dominance);

4. Remembering how collectively certain racial groups have nearly always ganged up together and scratched one another's backs;
5. Waking up to the ominous reality of 'superior' races giving one another calculated, selective entry points over the centuries whenever it came to do with minorities and vulnerable people groups, from whom even those with ulterior, even inhuman, motives might be granted such entry points by their straight-faced 'superiors;'
6. Knowing for sure that present African political leaders have largely failed the test, behaving like grandfather rulers of yore, who sold their people for pittance after pittance into slavery, and
7. Seeing how African politicians have unashamedly assimilated the culture of perpetual dependence on foreign aid and remain ready to kill one another to prove their bootlicking proficiency within their evidently short-sighted survival acumen (if at all), all while whipping their 'local' people into inter-community hyper-sensitivity and anarchic reactions, self-incriminatingly and self-derogatorily dubbed *tribal clashes*, one must observe and strongly propose that:

There is a dire need for a shift in the current paradigm, whereby and because:

1. The majority of political leaders in Africa and much of the 'black and coloured world' lost their capacity to further maintain and sustain the drives towards total fulfilment of independence a long time ago. By that token, they cannot and will not be able to face the powers that be, including racial, cultural, social and commercial eugenicists.
2. Africans must no longer invest in ill-defined, ill-perceived political power when it comes to development and international (inter-racial) relations.

3. Smart and serious African scholars must shun population-based studies sponsored and patronized from 'outside,' because of emerging fear of harmful population engineering. Any such studies should be consciously and conscientiously funded and controlled, if need be, by nationalist institutional frameworks from local budgets, not from foreign aid.
4. Erstwhile traditional diplomacy and international relations should be critically reviewed, re-evaluated and streamlined by Africans themselves, and by the African Union (if uncompromised), or any new similar grouping.
5. There is a dire need to redefine, even reinvent the United Nations Organization, based on the future and not the past (like the First and Second World Wars), with a view to meaningful, harmonious and wholesome human evolution and development, as well as commitment to prevention of a flagrant Third World War, or its semblance!
6. **TOLERANCE** should be the new vocabulary for mankind and our attendant dynamics of 'human relations.' One is compelled to propose that, because there are so many celebrated and marked days in a year, UNESCO's "International Day of Tolerance" on 16th November be merged with New Year celebrations on 1st January to highlight the need for hope, peace, understanding and tolerance for the ensuing 365 days as humanity starts yet another year of unavoidable human relations and human interaction. The existing cycle of the Christian calendar would then appear to be a natural reminder that we all need each other.

EPILOGUE

I

FIFTY-FIVE YEARS AS A MEDICAL DOCTOR (1968 – 2023)

ON 5TH DECEMBER, 2018, my family and I held a humble celebration at Taifa Hall, University of Nairobi, to mark my fifty years as a medical doctor. We simply cut a cake to mark the occasion. But the highlight of the event was the line-up of guests and the speeches.

2018:Marking 50 years as a medical doctor. My daughters assist me in cutting a cake. To the left, in the rear, is my eldest sister Truphena Anyango.

The guest of honour was the Vice-Chancellor of the University of Nairobi, Professor Peter Mbithi, represented by his Deputy in charge of Academic Affairs, Professor Julius Ogeng'o, himself a renowned author and the third-highest Kenyan anatomist after Professor Joseph Mungai and James Kimani, both of whom are deceased. Special guests included Professor Raphael Munavu (Chairman of the Kenya National Academy of Sciences - KNAS), Professor Shem Oyoo Wandiga (former Chairman, Department of Biochemistry and long-time Kenyan Representative to UNESCO as part of the Climate Change Forum, as well as former Deputy Vice-Chancellor in charge of Administration and Finance at the University of Nairobi), and Professor Gideon Barak Agembo Okelo (former Chairman, Department of Internal Medicine; former Dean, Faculty of Medicine; former Director of Medical Services - Ministry of Health, and Secretary of the African Academic of Science).

Other distinguished guests were Professor Julius Kyambi (pioneer paediatric surgeon); the late Dr. Peter Ochola Abila (former Chairman, Department of Surgery, and former member of Nairobi University Council, representing the College of Health Sciences); the late Professor Charles Odidi Okidi, Professor of Environmental Law; Mr. Jorim Otieno Guya, Principal, Ramogi Institute Of Advanced Technology (RIAT), and his Deputy, Mr. Ken (this is the same institute where I served as Chairman of the Board Of Governors).

This book was earmarked for launching on that occasion, but the printer delayed. When he eventually delivered the first copies, I found that he had committed gross errors in the production! He agreed that the mistakes warranted a repeat job, but quickly disappeared with all drafts and soft copies. Fortunately, I had backups, but it took me time to redeem all content! That 'extra time' enabled me to include this additional epilogue.

All said and done, perhaps this expanded compilation is better than the original draft! What I must do now is to apologize to all my readers and well-wishers, and to thank one and all for your patience while I seemed to have gone underground myself!

In the two years that followed, I was favoured with renewal of my contracts! I did one year's contract at the new School of Medicine at Masinde Muliro University of Science and Technology in Kakamega town, Kakamega County, courtesy of the generosity of the council and senate of that university, but even more specifically, the Founder Dean of the School, Professor Charles Chunge and Founder Chairman, Dr. Dominic Marera.

Upon completion of that contract, I got the rare privilege of being re-granted another contract of one year, from April 1, 2020, up to March 31, 2021, at the University of Nairobi's Department of Surgery, in the Thematic Unit of Thoracic and Cardiovascular Surgery.

By that 1st April 2020, of course, the Covid-19 pandemic was already with us, with its many variables, demands, equations and challenges! But I sincerely thank the Chancellor, Dr. Rattansi, Chairperson of UoN Council, Dr. Julia Ojiambo, Acting Vice-Chancellor, Professor Isaac Mbeche and the entire medical school management (Surgery Chairman, Dr. Julius Kiboi, School of Medicine Dean; Professor C.F. Otieno and College of Health Sciences (CHS) Principal, Professor Joseph Machoki).

As fate, luck, goodwill and trust would have it, I was accepted back at SOM, MMUST, from April 1, 2021.

II.
THE PLANET EARTH NAMED ENVIRONMENT: MY TAKE (TRANSLATING POLICY INTO PRACTICE)

One hears many powerful words about the entity called 'environment.' It is a word that has been in global use for a while now. Pronouncements regarding it are so rhetorical that they now render the whole subject a 'third-party' phenomenon, almost a cliché!

And yet, we are all 'environments' to one another. One person's take, view and actions are another person's environment, indeed multiples of environments, and to many.

The landscape is full of rivalries, contradictions and 'non-ownerships' (my coinage). In the end, the universality of the environment eludes all of us.

The Western world does this, the Eastern one does that. Africa and many third-world countries wait in the middle for the silver (shiny but short-lived), rather than the gold of the future, almost making it seem that real invention (even toned down to "innovation") is not for them to contemplate locally, or even from another part of the same continent! To be "original," to be "genuine," it must come from 'out there.' The complex combination of gullibility and denial is amazing! Hence policies are put in place to accommodate thoughts from 'out there.' One ends up with beautiful policy documents, even if some are not properly or appropriately 'domesticated,' which are never translated into truly useful practice or reality, and end up domiciled in lockers, shelves, and drawers, sometimes tainted with elusive and ethereal egos.

The missing link is the simple appreciation that everything happens in an environment. Even a given context fits into an environment. Hence the importance of grasping the gist of the policy and its intended follow up action, as a vision, a mission and an outcome!

The matrix below was a part of my unrelated lecture to a Clinical Epidemiology Unit (University of Nairobi School of Medicine) class in a course sponsored by the World Health Organization (WHO), entitled "TRANSLATING POLICY INTO PRACTICE" (see diagram at the end of this section below).

These things do not happen in a vacuum! The state of the environment is of utmost determinant relevance! That is why the poor leadership in Africa makes it look like our political leaders are merely on a joyride to ethereal, short-lived, earth-bound greatness, and have no idea where the continent (as it is today) came from and where it ***should*** be going! Prosperity for them is exclusively personalized and **body languages of the living** are, at best, merely excitements with skin-deep (political and politicized) success against other individuals, not against the ominous scourges like mass poverty, diseases and other suicidal paradigms, like neglect, degradation and destruction of the environment, not to talk of innate challenges of the environment itself!

My template is based on health training, service, outcome and job satisfaction, but may be adopted into any and all other sectors, with due acknowledgments!

Cheers! From my home in Ong'eche.

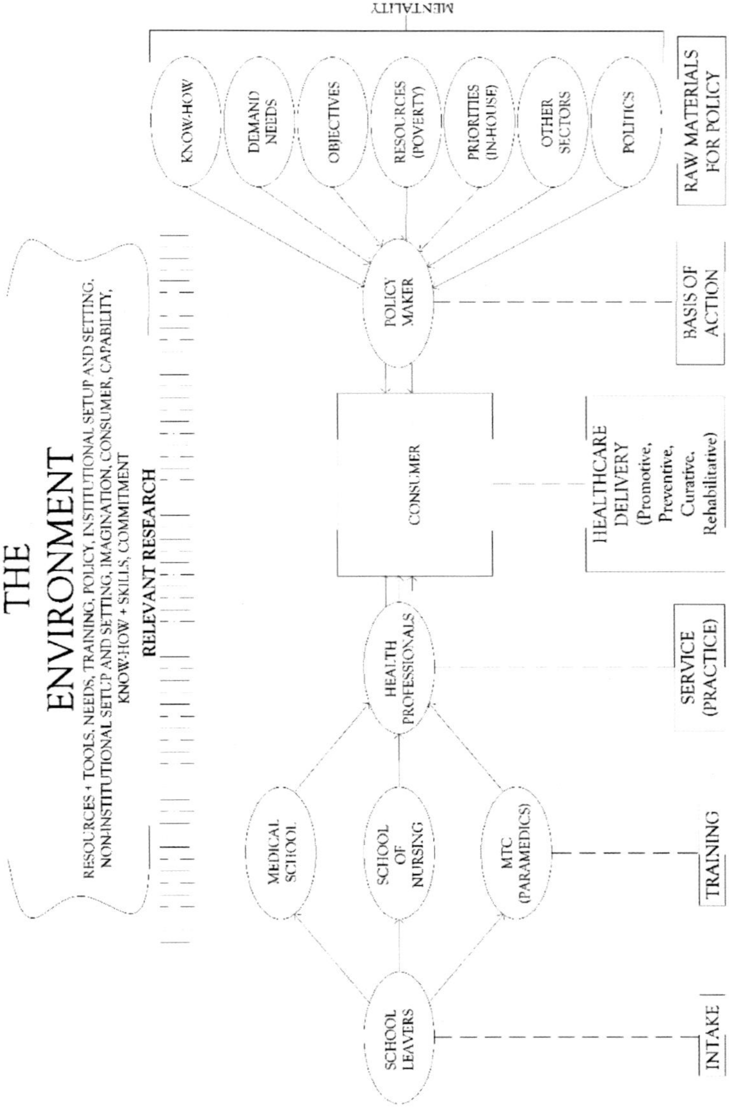

RESEARCH - POLICY-PRACTICE BRIDGE BY P.A. ODHIAMBO

III.
LEADERSHIP IN HEALTH

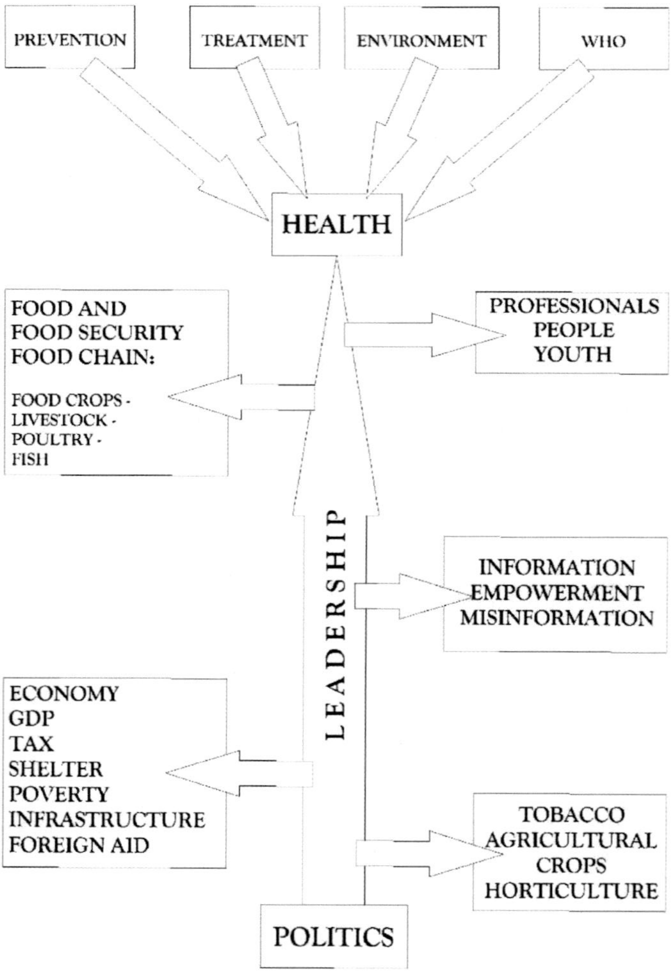

SUMMARY

Born: September 2, 1940.

Schools:

1. Omboga Primary School (1948-9)
2. Dudi Primary School (1950-1952)
3. Gendia Intermediate School (1953-1956)
4. Kisii High School (1957-1960)

College, University, Work, Achievements:
December 1960 – June 1962: Trainee Clerk Grade 2A, East African Railways and Harbours, Nairobi.

June 22, 1962: Steamship (SS Kampala) journey to India; back by Air India Feb. 28, 1971. While in India I attended Hindu College, University of Delhi, and Calcutta Medical College, University of Calcutta.

1968: MBBS (University of Calcutta).

1971/2: District Surgeon, Murang'a District.

1975: M.Med.(Surgery), University of Nairobi (1st batch).

1976:

January 1: Lecturer, Cardiothoracic Surgery, University of Nairobi at KNH.
September 1: Wedding.

September 30: Guy's Hospital, London.

1977: March – August: Charing Cross Hospital, London.

1978:

February: Fellowship, Royal College of Surgeons, Edinburgh – pass: FRCS-Ed.
March–September: United Hospitals of Wales and Llandough Hospital, Cardiff.
June-December: Visiting Lecturer, McGill University (at Montreal General and Montreal Children Hospitals), Canada.
December: Back to University of Nairobi (Lecturer)

July 1979: Founded *MEDICOM – The African Journal of Hospital and Scientific Medicine.*

1980: Senior Lecturer, UoN.

1981: Founder Chairman, Kenya Cardiac Society (KCS).

1982: Head, Thoracic and Cardiovascular Surgical Unit, KNH.

1984: Listed among Cambridge Biographical Library's"MEN OF ACHIEVEMENT."

1985 – 1989: Secretary-General, PASCAR.

1987: Member, New York Academy of Sciences.

1988: Associate Professor, UoN.

1989-1993: President, PASCAR.

1989-1993: Chairman, Division of Surgery, KNH.

1990: Giants Federation Award for outstanding service to community in Medicine.

1990-1991: Acting Chairman (Academic) Dept. of Surgery, UoN.

1991-1995: Vice Chairman, Surgical Society of Kenya (SSK);1994-1995 Ag. Treasurer, SSK.

1991-2006: Chairman Omboga High School Board of Management.

February,1992- May, 1996: Dean, Faculty (School) of Medicine, UoN.

1996 -2000: Chairman, Kenya Cardiac Society (separate 2nd term).

2000: (Full) Professor, Thoracic & Cardiovascular Surgery, University of Nairobi.

2000 -2008: Chairman, National Tobacco-Free Initiative Committee, (NTFIC), Ministry of Heath, Kenya.

2005: Elected Fellow, American College of Cardiology (FACC).

2000: Fellow, College of Surgeons of East, Central and Southern Africa, FCS(ECSA).

2006: Founder Chairman, Kenya Tobacco Control Alliance (KETCA).

2008 -2012: WHO 'World No-Tobacco Day' Award.

2009 – 2017: Chairman, Tobacco Control Board (TCB), Ministry of Health.

2009 – 2013: Member, BOG, Pangani Girls High School.

2012: Mater Hospital Recognition and Appreciation (Trophy) Award.

2013: SSK Award for "Outstanding Role in Medical Education and Teaching."

2014 -2020: Chairman, BOG Ramogi Institute of Advanced Technology (RIAT).

2015: Member, Kenya National Academy of Sciences.

2016: WHO World No-Tobacco Day Award to Board and Chair.

1994-2017: Chairman, UoN Teaching Hospital Project (UNTH).

2019-20: Teaching contract, School of Medicine, Masinde Muliro University of Science and Technology (SOM, MMUST).

2020-2021: Teaching contract, Department of Surgery University of Nairobi.

June 2021 – June 2022: Teaching contract, SOM, MMUST and Chairman, Department of Internal Medicine, SOM.

BOOKS:

1. *Cardiology in the Tropics* (Proceedings edited in1984);
2. *Tobacco Versus Health*, 2004;

3. *Making Sense of Cessation of Smoking,* 2010;
4. Forty Years of Editorials in *MEDICOM – The African Journal of Hospital and Scientific Medicine* (Bound volume), 2018.

COMING:

History of Heart Surgery in Kenya

Facing Up to Heart Surgery

Collected Works (Speeches, Lectures, Memorial Lectures, Keynote Addresses, Essays, Features - published and unpublished).

Made in the USA
Middletown, DE
28 August 2024

59672973R00254